The Cinematic Misadventures of

Ed Wood

by
Andrew J. Rausch
and **Charles E. Pratt, Jr.**

Foreword by
Ted Newsom

Introduction by
Tony Schaab

Afterword by
David C. Hayes

The Cinematic Misadventures of Ed Wood

©2015 Andrew J. Rausch and Charles E. Pratt, Jr.

Published in the USA by:

BearManor Media
P.O. Box 71426
Albany, Georgia 31708
www.BearManorMedia.com

ISBN-10: 1-59393-807-1 (alk. paper)
ISBN-13: 978-1-59393-807-9 (alk. paper)

Design and Layout: Valerie Thompson

Table of Contents

This book is dedicated to
Edward D. Wood, Jr.
and the cast and
crews of his films.

Thank you for all the great movies.

Foreword
by Ted Newsom

"I have lived too long among the Woodites."

So saith my late acquaintance Mark Carducci, the mastermind behind *Flying Saucers Over Hollywood*, the two-hour celebration of the 79-minute *Plan 9 from Outer Space* and Ed-Wood-mania in general. He spent several years putting the documentary together with research, video interviews and editing, then several more years trying to find an honest distributor. He never did, but he found a distributor. In corralling a network of loony fans, loonier Friends of Eddie, and people who wanted to downplay their association with Wood the way one would avoid mentioning a pedophiliac grandfather, he could not seem to get the stink off his boots.

I, too, have lived too long among the Woodites. I have spoken to Criswell, I have received Kathy Wood and Delores Fuller as guests into my home. I have conversed with Ed's dapper collaborator Steve Apostoloff, and hardcore gay-porn film maker Joe Robertson, been blitzed by Conrad Brooks' irrepressible rabid puppy-dog enthusiasm, and managed intentionally to avoid dealing with Paul "Kelton the Cop" Marco, primarily because I knew he went through a period during which he knew the world was populated by people with dog heads; however, I did arrange to drop an armored car on him in my spoof of sci fi movies, *The Naked Monster*. The one thing I never did was experience Ed Wood in person, but I figure I also saved myself the experience of being chased around a filthy apartment by a drunk with a knife, and getting a rambling call at three in the morning which ended in him calling me a shitbird.

His friends who knew him from the 1950s described him as movie-star handsome. Though it's true that his later mustached appearance gave him a sort of Kent Taylor/John Carroll look, I always thought he resembled a baffled Alan Young from *Mr. Ed.* Which seems appropriate.

How much can you say? He tried, mostly failed, and died.

A guy I worked for once gave me a soft cover Citadel Press film book, on horror movies, or westerns, or whatever, something he picked up cheap at a yard sale. I had fancied it because I'd noticed the inscription in the fly leaf: "From the library of Edward D. Wood, Jr." in Ed's own quite legible, even beautiful handwriting. I treasured it for a couple months, then gave it to director Joe Dante as a gift. I expect Joe treasured it for a while then gave it to someone else, who then treasured it for an appropriate period, then...you know. Sort of like a Christmas fruitcake: the Gift That Keeps On Getting Given.

As a writer and film maker who did more than his share of hack work, I relate to Ed Wood and do not envy him. Imagine for no reason I'm speaking in a broad Scottish burr when I say, "It's *crrrappp*. It's all *crrrappp*." 'Cause t'is. The best of the worst is fun *crrrappp*. The medium worst is amusing *crrrappp*. The worst is just damned dull. And the damnable paradox with Wood is, the "better" the film in production value, script or competency, the less enjoyable it usually is.

Can we get a few stupid misapprehensions out of the way? Most of them stem from the Wood revival inspired by *The Golden Turkey Awards*, by the brothers Medved. You may know one of them, Michael. He's the Gene Shalit clone (or a well-dressed Ron Jeremy) who rants in print and on TV talk shows how all Hollywood movies are perverted commie-symp propaganda. It's a wonder he doesn't say they turned him into a newt. That book was a follow-up to *The 50 Worst Films of All Time*, which does not even mention Ed Wood or any of his films. Ron Jeremy (or Gene Shalit) gave up writing this after screening a mere 200 pieces of *crrrappp* and his 17-year old brother Harry finished the project, along with his cousin Randy Lowell, alias Randy Dreyfus (also a cousin to Richard, or maybe Harry Reems) alias Bag Man McGurk, alias The Green Lake Peeper. *50 Worst Films of All Time* requested readers to nominate their own favorite cinematic piles of *crrrappp*. The overwhelming majority of responses nominated Ed Wood, whose person and work was apparently unknown to the Medveds, or at least unworthy of original inclusion. They actually interviewed a few drunks and liars to get background on Wood, hence worldwide mistaken impressions in general and specific (*i.e.* that *Plan 9 from Outer Space* is the worst movie ever made), including uncountable errors about the films and the man. Harry has more than atoned for his sins by working vigilantly for the Screen Actors Guild for many years, protecting the solidarity of SAG, and the rights of thousands of actors. Randy Lowell went on to a stable three-decade career as a performer. Michael, the elder and malcontented Medved, still hates commies, liberals and deviates. Especially Ron Jeremy.

There really is no big filmic idiocy involved in intercutting of real night shots and day-for-night shots, as in *Orgy of the Dead, Violent Years* and famously, *Plan 9*. In those films, many of the day-for-night shots are incorrectly printed. You expose the shots as best you can for the sunlight, then the editor or director orders that portion stopped down in the printer to make it look darker. When you forget to tell the lab which is striking your print, or if they just ignore the notation, it looks like regular daylight, because it is. There are tricks to make *good* day for night shots, like using a red filter when shooting in black and white (which makes the blue sky go dark) and using natural shadows whenever possible, and avoiding showing the sky if you can, but these "bloopers" were commonplace back then. I just saw a 60s *Dragnet* episode last night with a "night" driving clearly shot at noon, then printed darker. John Ford did it all the time, especially in westerns. Don Siegel's Elvis movie *Flaming Star* has beautiful examples of the technique, in color (blue filter instead of red). Ida Lupino's classic noir *The Hitchhiker* seems 80% day for night, all shot in full sunlight. Today, you'd CGI the hell out of the shot and it'll look like a perfect midnight. When you're trying to make a picture on a buck ninety-eight, especially in the 50s or 60s, you don't have the option of repeatedly kicking the thing back to the lab to demand perfection.

Okay, Ed Wood substituted his chiropractor for additional necessary "Ghoul Man" shots in *Plan 9*, but holding the cape over the bottom half of his face was perfectly appropriate, in fact, an ingenious tribute. Lugosi had done exactly that in *Abbott & Costello Meet Frankenstein* nine years previously, plus, in my opinion, about half the graveyard long shots in 1943's *Return of the Vampire* are probably a double. Had Eddie popped in some stock shot inserts of Lugosi's eyes from *Bride of the Monster*, and varied the blocking (with his back to camera the chiropractor would not have had to hold both hands in front of him), it might've sold the sequences a bit better, maybe even competently. And the movie would not be as perversely funny.

No, Lugosi didn't hate Karloff, nor was he a foul-mouthed old geek, as shown in the Tim Burton film. In the fascinating book *Nightmare of Ecstasy*, Wood historian Rudolph Grey collected a series of lengthy interviews, which were then rearranged by topic by editor Adam Parfrey of Feral Press, but neither felt fact-checking was necessary. The multiple, conflicting recollections was one of the fun aspects. One of the interviewed Woodites was a half-crazed drunken street person named John Andrews, who vaguely knew Wood in his last years. He's one of the dire masked monsters in *Orgy of the Dead*, and I don't care which one. Andrews' normal speech was peppered with expletives, and so were his third-party anecdotes, like Wood's recollections of Lugosi. Andrews never even met Lugosi. Given Andrews' potty mouth, everyone in his stories swore like a sailor. The boys who wrote *Ed Wood* simply used Rudolph Grey's book as if it were all true.

No, Bela Lugosi does not say, "Don't be afraid of Lobo. He is as harmless as a kitchen," although the *Bride of the Monster* scene does take place in a kitchen, which doubles as an atomic laboratory and basement aquarium. He says "kitten," just like in the script. I repeated that canard in the very first article I ever had printed in a national magazine; I was wrong.

No, Ed Wood did not use pie plates or hubcaps to create the saucers for the *Plan 9* special effects. They were 6-inch wide plastic models painted silver. I know; I built one when I was a kid. The scenes might well have worked better if Wood had the two-foot long metal saucer from *This Island Earth* and an entire soundstage at his disposal, plus a crew of twenty. But he didn't.

Wood was not the worst writer in history, nor even the worst ever to work in Hollywood. His ideas—*Glen or Glenda?* being the weird exception—were relatively mainstream and semi-comprehensible. Had he been working in the legitimate studio system, his stuff undoubtedly would have been rewritten by betters, but the concepts were mainstream. *Violent Years* and *Sinister Urge* could have been low-end Universal or Paramount or Allied Artists programmers. His unmade *The Ghoul Goes West* is not all that much different from Universal's *Curse of the Undead*, or Embassy's *Billy the Kid Meets Frankenstein's Daughter*. *Bride of the Monster* is an anachronistic anomaly more like a 1940s Lugosi films for Monogram, but, hell, *The Human Centipede* is the same thing on shit-eating steroids, and that's fifty years later. *Plan 9* is a combination of ideas used in *Day the Earth Stood Still, Earth vs. The Flying Saucers,* and the old *Weird Tales* pulps. *Night of the Ghouls* lifts the oft-used "phony spiritualist" set-up popular from the Houdini era through *Scooby Doo*, but pays off with a scene and a scream that is genuinely horrific.

As for competency: two of the most "competent" Eddie Wood films I've seen are the feature *The Sinister Urge* and the half-hour TV film *The Sun Also Sets*. *Sinister Urge* was made in 1960, *The Sun Also Sets* a decade before that, and both have production values comparable to other films of their eras, both have relatively decent performances, and both have Wood scripts which actually go from Point A to Point B and eventually arrive at Point C. The studio lighting and set design is passable, the stock music is appropriate and correctly placed (the *waa-waa* saxophone in *Sinister* is evocative of *noirs* of the time, and the ten zillion detective shows then on TV). And both films show the same dilemma: they're dull. They're without the surreal zaniness brought on by a lack of funds as with *Bride of the Monster.* There's little of the idiosyncratic dialogue of *Glen or Glenda?* They don't even have the occasional "WTF!?!" scenes like *Night of the Ghouls'* séance, with its eerie Looney Toons slide-whistle accompanying the wire-operated dancing tambourines and the bug-eyed guy in the Devo hat mouthing "Wah-oh, wah-oh, wah-oh." None of that. They're just dull.

There were less talented, even less coherent contemporary movie makers than poor old Woody. Wyatt Ordung comes to mind, a guy with a name that sounds like a question from Satan, or a psychotic farmer. Ray Dennis Steckler. Phil Tucker. Ronnie Ashcroft. Andy Warhol, whose entire personal *oeuvre* was a smarmy "Fuck you" to the deluded artsy audience. For sheer audience insult, any movie hydrant or cinematic tree Jerry Warren pissed on. Oh, yeah, there were worse directors. At least Ed Wood actually tried to shoot coverage, unlike Vincent Minnelli, who, unaccountably, was absent from either Medved book.

I think many of us laughably-classified "artistic" types want in their hearts to make movies like those which so affected us as children. But you have to adapt this nostalgia to a contemporary style. With Ed, though, he had no luck convincing genuine movie companies that audiences would shell out scheckles for updated variations on Dwayne Esper schlock or Bob Steele westerns. Even AIP's Sam Arkoff, who released some real *crrrappp*, referred to poor Ed as "a one-lung producer." And this, coming from the guy who distributed *Invasion of the Star Creatures* and *Reptillicus*...pshew!

Wood's last ten years had little to recommend them as regards artistic output. The soft-core scripts he wrote for Steve Apostoloff stunk on ice while simultaneously managing to be stultifying, though Steve thought to his dying day that the world would adore a sequel to *Orgy of the Dead*. Wood's hardcore porn screenplays were indistinguishable from anyone else's.

Incidentally, his literary work was one of the cornerstones of my early sex education. A relative gave me a half-dozen dirty paperbacks when I was 16, already not a virgin but still unwise in the ways of the bedroom. Among these included something depressingly bleak called *The Itch* and a charming novel titled *Sally in Black Bondage*, with the titular virgin defiled by a humongously endowed and repulsive black dwarf. Memorably, there was *Love of the Dead*, about necrophilia. The early chapters were an overwrought history of death and funeral trivia, with hard core anecdotes involving necrophiliacs feigning death, and the joys of screwing in a coffin. As it progressed, it got ickier. There were graphic chapters on making love to real corpses in mortuaries, funeral homes and morgues. Detail by detail, erotic revulsion after revolting erotica. I never felt that creeped out until I read a book on Ed Gein. I wanted to wash my brain with Clorox and gouge my eyes out for betraying my soul. The book was written by Ed Wood, one of dozens, maybe hundreds he wrote in the 1960s and 70s. And honestly, it was given to me by my Aunt Shirley. When you finish Andy & Charlie's book, you will understand the synchronistic significance.

A couple of Criswell anecdotes. Criswell was the phenomenally inaccurate "psychic" who appeared in both *Orgy of the Dead* and

Plan 9, as well as his own LA TV show, on which he always used the catchphrase which crops up in *Plan 9*: "We are *all* interested in the *Future*, for *that* is where we will spend the *rest* of our *lives!*" Every New Years, he appeared on Johnny Carson's *Tonight Show* prognosticating things like "I predict—in April, Captain Kangaroo will be assaulted by wolverines!" and "I predict—this year, Pasadena, California, shall become the homosexual capital of the world!"

I attended a goofy psychic fair with my ex-wife about 1980, and among the kiosks of crystal-hawkers and sellers of cure-all bottled water, there was a big carnival-style striped tent and a huge photo portrait of Criswell! I got in line to meet the man himself, who was telling fortunes with Tarot cards, in his resplendent tuxedo and yellow-white Gumby pompadour. I could hear him with the enraptured client just ahead of me.

"*Cut* the cards *three* times to the left with your *left* hand," cooed Criswell, who then flipped the cards over and studied them seriously. "I see a *marriage* in your future. Are you *planning* to get *married?*" The woman shook her head. Criswell said, "*Someone you know* is planning to get *married.*"

I sat down and explained I didn't need my future told, I wanted to talk about the old gang. "Oh, Eddie was a nice man," Criswell said, dropping his stentorian tones. "Full of energy, very good-humored. The pictures he made were not very good, but I enjoyed myself with Ed." I asked, And Lugosi? "He was also a very nice man. Dignified, but not stuffy, very Old World, and courtly. I remember one Christmas, at Eddie's home or maybe Paul Marco's, the tree was decorated in his honor with black snowballs hanging from the branches! Festive and macabre in equal measure. He got quite a chuckle out of that." We spoke for a few more minutes and I excused myself, "I'll make way for the paying customers." He shook my hand and went back to the booming professional tones. "Thank you so much, and good luck. Next, please."

As the next customer sat opposite him, Criswell said, "*Cut* the cards *three* times to the left with your *left* hand. I see a *marriage* in your future. Are you *planning* to get *married?*" The man shook his head. Criswell said. "*Someone you know* is planning to get *married.*"

The other time I saw him was a couple years later, at an all-Wood film festival at a small neighborhood theater in the same building in which Ed Wood and Alex Gordon shared an upstairs office thirty years before. The place was packed, the height of post *Golden Turkey* Wood-mania. The show featured special guests, like Paul Marco, in his invariable "Kelton the Cop" uniform. No longer seeing the world population as mutants with dog heads, he'd exchanged that delusion for one in which he was a cult movie star, a mistake he made by taking a joke from director Joe Dante seriously.

Parenthetically: Marco frequented the home of my friend David del Valle, campy film archivist, acidic raconteur, and wrangler of such Hollywood fringies as *Beyond the Valley of the Dolls* psychotic John Lazar, the dapper and hideous Reggie Nalder (whom David's friend Barbara Steele referred to as "that ghoul") and mystic nut bar Kenneth Anger. Marco would drink himself maudlin and whine, "Oh, I'm so lonely! I need a trick. David, please, buy me a trick. A pretty boy, oh, please." On slightly more sober occasions, Marco showed the new *chotskies* he planned to sell to all the potential members of his make-believe "Kelton the Cop" fan club: "I Love Kelton" bumper stickers, buttons featuring him in his legendary police uniform, and official membership certificates suitable for framing.

"We'll have meetings every week and watch all my films!" Marco told those around him, real or imaginary. "We can look at *Bride of the Monster*, then the next week we can see *Plan 9*, and then we can all watch *Night of the Ghouls!*"

"Paul-l-l-l...," drawled David, "what are we going to do the *fourth* week?"

At the film festival, irrepressible Wood crony Conrad Brooks introduced a short subject he made himself in 1960, *Mystery in Shadows*. "If you think *Plan 9* is lousy, wait til you see this!" he shouted, enthusiastically and accurately. Finally, the guest of honor was called up to the front of the theater. Rolled out, actually. Criswell was trapped in a wheelchair by then. He was still the pink-faced, white haired apparition in his decades-old spangled tuxedo, but clearly frail. They pushed his chair up to the microphone and he leaned into it. In a thready but still theatrical voice, he said, "Thank you, my friends. As I always used to say...on my television program..."

And then he went silent. He looked out into the audience steadily, as if into the distance, or the past. Everyone felt uncomfortable.

Some of us thought of finishing his sentence for him. Others worried that he'd simply blanked. Or had a stroke. Or died. The theater was silent as night, three hundred people waiting. The absence of sound was frightening. No one rustled even a kernel of popcorn. Oh, God. No.

Then, loud and firm as ever: "We are *all* interested in the *Future*, for *that* is where we will spend the *rest* of our *lives*."

The relieved mob sighed, and cheered.

My other brush with the Woodian world was accidental, shortly after the Wood revival began. I saw a man in his 60s in a copy store paying for his Xerox order and sneaked a peek at the receipt to verify this was indeed Greg Walcott, stalwart "Jeff Trent" of *Plan 9*. Politely, I expressed interest in his one film for Eddie. He smiled indulgently and chuckled. "Oh, that awful thing." He had a Southern lilt to his voice, like Randolph Scott, also a native North Carolinian. "Of all the pictures I've made, that's the only one anyone ever asks about." He did indeed work a lot, and in major films nearly from the beginning of his career. *Mister Roberts, Perry Mason, Maverick, 87th Precinct* (he was a regular for two seasons), *Every Which Way But Loose* and three other features for Clint Eastwood, *Norma Rae, Midway, Dallas, Murder She Wrote*.

"I was young 'n' wanted to work," Walcott said, "and through my pastor, I got the lead in this science fiction picture. I read the script and thought, okay, this might work. Then I got to the studio, this tiny little ol' place off an alley, and saw the sets and thought, 'Ho-ho, oh, boy, what have I gotten myself into?' But we did it. And here it is a long, long time later and people still watch that thing. You just never know."

I wrote and directed *Ed Wood: Look Back in Angora* at the suggestion of my friend Arny Schorr at Rhino, to whom I'd sent Mark Carducci's film for potential distribution. They thought it was boring and overlong, but liked the basic idea of a Woodian video, since they'd made money distributing *The Violent Years* and *Orgy of the Dead*. Indeed, I'd always needle Mark about the two hour length of his *Plan 9* documentary, telling him my mine was twice as good as his, because it was half as long. I wanted to do mine in an entirely different way from Mark's, which was talking head, film clip, talking head, talking head, film clip. Instead, in my first cut, I used as much film footage and movie dialogue as I could, letting Wood's own words tell the story with minimal narration and no interviews.

A lawyer representing Wood's widow Kathy approached Rhino, and then so did ex-gal pal Dolores Fuller, each volunteering for an interview, on one condition: I had to edit out the clip from *The Photographer* in which a greasy, bloated Eddie, held on a leash by some unsexy hookers, licks the dirt off the bottom of a woman's dominatrix boot. It showed just how low Wood sank in his career and his life. I grumbled, then acquiesced to adding interviews, avoiding repetition of anyone Mark used: Steve Apostoloff, gay-porn director Joe Robinson, Dolores & Kathy, and in so doing, had to cut a corresponding twelve minutes out of the original show.

I'd first tried to get John Waters to narrate, but I could not get through. Next on the list was Johnny Depp, but a wall of secretaries, agents and flunkies effectively threw up a barricade. Then I had a brainstorm: the narrator of *The Final Curtain*, the alien philosopher-soldier of *Plan 9*: Dudley Manlove! Yes, that's his real name, though heaven knows he must've suffered for it when he was a kid. Can you imagine? It's like growing up with the name Alfredo Dickjuice or Morry Buttbanger.

Somehow I got his phone number in Palm Springs, and called one Saturday morning. Dudley was already in the bag and it was only 10:30. Luckily he was affably plastered and we spoke for a half hour. I have a tendency to speak quickly, and he chided me, sounding just like Eros admonishing the Earthlings. "Young-g-g man-n-n-n," he said, "you must LEARN to e-NUN-ciate clearly. It is es-SEN-tial to communication. I-I-I was the VOICE of Lux Soap on the AIR for over twenty YEARS." I wanted that voice. Rhino overruled me and got Gary Owens, who did a wonderful job for a reasonable price.

Rhino hit the streets with *Look Back in Angora* exactly one week before Tim Burton's movie with Johnny Depp premiered. We coasted on a multi-million dollar ad campaign for not one cent. Take that, William Castle.

Several years later, film collector Jeff Joseph called me with a notion for yet another Ed Wood show. It was already past the Woody saturation point by then, but he did have tapes of some fascinating stuff. He had all sorts of rare films, so perhaps we could package them for release—assuming I could find some sucker company to shell out the price Jeff thought his stuff was worth. He had the competently morose *The Sun Also Sets*, with Tom Keene and Lois Lane, a.k.a Phyllis Coates (both just fine). There was a series of interminable spec' "commercials," all shot in a single-take wide shot, with the ingenious idea that they would be generic, each one targeting a different sort of local store or service: a car repair commercial, a bakery spot, a supermarket version, haberdashery. The theory was to cut in the local sponsor between the "comedic" set-up and the final gag. They proved two things: 1) it was a lousy idea badly executed, and 2) Eddie Wood was as good at comedy as he was with drama, westerns or sci-fi.

Jeff also had the original half-hour version of *The Final Curtain*, most of which was incorporated into the feature *Night of the Ghouls*. I saw the stupid thing twenty-five years ago. No, Bela Lugosi didn't have the script in his hands when he died, and he was lucky to die five years before it was made.

The most fascinating rarity Jeff Joseph had was a reel of 8mm home movies. Understand, old 8mm film was 16mm wide and 25 feet in length, about two minutes running time. It was run through the camera twice, first exposing on one side of the film, then carefully opening the camera (not in the sunlight or you'll ruin everything), flipped the now-full take-up reel around and put it on the feed reel, re-threaded the film through the aperture, then shot on the unexposed side. In processing, the lab would split the film down the middle and splice it together, making one small 50-foot reel.

In final form, the brightly colored Kodachrome footage, eerily silent, showed Ed, not in his prime but at least not the tub of guts he'd later be, grinning and mugging on a suburban front lawn, playing Fetch with someone's dog. Assorted friends or relatives or who-gives-a-shit smiled motionlessly at the camera, as if holding still for a Kodak Brownie snapshot. Standard stuff for amateur home movies.

Then a magical thing happened. There were weird flashes and arbitrary light splotches, swish-pans of table lamps inside the house, new and cockeyed angles of waving relatives. The interior shots were too red-orange and dark (Uh-oh. Someone didn't remove the yellow Type A sunlight filter), which were all superimposed with extended uncut takes of dogs romping out in the front yard—*upside-down*. Someone threaded the 8mm film into the camera backward and it exposed twice on the same side, but reversed top to bottom, bottom to top.

There was Edward D. Wood in a living room, laying in a leather recliner, napping and drunk, or napping and not drunk, his face turned toward camera. He was dead to the world, completely slack and gloriously relaxed. And over him, across him, around him were the upside-down jumping dogs out on the lawn. A little dog, a bigger dog, a really big dog, all running and romping with each other. They chased each other, frolicked freely, snapped at each other and bounced, all superimposed and upside down over the continuous shot of unconscious Ed on someone's recliner. Was he dreaming of dogs, or simply exhausted? Were the carefree mutts playing or arguing, or both? Would he ever open his eyes and look at the camera? The double images were hypnotic, arbitrary, and baffling. There was a quick, bright flash of light—an overexposure caused by removing the film clumsily from the camera—and the home movie flickered to black.

The sequence at once conjured memories of the amateur Lugosi *Dracula* footage inserted into *Plan 9*, the incongruous buffalo stampede stock shot in *Glen or Glenda*, the surreal cinema of Kenneth Anger and the intentional extended-take boredom of Warhol—and in a weird way, even the brilliant theme of Welles' *Citizen Kane*. Was I seeing Eddie's personal Rosebud? Did the moving pictures mean something, or nothing? It was home movies transformed into art by accident.

Now you're prepared to read this book, everything explained in loving detail. But bear this in mind. No one can tell the story. Mistakes are made. But there is no mistaking the thoughts in a man's mind.

That, and the movies are all *crrrrap*.

Introduction
by Tony Schaab

Greetings, my friend.

If you're anything like the "average" sci-fi or B-movie fan, you're more than likely familiar with Ed Wood by name—and perhaps by his most well-known film, *Plan 9 from Outer Space* (1959)—and not much else. Certainly, get ready for this book to open your eyes to a world of bizarrely entrancing entertainment that your feeble human mind never knew existed!

I'm honored (and a little concerned for my own mental faculties) to be included in a fairly elite circle of folks who might be considered "experts" on part or all of Ed's legacy. I'm in the process of writing the novelized version of *Plan 9 from Outer Space*, working directly for a reputedly-authentic original copy of the film's script, with my end goal being to bring to life the incredible story that Ed wanted to tell with the film, the story that didn't quite translate to the silver screen due to a variety of factors. I can see the tale in its fully-envisioned grandeur in Ed's script and liner notes; with unlimited resources (or at least the backing of a semi-reputable film studio), he could have created a truly enjoyable blend of visual feast and thought-provoking tale, but as we all now know, that was not destined to happen.

Everyone has to start somewhere when learning of Ed's legacy, and as an avid Wood fan myself, I must admit that I started out much like you in the knowledge (or lack thereof) of this very quirky and tirelessly motivated individual. In college, when I saw *Plan 9* for the first time, the movie initially seemed to me as it probably did to the vast majority of its viewers: some chintzy B-movie from the black-and-white era, plagued by a bad script, wooden actors, and a budget that was likely smaller than what I was paying for my tuition in that year alone.

To be fair, a large chunk of people who sought out *Plan 9 from Outer Space* did so because, like myself, they heard about it as being labeled "the worst movie ever made" by someone, somewhere, and they wanted to watch it to see if that title held true. And most viewers probably came to the same conclusion after the end credits started to roll: it was pretty bad, yes; but was it THE worst movie of all time? Definitely not.

Amazingly, something else also happened at the end of a first *Plan 9* viewing for a good-sized portion of the viewership: they couldn't shake an odd feeling in their brains. A feeling of strange intrigue. A feeling of piteous reverence. A feeling of backhanded respect. Were these feelings due to the subliminal backlash of having seen a movie unfairly branded as the worst of all time, or did viewers just simply *know* that, on some level, there was more to this movie (and its creator) than meets the eye?

When I first watched the film, in the mid-1990s, I was at a point in my life when I was intentionally seeking out bad movies. The mesmerizing allure of *Mystery Science Theater 3000* was in its prime, and I had caught the *MST3K* fever big-time. I had seen the other "worst movie ever" front-runners: I bravely and willingly sat through viewings of *Manos: The Hands of Fate* (1966) and *Santa Claus Conquers the Martians* (1964), both the joke-tracked *MST3K* and the original versions. (Growing up as a sci-fi and horror fan in the 1980s, I had also seen plenty of other really bad movies, but the haze of time passing mixed with the blur of nostalgia meant that I didn't truly realize that those movies were *that* bad until at least twenty years after the fact.)

After my first viewing of *Plan 9 from Outer Space* all the way back then, I wish I could tell you that I was instantly enamored and spent the rest of my days between then and now learning everything I could about the quirky film and Ed, it's even quirkier director; alas, it was not quite "love at first sight" as a romanticized Hollywood might have you believe. I put the movie in my mental repository of B-movies and left it there, untouched, for years.

Remember those feelings I spoke of earlier—the nagging suspicion some *Plan 9* watchers had that there might be more to the story of this film that simply what was captured on camera? I was a victim of these sentiments as well, and in 2003 I had a chance encounter with a book in a secondhand store that brought things full-circle for me: the Medved Brothers' *The Golden Turkey Awards*.

The Medveds, you see, had been judging Hollywood's worst of the worst in movies, actors, and directors for some time, and *The Golden Turkey Awards* was a collection of "honors" given to the most god-awful, as judged by the brothers themselves and a write-in campaign they held prior to the book's release. It didn't take long in flipping through the book to recognize many of the names and films sprinkled throughout the pages.

Then, as if by divine providence (or just the fact that I had seen a lot of really bad movies in the last twenty years), there were the names of the appointed Worst Director and Worst Film of All Time— names I recognized instantly from watching that oddly-enthralling movie so many years before.

Ed Wood. *Plan 9 from Outer Space*.

That essentially sealed it for me. As I mentioned previously, I had heard that someone, somewhere had given *Plan 9* this dubious moniker, but I never knew the "who" or "how" until that moment. I couldn't fathom how a pair of writers (let alone their fans via the write-in campaign) could assign *Plan 9* that title—even though at that time I hadn't seen the movie in years, I remembered it being more...*cheesy* rather than outright-bad.

Soon after the bookstore, I found and bought *Plan 9* on DVD and watched it again.

And again.

And again.

I was officially hooked.

Every time I watched the film, I saw something new in the action that made me think "if the budget had only allowed for _____, then that would actually be a really awesome scene." Or "if the actor had only delivered that line differently or had said _____ instead, then this whole part would make a lot more sense." Or "if only Ed had included a scene about _____, then the whole movie would have flowed together so much better."

The list goes on and on, but the point is this: through the layers of muck and grime, I saw the *true* story that Ed Wood was trying to tell—and I thought it was a damn good one.

Now it's true, to an extent, that you could probably say this about most films: "if only the director had more money and better actors and done a better job telling the story, then the movie wouldn't be so bad." I get that. But what I think makes Ed Wood's story so compelling is how much he *cared* about the projects he created: he firmly believed that *Grave Robbers from Outer Space* (the original title of *Plan 9* before, allegedly, the Baptist church that funded part of the film demanded that the title be changed to something less "highly offensive") was the best story he had ever written—even if it didn't translate as well on film as he had hoped.

Anyone who has seen the movie has seen the gloriousness of its ineptitude. The questionable dialogue delivered by wooden and emotionless "actors" (some of whom who were members of the aforementioned Baptist church, given starring roles in exchange for the church's funding of the film). The flying saucers on strings and other effects that are a far cry from "special." The scenes that switch from night to day back to night again due to a serious lack of editing (or attention to detail in general).

Yes, the film *Plan 9 from Outer Space* is bad.

But is the story itself so bad?

Well, my friend, if you find yourself as intrigued as some with this particular Ed Wood film, you now have the chance to decide for yourselves. I've made available a copy of the script I have in my possession for anyone interested in giving it a read (a quick search on Amazon for "Plan 9 screenplay" or my name should help you find it), and of course my novelization of the story is certainly going to be my heart-felt attempt at helping Ed's "true" story reach the masses. My goal is to—hopefully—create the narrative version of the story that Ed was unable to bring to life on film due to constraints with his budget, acting talent, and production timetable.

If you've bought this book, are reading through this introduction, and are finding yourself getting more and more excited to read all of the intricate details of Ed Wood and his films that wait in store for you here, I want you to know that even though this is not an officially-recognized support group (mostly for tax and legal reasons), you are not alone! Ed's cinematic creations are so alluring and mesmerizing that many folks have created new fictions entirely based on or inspired by Ed's works. I myself compiled and edited a fiction anthology, Before *Plan 9: Plans 1-8 from Outer Space,* that tells the tales of the first Plans enacted by the aliens prior to the events shown in the *Plan 9* film. "Yes, but Tony," you're saying to yourself, you appear to be bonkers over this film, and you're like a man in public not wearing any pants, because I can clearly see you're nuts." That's a fair assessment, but what if I told you again that you (and I, **we**) are not alone: the authors of the tales of the first eight plans include a *New York Times* best-seller, a Marvel Comics writer, and multiple literary award winners. People from any and all walks of life find it very easy to recognize Ed Wood's passion and eccentric idiosyncrasies. You are not alone.

I sincerely hope that, if you enjoy the zany wonder of Ed Wood and specifically the odd allure of *Plan 9*, you will enjoy not only this painstakingly-detailed reference from Andrew Rausch and Charles Pratt that you now have before you, but you may also give a read to my take on Ed's story as well.

All we want to do is help bring his visions to the masses.

I just hope our stupid, stupid human minds are up to the task.

Author's Note

Ask ten different cineastes whom Edward D. Wood, Jr. was and you're likely to get ten different responses. He has become something larger than life, more than a man. He represents different things to different people. To some, he is the much-ballyhooed "Worst Filmmaker in History"; a hack, if you will. To others, Wood was an artistic genius whose work contained layers of subtext and profound artistry. The truth, as usual, likely lies somewhere in the middle.

Was Wood the worst filmmaker in history? Definitely not. That title easily goes to the hundreds upon thousands of workmanlike directors who toiled on films that are now forgotten. We do not speak of them today as we speak of Wood. They are the gentlemen who helmed the comedies that weren't funny and the dramas that lacked drama. Were they more technically proficient than Wood? In most cases, yes, they probably were. But they lacked the passion that Wood carried with him on each of his projects. They lacked the singular vision and hunger of Ed Wood. They were given larger budgets with which to conceal their flaws.

Ed Wood's passion was his driving force. He had very little training in filmmaking, and it didn't matter. Things like that couldn't stop the indefatigable Wood. By god, he wanted to make motion pictures and he did. They may have lacked the sophistication and excellence of something like *Citizen Kane* (1941), but by and large they contained Wood's blood, sweat and tears in each and every frame.

For most film buffs, Wood is beloved for overcoming his own shortcomings. He didn't always have the talent to make the pictures the way he wanted to make them, and he definitely didn't have the budget to fully realize his dreams. But nevertheless he persevered. Like thousands of other people (many of whom may have actually possessed more talent than he), Wood went to Hollywood with the dream of making movies. Was he successful during his lifetime? Not in terms of artistic acclaim or financial reward, but he was successful because through all of the trials and tribulations he found a way to continue making movies. The truth is that he probably didn't make the movies he truly wanted to make in a way that he envisioned, but he was too stubborn to back down. Through a mixture of naivety, ignorance, and flat-out obsession, Wood created films that have stood the test of time and are beloved by millions.

There is an innocence in Wood's work that shines through as brightly as his passion. His views on the world and the way things worked weren't always accurate, and his often child-like perceptions show through in his films. But his films are somehow more than the sum of their parts. Sure, they can be dissected and picked apart piece by piece; flaws abound. But somehow those flawed pieces came together to make something memorable and special.

As we will discuss in this volume, Wood loathed filmmakers who peddled in smut, and yet he himself would later become associated with such pictures. He wrote a handful of soft-core sex pictures, as well as nearly one hundred lurid novels, and even directed a hardcore porno film. It's likely that he loathed himself for doing so. We'll never know exactly how Wood viewed himself and his work during this period, but it might be said that his excessive alcoholism may well be an indicator of his self-loathing. But he shouldn't have loathed himself. He continued writing screenplays he was passionate about during this period. They didn't find financing, which no doubt brought him great distress, but his perseverance in these endeavors indicate a man with an undying passion. Perhaps this drive was unhealthy as it seems he cared more about his art than he did his own well-being. And maybe the porn films weren't exactly the movies he longed to make, but the undeniable truth is that he was a success because he found a way to continue making movies of some sort even when the deck was stacked against him.

Ed Wood is a legend and deservedly so. He earned that right by fighting tooth and nail for decades to make motion pictures. He was a filmmaker, and no one can take that away from him. He was also an auteur in the truest sense of the word; unlike other filmmakers who had larger budgets, Wood was forced to do almost everything on his pictures himself.

Ed Wood loved motion pictures perhaps more than anything else, and that love behind the camera is what makes his films endure today. Audiences can feel his passion, his motivation, and his desperate desire to succeed.

This volume is dedicated, with love, to the man and his many achievements.

Author's Note #2

In the course of writing this book we discovered that some people revere Edward D. Wood, Jr.'s work in a different way than we do; they don't revere it more, just differently. While we are huge fans of Wood and his work as both a filmmaker and as a novelist, we find unintentional humor in them. We find Wood to be naïve at times in terms of the way he viewed people, their actions, and the world around him. We found his sense of logic to be, at times, skewed. We find him to have been, at times, somewhat inept in the creation of these works. This is not to say he was a stupid man; by no means do we believe that notion. Again, here was a man who loved movies and found a way (with no real training to speak of) to write, direct, and produce films for the better part of his life. That is a substantial feat which cannot be ignored.

We are not in the camp who laughs at Wood and labels him a failure, nor are we a part of the camp who labels him a misunderstood genius and a genuine artist. We tend to fall somewhere in the middle on that scale; more than anything we admire Wood's endless passion for creation, be it personal films, pornographic films, or lurid paperback novels. We are not here to mock the man, and that is not the purpose for this book. Again, this book falls somewhere in between those two premises; our book holds Wood in great regard as a creator, but also acknowledges his missteps and the unintentional comedy to be found as a result of them.

Our beliefs regarding Wood's work tend to be somewhat different than the more academic writers like Rudolph Grey and Rob Craig, who have preceded us in writing tomes on him. We have the utmost respect for both of those great writers, but we look at things differently than they do. For instance, many Wood aficionados hate the posthumously-produced film *I Woke Up Early the Day I Died* (1998) because either a) they feel it was too slick and too polished for a Wood film, b) they feel it makes fun of Wood in some way, or c) because it's a more intentionally comedic film than Wood's own offerings were. We, on the other hand, see that Aris Iliopulos-helmed film as being the single greatest achievement in the Wood canon; we believe it is the sort of quality production that Wood always wanted to make but could not due to deficiencies in talent and/or budget. (This is not to say Wood was completely devoid of talent, either. There are different levels of talent and we simply believe Wood to have been more than few rungs beneath that of guys like Orson Welles, John Ford, or Budd Boetticher.)

Rudolph Grey advised us not to include the three posthumous films (*I Woke Up, Devil Girls*, 1999, and *Tomb of the Vampire*, 2013) as he felt their inclusion might help to diminish Wood's legacy. Because we wanted to be as thorough as possible we include them here, be they good, bad, or ugly (which is actually sort of the order in which they fall). It is certainly not to diminish or in any way harm Wood's good name and legacy. This book was intended as a celebration of Wood the filmmaker and all of the films on which he was either a writer or director.

So where do you draw the line? Well, we chose to not include films Wood is merely rumored to have been involved with, such as *Revenge of the Virgins* (1959); if we couldn't verify his involvement, we left it out. We also chose to omit the film *Hot Ice* (1978), which Wood appears in and worked on as assistant director, because he was not the picture's writer or director. Finally, in terms of posthumously made films, we left out films that are simply homages or fan-made sequels to his work; we included only the three films on which he is credited as a screenwriter. (A fourth, John Johnson's *Plan Nine*, 2014, was in the works but was not completed in time to be included in this volume.)

So, in the end, we love Wood's films as much as anyone else does. Maybe some will believe that we love them for the wrong reasons. We love and respect these films for what they are and what we see them as. Many of them are undeniably classics, but are they really art? Or, even more to the point, are they really *artless?* We don't really support either of these positions. But, in the end, do our motives really matter? After all, we're all here for the same reason—to celebrate the life, art, and passion of Edward D. Wood, Jr.

Glen or Glenda? (1953)

Originally titled *I Changed My Sex!*, *Glen or Glenda?* was to be an exploitation film based on the famous transgender surgery of Christine Jorgensen. However, Jorgensen threatened to sue if her name was used in the film, so producer George Weiss hired then-unknown Edward D. Wood, Jr. to write the screenplay and then shoot it in four days. Wood, a cross-dresser himself, ultimately changed the premise, turning it into a film about transvestism. In order to appease Weiss' demands that the film be a sex change picture, Wood tacked on a short second story, titled "Alan or Anne?," dealing with the operation. Thus was born the single weirdest cinematic PSA announcement and plea for acceptance of all time. One can only imagine what the reaction from the theatrical crowd was.

Glen or Glenda? is probably Wood's most important film—important because Wood had the opportunity to make an exploitation film and turned it into a chance to communicate directly with the audience. Yes, his skills were inept, but Wood's message comes across loud and clear. There has never been another film like this one, where a filmmaker has tried so valiantly to pour out his heart and plead for understanding. It took courage for Wood to craft such a personal film, even taking the lead role himself. Unfortunately all of that comes to naught for casual viewers and schlock hounds who enjoy the film for its plethora of WTF? moments, while failing to consider what Wood was trying so hard to communicate. One wonders what today's filmscape might look like if some of our talented independent filmmakers possessed Wood's fierce drive and sincerity.

Despite Wood's changing the nature of the film, the film's misleading trailer would still tout it as being primarily about a sex change operation.

With *Glen or Glenda?* Wood first proved his unique inability to tell a coherent story. Here, he utilizes narration by multiple sources including a god-like mad scientist, a psychiatrist, the title character himself, and maybe strangest of all, an occasional dream-like manifestation of his own subconscious. The film swings willy-nilly from one viewpoint to the other and the goings on are convoluted—to say the least. The film begins with the following warning, letting us know that Wood means business:

In the making of this film, which deals with a strange and curious subject, no punches have been pulled—no easy way out is taken. Many of the smaller parts are portrayed by persons who actually are, in real life, the character they portray on the screen. This is a picture of stark realism...taking no sides...but giving you the facts...all the facts...as they are today... You are society... Judge ye not!

One of the biggest problems with the film—and there are a great many to choose from—is the film's thin plotline. The majority of the film is about a transvestite, Glen, who is afraid to tell his fiancée, Barbara, about his dirty little secret. As their wedding day grows nearer and nearer, Glen knows he must tell her. However, he is afraid he will lose her once she learns the truth. Eventually he tells her, and in a scene that was surely Wood's own fantasy, she is accepting; so much in fact that she takes off her angora sweater and hands it to him to wear.

Also telling that this is, in many ways, Wood's own story is his constant insistence that he is not homosexual. This point is needlessly made repeatedly throughout the film. It is sadly ironic that Wood, who longs for the world to understand his situation as a transvestite, seems to look down at homosexuals.

As one might expect, Wood's logic and reasoning in the film is often silly. In one scene, he implies that there is a little bit of Glenda in every man. "Little miss female," the narrator says, "you should feel quite proud of the situation. You of course realize it's predominantly men who design your clothes, your jewelry, your makeup, your hairstyling, your perfume."

The high or the low point of the film, depending on your

particular viewpoint, is a ten-minute long surreal sequence that feels like the cinematic equivalent of an LSD trip. The scene, which features Bela Lugosi stoically observing such unexplained scenes as a man whipping a woman, a woman performing a striptease, and a strange S&M act between two women, is difficult to make heads or tails of. No doubt a psychoanalyst would have a field day with this sequence, but for the average viewer it is incomprehensible. Then the devil, which may or may not be Glen's father, shows up, and more indescribable strangeness occurs.

What is little known about the dream sequence in *Glen or Glenda?* is the fact that producer Weiss was the person responsible for adding in the nonsensical bondage and S&M bits from one of his previously unreleased films (directed by Merle Connell). Weiss did this to pad out the picture and bring its running time up to the minimum time for a feature film.

By 1953, actor Bela Lugosi, best known for his turn in *Dracula* (1931), was at the end of his life and the end of his career. Down on his luck, the former star agreed to appear in Wood's semi-auto-biographical *Glen or Glenda?* as a type of narrator (who appears to be a god of some sort), here credited as "The Scientist," who says nothing specifically about the plot or any of the events in the film. Instead, he dramatically says: "Beware! Beware of the big green dragon that sits on your doorstep. He eats little boys... Puppy dog tails, and big fat snails... Beware! Take care! Beware!" This dialogue makes absolutely no sense, but as performed by Lugosi, it does have a sort of simple lyricism to it. (When he says it, it sounds like "*bevare.*") This same ridiculous dialogue will be delivered three times in the film; twice by Lugosi, and once by the devil character.

Despite the madness which surrounds him, Lugosi gives a credible and fascinating performance. He is as elegant and transfixing as ever, and is easily the finest performer in the film. Also decent (despite extremely wooden dialogue) is veteran performer Lyle Talbot, who plays police inspector Warren. The rest of the cast displays the lack of acting chops that would ultimately become a trademark of Ed Wood's films. Leading the way here is Wood himself, who appears in the lead role. Judging from his performance, Wood may well be the worst actor Wood would ever work with, and that is saying a great deal.

Also extremely dull and robotic is Wood's then-girlfriend Dolores Fuller, who naturally appears here as Glen's girlfriend, Barbara. Scenes between Wood and Fuller are cringe-inducing and rather painful on the ears. In real life Dolores had learned of Wood's transvestism just before the production of *Glen or Glenda?* and was appalled at her boyfriend's splashing their private lives and problems across movie screens for everyone to witness. It's not difficult to imagine her heart not being in this production. Fuller would soon leave Ed Wood after the completion of the film.

It must also be noted that Conrad "Connie" Brooks, an actor Wood would later work with again on three more features, appears here in four different roles (Banker, Reporter, Pickup Artist, and Bearded Drag Queen).

The film also features interesting cameos by cinematographer William C. Thompson (as the judge), producer George Weiss (as an onlooker at the scene of a suicide), and Conrad Brooks' brother, Henry Bederski (as a man whose hairline recedes because of his hat—and yes, this *is* as ridiculous as it sounds).

Copious amounts of stock footage are used in the film. This would later become another staple in Wood's films. Here he uses much more stock footage than he would ever use again, utilizing nearly fourteen full minutes of it. Footage of New York City pedestrians appears numerous times throughout the film. Other uses of stock footage "integration" include World War II battle footage and a stampede of buffalo, which makes absolutely no sense in the context in which Wood places it in the film. Wood uses stock footage of lightning an astounding six times in the film.

One of the elements of Wood's films that he would ultimately be most remembered for is his dialogue, which is often absurd, wooden, awkwardly phrased, and/or redundant. As Wood collaborator Stephen C. Apostolof would later explain, Wood would write screenplays in a stream-of-consciousness manner, spilling words onto the page as quickly as he could type them. This will come as no surprise to anyone who's ever heard Wood's dialogue, but it does explain a lot. *Glen or Glenda?* features a lot of Woodian dialogue, most of which falls under the category of awkwardly phrased, such as "Here's a story from fact."

Then there's the silly and the redundant, such as "People...all going somewhere...all with their own thoughts...their own ideas...all with their own personalities."

Later the Scientist says almost the same thing: "The world is a strange place to live in. All those cars. All going someplace. All carrying humans, which are carrying out their lives."

In another scene, the psychiatrist, Dr. Alton, says, "Only the infinity of the depths of a man's mind can really tell the story." This of course makes no sense, but then this is an Ed Wood film... Later Glen will explain that he "can't make sense to myself sometimes."

Then there are the unnatural phrases like Inspector Warren saying, "you men of medical science." All of this dialogue is ridiculous, but it's a big reason why we all love the films of Edward D. Wood, Jr.

It should be noted that this is the only film Wood would ever direct that he did not also produce.

CREDITS: Producer: George Weiss; Director: Edward D. Wood, Jr.; Screenplay: Edward D. Wood, Jr.; Cinematographer: William C. Thompson; Editor: Bud Schelling.

CAST: Bela Lugosi (Scientist); Lyle Talbot (Inspector Warren); Timothy Farrell (Dr. Alton/Narrator); Dolores Fuller (Barbara); Tommy Haynes (Alan/Anne); Edward D. Wood, Jr. (Glen/Glenda); Charles Crafts (Johnny); Conrad Brooks (Banker/Reporter/Pick-Up Artist/Bearded Drag); Henry Bederski (Man with Hat); Captain DeZita (Devil/Glen's Father), Shirley Speril (Miss Stevens); Harry Thomas (Man in Nightmare); William C. Thompson (Judge); Mr. Walter (Patrick/Patricia); George Weiss (Man).

Jail Bait (1954)

When you first learn that Edward D. Wood, Jr. wrote and directed a film titled *Jail Bait*, you expect an exploitation film about reckless youth. Well, don't get your hopes up, because that's not what this movie is. In this instance, said "jail bait" is a gun. This isn't an exploitation flick, but rather a melodramatic public service announcement about the evils of firearms. Co-written with Alex Gordon, with whom Wood would later collaborate on *Bride of the Monster* (1955), this is the director's first truly competent production. Sure, it has the wooden acting that one expects from a Wood film, but the dialogue is better than the average and the plot, while still silly, is far more effective than what we find in most of his films.

If the credits didn't inform you that this was a Wood-helmed picture, you'd never even guess he was involved. This is perhaps a hint that Wood could have produced really solid work had anyone ever given him an "A" movie budget. Think about it—money would have given way to more realistic props, soundstages, and more takes for each scene, as well as better actors who would have given more convincing performances. But that never happened. However, Wood fully utilizes the low budget in *Jail Bait* and creates something credible. Was *Jail Bait* astonishing? Was it a profound work of art? No and no, but it's at least an average crime melodrama that wouldn't have embarrassed anyone involved with it. (Saying that Wood, at his best, was average is no insult; after all, *most* Hollywood directors are merely average.) So why does no one talk about films like *Jail Bait*, where Wood did competent work? Likely because it does little to further the misconception that Wood was an untalented hack, or, even worse, the "worst filmmaker in history."

Jail Bait features a cast that is rather impressive for a minor production with a low budget. For every Dolores Fuller or Mona McKinnon in the cast there is a more accomplished actor like Lyle Talbot or Bud Osborne. The film also features an early performance by former Mr. Universe Steve Reeves (this was his first credited performance in a feature film).

The film's trailer promises that it will be a "siren-screaming bullet-blazing thriller," and *Jail Bait* delivers on that promise.

Don Gregor (played by Clancy Malone, whom Wood met when Malone delivered his groceries) has just been arrested for carrying a gun without a permit. Inspector Johns (Talbot) and his partner, Lt. Lawrence (Reeves), believe Don is keeping company with a low-life thug named Vic Brady (Timothy Farrell). After Don is released from police custody, his sister, Marilyn Gregor (Fuller), warns him that guns are "jail bait." Nevertheless, Don leaves the house with his back-up pistol.

Don's father, world-renowned plastic surgeon Dr. Boris Gregor (played by silent movie star Herbert Rawlinson, who died from lung cancer the day after filming on *Jail Bait* wrapped), comes home and tells Marilyn that the police have informed him of Don's illegal gun toting. (We know Boris is a doctor because he carries a black medical bag with him wherever he goes. After all, you never know when or where an emergency facelift might be required.) The doctor discusses an accident victim from earlier in the day whose face he had to remodel. (Could this seemingly pointless discussion be fore-shadowing? Hmmm.) Both Don's father and sister believe his hanging around with Vic Brady will get him into trouble.

We then see Don, once again "carrying a rod," and hanging out with Vic in a bar. Off-duty cops Inspector Johns and Lt. Lawrence just happen to show up at the same bar, and a minor altercation takes place in which Don threatens to punch Johns. Once Vic and Don have left the bar, Vic advises Don not to treat police officers in such a manner. "He was out to get you sore," Vic says.

It is soon revealed that Vic and Don are planning to heist the $23,000 Monterey Theater payroll. Don is hesitant, saying, "That cop has me rattled. I might get trigger-happy." But Vic convinces Don to go through with the crime anyway.

In the film's one true Woodian moment of ineptitude, the audience is treated to a stock footage performance of Cotton Watts (himself), a nightclub performer in black face. The scene, in which Watts refers to himself as a monkey, shucks and jives while speaking in Ebonics, and dances around while suggestively grabbing his crotch is offensive to say the least. While it's true that 1954 was a much less politically correct time, Wood should have known better.

As Vic and Don are about to bum rush the theater's night watchman, Vic advises Don to shoot first and ask questions later. The two of them then accost the night watchman (Osborne) and tell him if he doesn't open the safe he will be killed. The guard ultimately does what he's told. But when a female employee of the theater walks in, he goes for the telephone and is gunned down by Don. Vic then chases the woman, shooting her. Humorously, sirens begin to wail in the far off distance at almost the exact second Vic fires his weapon. These cops in Wood's world are extremely effective, to say the least!

The audience is next treated to a car chase between Don and Vic and several police cars. The cars shoot back and forth at one another, and Vic ultimately loses the cops by turning into an alley. (Maybe these cops aren't so effective after all...)

It is soon revealed that the woman, Miss Willis (McKinnon), survived the shooting and can pick the shooters out in a line up. Soon there will be a second revelation: the night watchman was a former cop, making Don and Vic "cop killers" (this phrase will be used *ad nauseum* from this point on).

Vic's girlfriend, Loretta (Theodora Thurman), observes, "That's bad business, cop killing." Don then declares that he wants to turn himself in for killing the night watchman. Vic is of course unhappy with this development, but when Don escapes, there is little he can do. Don goes to his father for help. This is where Wood's usual illogical thinking once again comes into play; Don says he will give himself up to the police, but not for another three days. The father agrees. However, it is never said what exactly Don plans to do for those next three days. More than likely this is just an excuse to further the plot by having Vic capture Don, which he does immediately. When Don keeps insisting that he's going to hand himself over to the police, Vic shoots him. The audience is then treated to an overly-long, extremely humorous, fake-looking dying scene in which Don flops around for a good minute or so before finally succumbing to the gunshot. (It seems that even here, in what is one of his finest outings, Wood could not help himself in some ways.)

When Vic hides Don's body in a closet just off the kitchen, Loretta complains, "I don't like dead men cluttering up my place." She then proceeds to call Vic a "has-been with a gun," which manages to bring his wrath down on her. He doesn't kill her, but he does give her a forceful smack in the kisser.

Vic Brady approaches Don's father with an offer—he will trade Don alive for a plastic surgery make-over that will give him the appearance of being someone else. Dr. Gregor agrees to do this, but ultimately finds his dead son's body—somehow standing, leaning on only a hanging sheet (this is an Ed Wood picture, don't worry about how implausible this is!). The good doctor then goes on with the charade, operating on Vic's face.

At the film's conclusion, the wraps come off and it is revealed that Dr. Gregor gave Vic his son Don's face, thus making Vic guilty of the night watchman's murder. "This is my son," Dr. Gregor tells the cops, "the man who killed the policeman." Vic tries to run, shoots at the cops, and is ultimately shot next to an outdoor swimming pool. At first we believe Wood has avoided the cliché by not having Vic fall into the pool, but Vic then takes awhile to die a long, goofy death, and he ultimately rolls into the pool.

It is interesting to note that, according to actor Lyle Talbot, the legendary James Cagney almost appeared in *Jail Bait*. Talbot says that Cagney wandered into their shoot and then agreed to appear in the film as he had nothing else to do. If we are to believe this story, Talbot says that the police then arrived and told Wood and crew to disperse since they didn't have a permit to shoot in the location, thus spoiling Wood's once-in-a-lifetime opportunity to direct Cagney.

CREDITS: Producer: Edward D. Wood, Jr.; Director: Edward D. Wood, Jr.; Screenplay: Edward D. Wood, Jr.; Alex Gordon; Cinematographer: William C. Thompson; Editor: Igo Kantor; Charles Clement.

CAST: Lyle Talbot (Inspector Johns); Dolores Fuller (Marilyn Gregor); Herbert Rawlinson (Dr. Boris Gregor); Steve Reeves (Lt. Bob Lawrence); Clancy Malone (Don Gregor); Timothy Farrell (Vic Brady); Theodora Thurman (Loretta); Bud Osborne (Night watchman Paul McKenna); Mona McKinnon (Miss Willis); Don Nagel (Detective Davis), John Robert Martin (Detective McCall); La Vada Simmons (Dorothy Lytell); Regina Claire (Newspaper Woman); John Avery (Police Doctor); Conrad Brooks (Medical Attendant/ Photographer).

Bride of the Monster (1955)

Bride of the Monster is an anomaly in that it's an Edward D. Wood, Jr. film that's so competently made that it's more entertaining on its own merits than for its inadequacies. Sure, it still contains some of the ineptitude that is associated with Wood's work, but there is very little of this in contrast with his other films of this era. In fact, most of the dialogue is competent enough to be considered adequate.

Most Wood aficionados credit producer and co-writer Alex Gordon with the film's higher quality. Gordon, who would later produce a number of highly-effective films for American International Pictures (AIP), seems to have reined in much of Wood's eccentricities for this film. What other reason can there be for this new-found competence? After all, this was four years before *Plan 9 from Outer Space* (1959), which in many ways exemplifies the worst of Wood's predilections.

But Wood being Wood, he cannot help himself from falling into a few of the old traps here. There is, of course, plenty of obvious stock footage "integration." Then there's the infamous inanimate rubber octopus, which the actors have to assist in their own deaths by waving its flaccid tentacles around to simulate movement.

The acting is typically bad in *Bride of the Monster* save for Bela Lugosi's performance as Dr. Eric Vornoff. Lugosi is actually quite watchable here. By this time Hollywood's forgotten boogeyman was addicted to morphine, ill, and more or less living off anything his burned out star status would afford him. According to Wood and many of his associates, Lugosi and Wood were the best of friends. However, Lugosi's family maintains that Wood simply capitalized on Lugosi's tragic circumstances. Whichever the case, it cannot be denied that Lugosi, though greatly diminished, throws himself wholeheartedly into the role of the mad, misunderstood doctor. He wrings as much over-the-top zeal as he can from his lines.

Who can forget the speech that Lugosi's Vornoff delivers to Professor Vladimir Strowski (George Becwar) as to why he won't return to his homeland? "Home? I have no home. Hunted, despised, living like an animal! The jungle is my home. But I will show the world that I can be its master! I will perfect my own race of people. A race of atomic supermen which will conquer the world! Ha, ha, ha, ha, ha, ha!" Who else could have given that speech the way Lugosi delivered it?

It's not a stretch to imagine Lugosi seeing a bit of himself in this role. Forgotten; washed up; living on scraps. However, unlike Vornoff, Lugosi would show the world that he wasn't quite finished. He had one more memorable performance left, and that's exactly what he gives here—one last truly remarkable turn.

One can easily picture Wood associating himself with Vornoff, as well. Like the mad doctor, Wood saw himself as a misunderstood genius exiled from the mainstream. Unfortunately, the similarities between Vornoff and Wood don't end there; most of Vornoff's experiments die on the table, and most of Wood's creations were stillborn, at best.

The lead actress, Loretta King, delivers her lines as Janet Lawton, brassy busy-body reporter, with all of the verve of a poorly-constructed text-to-speech application. King insisted that stories of her being cast by Wood in the hopes that she would finance the film are greatly exaggerated, but there is no evidence in her performance to indicate she had been cast for any reason remotely linked to having talent. Also atrocious is the male lead, Tony McCoy, who doubles as an associate producer. Unlike the Loretta King situation, no one denies that McCoy landed his role after his daddy agreed to bankroll the picture.

The film's story centers around Lugosi's mad scientist, Vornoff. After having his theories rejected and scoffed at in his own unnamed country, Vornoff has exiled himself from the outside world. He now lives in a ramshackle house in a "jungle hell" located just outside a small American town. It should be noted here that this jungle, also identified as a swamp, inhabited by dangerous rubber snakes and stock footage alligators, appears to be just a normal, run-of-the-mill wooded area. Exaggerated dialogue like "this swamp is a monument to death" are also fun.

Vornoff is assisted by Lobo (Tor Johnson), a monstrous hulk of a man the doctor "discovered in the wilderness of Tibet." Vornoff and Lobo kidnap whatever unfortunates happen to wander into their domain. (Twelve people have come up missing in only three months.) They then conduct experiments on their captives, with Vornoff attempting to create atomic supermen as "big as a giant" with the "strength of twenty men."

It's a riot to watch each victim wake up on a gurney with his or her hands strapped at their sides, wearing on their heads what has got to be the most guffaw-inducing prop of all time—*an aluminum salad bowl with three spark plugs on top, strung together with chicken wire*! This contraption also comes with a chin strap so that when the atomic ray beam is turned on, the victim can thrash fitfully and shake their head without dislodging the spark plug bowl.

As the film progresses, the intrepid Janet Lawton makes her way out to the old Willows place to investigate claims of a horrendous monster who lurks around a small pond, frequently referred to in the film as being a lake or marsh. (Wood actually names this small body of water Marsh Lake.) Lawton decides to conduct this investigation at night during a cataclysmic storm (naturally). She then wrecks her automobile near the house. Dazed and confused, she vacates the vehicle only to be menaced moments later by a large rubber python resting in a fake tree. Cue the stock footage of a snake slithering around on a dry tree branch in broad daylight. Thankfully for Lawton, Lobo just happens to be out wandering aimlessly around the lake, and saves her by smacking the rubber snake's head into the fake tree trunk.

Lobo delivers the unconscious reporter to his master, but keeps her angora hat for himself. He then pulls the fuzzy hat from his pocket throughout the film, stroking it in a sexually suggestive manner. Apparently Lobo, like Wood himself, has an angora fetish. Another what-the-hell moment occurs when Vornoff, weary of bantering with Lawton, waves his hand in front of her face (in a very Dracula-esque sort of way) and hypnotizes her to sleep. He then instructs Lobo to carry her to his chamber. This begs the question we're not sure we want the answer to—what do you suppose the evil doctor is going to do with that woman secreted away in his chambers? One shudders to think.

Tor Johnson is priceless in this film. He does what he always does, which is hulking around with his arms raised over his head, ready to wave somebody into submission at the earliest beckoning from Dr. Vornoff. But this time Tor really gets to emote. Mercifully, he has no dialogue. In *Bride of the Monster*, if he's not leering at Janet Lawton and pawing lasciviously at her fuzzy cap he's commiserating with Dr. Vornoff when another one of his experiments is lying dead on the table. This movie shows Tor at his most emotionally unhinged. Tor is sad; *very* sad. Tor is horny; Tor is *very* horny! Tor is in a rage! Yes, no Tor Johnson fan can walk away from this film without feeling like they've been on a seventy-minute emotional roller coaster.

Humorously, throughout the film the cops say they have combed the Marsh Lake area thoroughly, but somehow they failed to investigate the only house in the area, which is right next to the body of water. Vornoff also keeps an oversized atomically engineered octopus in the pond. It is, of course, unlikely that an octopus, atomic or otherwise, could survive in a freshwater pond, but this is an Ed Wood picture, so who cares?

Vornoff's laboratory is as crappy a creation as anything that appears in Wood's work. The tiny lab, made of obviously-fake stone, inexplicably contains a full kitchen. (Perhaps Vornoff wanted to be prepared in case he and Lobo got the munchies while experimenting on some poor unsuspecting townsfolk.) Perhaps cheesiest of all here is Vornoff's atomic ray gun, which is actually nothing more than a photograph enlarger.

Again, there is much to poke fun at here, but this is clearly one of Wood's most mature, most competent efforts. One wonders what Wood's legacy might have been had he continued collaborating with Alex Gordon. Instead of being remembered as one of the worst filmmakers in history, he might have been forgotten as just another of many boringly competent B-movie directors.

CREDITS: Producers: Donald E. McCoy; Tony McCoy; Edward D. Wood, Jr.; Director: Edward D. Wood, Jr.; Screenplay: Edward D. Wood, Jr.; Alex Gordon; Cinematographer: Ted Allan; William C. Thompson; Editor: Warren Adams; Igo Kantor.

CAST: Bela Lugosi (Dr. Eric Vornoff); Tor Johnson (Lobo); Tony McCoy (Lt. Dick Craig); Loretta King (Janet Lawton); Harvey B. Dunn (Capt. Tom Robbins); George Becwar (Prof. Vladimir Strowski); Paul Marco (Officer Kelton); Don Nagel (Det. Marty Martin); Bud Osborne (Lafe "Mac" McCrea); John Warren (Jake Long); Ann Wilner (Tillie); Dolores Fuller (Margie); William Benedict (Newsboy); Ben Frommer (Drunk).

The Violent Years (1956)

In many ways, *The Violent Years*, Edward D. Wood Jr.'s take on juvenile delinquency, tells us as much about the man behind the typewriter as any of his films. After watching this, one must conclude that Wood was somewhat of a conservative man (startling considering the number of pornographic films Wood would later make or be associated with). The plot of this film, which takes place in the real world, is perhaps even more ludicrous than the artist's most far-out science fiction fantasies. Wood obviously saw such mundane social infractions as ignoring common courtesies and a lack of carrying out the unspoken rules of general decency as being a slippery slope that could ultimately lead to crime, promiscuity, murder, and even affiliations with foreign Communist factions. His rather naïve take on these societal nuisances were clearly the fantasies of a paranoid, out-of-touch conservative. His simplistic assertion in the film that leading children "back to God" would ultimately put an end to juvenile delinquency (and, it is hinted, preserve the "American way") is equally naïve.

The Violent Years was the first film of Wood's career in which his screenplay would be shot by a director other than himself. Despite his absence from the director's chair, this film is ultimately as Woodian as anything he would helm himself. The film was directed by William Morgan, a filmmaker who had already directed a dozen or so films, but had made a name for himself as an editor on features such as the 1934 Bette Davis vehicle *Of Human Bondage*. It would also be Morgan's final film as director (read into that what you will). The film was based on an original story by B.L. Hart entitled *Killers*, and its working titles were *Girl Gang Terrorists* and *Teenage Girl Gang*.

The Violent Years stars former *Playboy* Playmate Jean Moorhead, who looks stunning here and turns in a surprisingly adequate performance. Although Moorhead had already appeared in a handful of motion pictures, this was her first credited appearance and she made the most of it. This is especially impressive considering the ridiculously bad/flat dialogue Wood puts in her mouth. Rounding out Moorhead's "gang" are actresses Theresa Hancock, Joanne Cangi, and Gloria Farr. For the most part, the cast does a remarkable job with what little they're given; wooden, yes, but not as profoundly horrific as performers in some of the other Wood entries (save for Bruno Metsa as Manny, who actually does a full flip in the air when he is punched by another character).

One thing about Wood's screenplay that is strange is that the gang consists of four girls who all have male nicknames (Paul, Phyll, Gerald, and George). This bizarre reversal of gender roles continues with the name of the male judge, Judge Clara. In other instances, a male character named Barney is referred to as a "sob sister" and female Paula (or "Paul") is referred to as a "guy." Wood's motivations for making these artistic choices is unclear (as many of Wood's decisions frequently were) but if the authors were to make suppositions we would guess that Wood intended to poke at the traditional roles of men and women and their conduct right under the noses of the censors, something like an inside joke that only Wood was aware of.

The film opens with a scene from the end of the picture in which Judge Clara (veteran character actor I. Stanford Jolley) gives a stern lecture to Paula's "incompetent" parents, as well as the viewing audience, which is the first of many heavy-handed Ed Wood public service announcements he will deliver in the film. Clara explains that a lack of love and attention can and will lead to juvenile delinquency, which, again, can then lead to such societal no-nos as cop killing, sexual promiscuity, and of course Communism. To say that Wood (and Judge Clara) oversimplifies matters a bit here would be a massive understatement, but this opening provides us with a glimpse of what we're in for during the next hour and five minutes.

After Clara provides us with the opening scolding soliloquy, we see beautiful honors student and would-be class president Paula Parkins talking with her mother (Barbara Weeks). During the casual conversation, Wood provides dialogue that less than subtly informs us that Paula's parents are too busy to pay close attention to her day-to-day activities. (And what are these awful so-and-so's doing that's so important? Is her mother a tramp who has lost herself in alcohol and low life men? No, her mother is busy with charities to feed hungry children! and her father? Well, he is busy working long hours as a newspaper publisher so that he may feed his family! Such terrible parents, indeed!)

Proving to be a hilarious contrast, Paula is sugary sweet during the conversation with her mother, but then turns icy and businesslike once her mother leaves the room. The light and schmaltzy stock music abruptly changes to something more menacing to let us know (in case we somehow missed it) that we are now witnessing a darker side of young Paula. She picks up the telephone, makes a call, and brusquely informs her criminal cohorts that she will see them soon so they may go and rob a gas station together.

The four beautiful young ladies take Paula's mother's car and rob a gas station at gunpoint. As if this scene isn't silly enough, one of the young ladies strikes the gas station attendant over the head, nearly killing him; never mind the fact that the girl couldn't possibly weigh more than a hundred pounds and wouldn't have the strength to bash a grown man's head in...

The audience is then given an update as to the health status of the gas station attendant, and also the police department's tracking of the young girls, through a conversation between newspaper reporter Barney (Glenn Corbett—and no, not the famous Glenn Corbett) and police Lt. Holmes (played by Timothy Farrell of Wood favorites *Glen or Glenda?*, 1953, and *Jail Bait*, 1954). Barney then reports back to his editor, who just happens to be Paula's father, played by Art Millan).

In one of the film's more absurd scenes, the girl gang drives up on a young couple necking in a car at Lover's Lane. The girls then harass the young couple, waving pistols in their faces. "Ain't love something?" they ask sarcastically. The surly girl gang then forces the woman to disrobe so they can steal her sweater and bound and gag her with her own skirt.

As if all of this weren't enough, the four girls then force the man into the woods so they can rape him. The young man is (naturally) horrified at the thought of being raped by a pack of gorgeous eighteen-year-old women, but goes along with their plans. *Really*?! Who in the world has ever heard of instance in which four model-esque young women (one of whom is a *Playboy* Playmate!) raped some sad sack in the woods at gunpoint? This makes no sense. This simply doesn't happen. Obviously Wood is trying to shock us here (and again he tries to switch the conventional roles of attacker and victim), but this scene is so bizarrely ridiculous that one can't help but laugh. Rape is a very serious, very unfunny thing. So leave it to Ed Wood to inadvertently make a mockery of it. This is yet another instance of Wood the outsider not really being grounded in the reality of the real world. Then one must also consider the innocence of the period in which this film was made and the audience's gullibility to believe such nonsense. This scene probably seemed quite shocking in 1956.

Here director Morgan utilizes one of Wood's favorite cinematic devices—a newspaper headline which boldly reads: "YOUNG MAN ROBBED, CRIMINALLY ATTACKED BY FOUR GIRLS!" There is, however, one key difference between William Morgan's use of this device and Wood's own; unlike in Wood's films, this film actually uses a newspaper with a full story about the girls' crime rather than a fake headline pasted on top of a real story. And again, this isn't mentioned to lampoon Wood's work, but rather to point out the type of cheapjack cheesiness that endears his work to so many people today. Whatever deficiencies he had as a filmmaker, there can be no denying that Wood was a genius at creating "his" type of motion picture. Numerous attempts have been made to copy Wood's style, and all of them fail miserably; only Wood was capable of creating a true Ed Wood picture, be it as a screenwriter or as a director.

We soon learn that Paula's father will not be able to be present for her birthday. She quietly laments this, never realizing the irony in that her own actions as a criminal are the very reason he must now work extra hours at the newspaper. (As an editor, her father is hell-bent on covering every one of these incidents as they occur.) Her mother will also miss her birthday as she has a charitable function to attend. We will later learn that Paula's "awful" parents only give her a brand new convertible for her birthday present. But this doesn't make her happy. No, Paula yearns for what every teenager yearns for... Hell no, she doesn't want a new car. What she wants is attention from her parents...

Let's be honest here: real-life teenagers by definition are self-centered and materialistic, and hanging out with their parents isn't exactly their idea of a swell time. This instance, again, is proof that Wood's views and beliefs were out of touch from reality. Given the number of films on Wood's filmography, it may be safe here to assume that he spent all of his time writing films rather than experiencing life. If this was indeed the case, then it stands to reason that Wood's artistic output would be as detached from the real world as he himself was.

Gang leader Paula soon does what any self-respecting criminal would do—she questions her father about what evidence the police have under the guise of hoping to one day stamp out juvenile delinquency when she becomes class president. So dad, being the naive softy that he is, tells her that the police plan to stakeout all of the gas stations open past ten p.m. This leads Paula to inform her gang that the "cops have pulled a sneak." The group then decides to stop robbing gas stations for the moment.

When Paula and the gang go to visit Sheila (Lee Constant), their fence, they smoke and drink, showing 1950s audiences that they really were bad characters indeed. Sheila threatens to blackmail the girls when they balk at the amount of money she offers them for their stolen goods, but they turn the tables on her and convince her to pay more. A booze-swilling Paula then brags that it's "the thrill [of crime] that gets me."

Sheila then informs Paula that she has "a connection who doesn't like schools." She goes on to imply that the group is comprised of foreign Communists and that they are willing to pay big money in exchange for the girls' vandalizing classrooms and tossing American flags on the ground. This is, of course, ridiculous, and goes to show just how paranoid and uneducated Americans (and, in this case, Ed Wood) were at that time regarding Communism. Why would Communists care if a classroom is vandalized? Presumably to destroy the American way of life, which is silly to say the least. No further motives are ever given, and the girls happily go forward to destroy a couple of classrooms.

But not before they've had a pajama party. As Paula's parents are away for the evening, these seemingly innocent young girls will drink, smoke, and make out with older men. This is the scene in which a character is punched, and then does a flip in the air before crashing to the ground. Who was this guy with such a knockout blow, you ask? Was it Mike Tyson or some great boxer of the 1950s? Not hardly. No, it's a scrawny little reporter buddy of Paula's father's. The scene is truly goofy, and a hell of a lot of fun to observe. Actor Bruno Metsa's reaction to the punch is as poorly acted as any of those melodramatic death scenes you've seen in a million bad movies. It's a sight to behold. It should be taught as a "what not to do" at acting schools around the world.

So the girls go and break into their high school to ransack the place. They even go so far as to erase the blackboards (!), and we know at once that they mean business. One of the girls exclaims, "I'm gonna smash everything in this joint!" As the girls are having quite a time destroying things, the cops show up and a shootout takes place (yes, you read that correctly) between the girls and the law enforcement officers. "Look at 'em jump!" one girl says. "Just like rabbits!" But then things predictably get out of hand and two of the girls and one police officer are killed in the ruckus.

When the police lieutenant sees one of the dead girls, he says sorrowfully, "I've seen dozens like her." Really, Ed Wood? Dozens like her? When exactly did this epidemic of pretty young girls getting in shootouts with police officers take place in the 1950s? Oh yeah, it didn't. This is once again an instance of Wood having preposterous ideas about what exactly went on outside of his drawn curtains. And again, that's not a knock; this is just one of the many reasons one can't help but adore the man's work.

The girls escape and head for Sheila's house to get their money for vandalizing the school. Things quickly go south, however, and Paula murders Sheila in cold blood.

Paula keeps complaining about having cramps. Perhaps no one in 1956 could guess what is being foreshadowed here, but contemporary audiences will see this "shocker" coming a mile away... Paula and her one remaining cohort crash in an automobile accident fleeing from police, and hey, guess what? It turns out that Paula is pregnant! And she doesn't know who the father is! And she's going to have her baby in prison!

Well, this being a crime movie from the 1950s, *The Violent Years* obviously becomes somewhat of a morality play with a blatant anti-crime message tacked on the ending. Here the message is delivered (again) by Judge Clara, who lectures Paula's parents for raising a criminal. The judge will then go on to deliver a ten-minute spiel (it may have only been five minutes, but it feels like ten) about proper parenting and how praying to God is the only thing that can ultimately put an end to all of this madness.

Paula is then sentenced to life in prison. She has her baby, but of course dies in childbirth, which one senses the screenwriter found fitting. Paula's last words ("SO WHAT?") can be seen as the summation of what Ed Wood fears all female teens will adopt as their motto if not shown the proper attention, made to say their prayers and eat their vitamins. (If only parenting were so easy!) After all, in the minds of upright citizens of the 1950s (and apparently Ed Wood himself), women who act like whores should die for their sins. It's all just part of that slippery slope.

CREDITS: Producer: Roy Reid; Director: William Morgan; Screenplay: Edward D. Wood, Jr.; Cinematographer: William C. Thompson; Editor: unknown.

CAST: Jean Moorhead (Paula Parkins); Barbara Weeks (Jane Parkins); Art Millan (Carl Parkins); Theresa Hancock (Georgia); Joanne Cangi (Geraldine); Gloria Farr (Phyllis); Glenn Corbett (Barney Stetson); Lee Constant (Sheila); I. Stanford Jolley (Judge Clara); Timothy Farrell (Lt. Holmes); F. Chan McClure (Det. Artman); Bruno Metsa (Manny); Harry Keaton (Doctor).

The Bride and the Beast (1958)

Coming two years after *The Violent Years* (1956), *The Bride and the Beast* was just the second screenplay Edward D. Wood, Jr. wrote for another director. This time out the script would be for veteran producer Adrian Weiss. Weiss wanted to make his feature directorial debut with a film he envisioned about a woman and her strange attraction to a gorilla. Wood was then brought in to pen the script based on Weiss' story idea.

The Bride and the Beast is an interesting film, especially in terms of Wood's involvement. The screenplay is easily one of Wood's finest in terms of dialogue. Gone is the clunkiness and redundancy normally associated with Wood's writing. In fact, the writing is actually quite competent; so much so that one must wonder if another writer had a hand in the screenplay. If anything, it's the ridiculously fantastic storyline that seems the most Woodian, and that was conceived by Weiss. The film's pacing is extremely slow in places, but Weiss' direction is more to blame than Wood's screenplay. *The Bride and the Beast* may well be Wood's finest screenplay. That's not to say it's good, but it is competent in a way that is unusual in a Wood-scripted film.

The film opens with Dan (Lance Fuller) and Laura (Charlotte Austin) Fuller on their wedding day. Once Laura arrives at her new home, she is informed that a huge gorilla named Spanky lives in the basement. (Why didn't she know this previously? Just how long did Dan and Laura date before tying the knot?) But Laura doesn't mind; she grew up with a pet monkey who treated her just like family.

"He's beautiful," gasps Laura the first time she sees the gorilla. Spanky, clearly a man donning a fake-looking gorilla suit with a plastic face, immediately falls in love with Laura. (Spanky was played by actor Steve Calvert, who made a career out of playing gorillas; *The Bride and the Beast* was the tenth motion picture in which he appeared as a gorilla.) He pulls her close to his cage and gently strokes her hair. This alarms Dan, who whisks her away from the gorilla and explains to her that Spanky is a savage creature capable of killing her. Laura, obviously feeling some sort of unnatural attraction to the animal, is left in a daze. Having had his love interest pulled from his arms, Spanky becomes enraged and begins destroying everything inside his cage. (When he bumps into the wall of his cage, it moves, revealing that it's a set wall.)

It's beginning to storm outside. Inside their wedding night bedroom, Dan is thinking about making love to his wife. Laura, however, is concerned about the well-being of the gorilla. "Do you think Spanky is afraid of the storm?" she asks. Dan tells her no and redirects her to a bout of unseen lovemaking. The two of them then return to their own beds (this was the '50s, kiddies, so Dan and Laura have separate beds) and fall fast asleep. Once she's asleep, Laura begins to dream about the gorilla.

Meanwhile, back downstairs Spanky is still enraged. In a fit of rage he bends the bars to his cage and escapes. He then makes his way up the stairs just as Laura wakes up. Spanky enters the room. Laura doesn't scream to wake Dan. The gorilla stares at her lovingly and begins to paw at her nightgown. He then tears it off of her just as Dan awakens. (Wood would later revisit the theme of gorilla male/human female sexuality in the film *One Million AC/DC*, 1969.) Dan pulls out a pistol and fires three times at point blank range into Spanky's chest, sending him reeling out into the hallway and crashing down through the railing to his death.

The whole "Spanky affair" leaves Laura feeling sad. She begins to experience *déjà vu* and explains that she feels like she has experienced all of this before. Once she goes back to sleep, Laura starts dreaming about stock footage jungle animals and has an epiphany that perhaps she was a gorilla in a past life. "Do you think we can come back after death?" she asks. Dan has no answers, but says he will bring family friend and psychiatrist Dr. Carl Reiner (William Justine) over to see her. (This character is probably not named after the famed writer and director of the same name. Having only written for the television show *Caesar's Hour* by 1958, it's unlikely Wood or Weiss would have known who he was.)

Reiner explains that he would like to hypnotize Laura. She believes hypnotism to be a silly party trick, but nonetheless agrees. Before putting her under hypnosis, Reiner explains, "Now in hypnotism we have things which lead us to believe that we have outlived many life spans. We might find through hypnosis where your dreams come from." He then puts her under and Laura starts to talk about her fascination with angora sweaters (natch!), explaining that they are "soft like kittens." Reiner says he is going to "send her back in time" and puts her into a deeper sleep. In her hypnotic state, Laura sees (stock footage of) leopards, zebras, and snakes. Then she sees giraffes and notes that they are all running away. "All the animals run when I'm near," Laura observes. She goes to a body of water and looks into it, seeing her own reflection. At this point she realizes she was indeed a gorilla. Just as she comes to this realization, two aborigines shoot her with a poisoned dart and kill her.

Before waking Laura, Reiner reiterates to Dan that she was likely a gorilla in a past life. "Her fixation for fur-like materials points to that," he explains. Dan just shrugs this off, choosing not to believe such a thing is possible. He declares that he and Laura are going on their honeymoon one way or the other. But where could they be going? Why, to a jungle safari in Africa, of course! And they will be accompanied by Dan's African man-servant, Taro (Johnny Roth). (Humorously, Taro is played by a white man pretending to be a black man who speaks like a Chinese man! Throughout the film Taro will speak in Charlie Chan-like "me-go-now" broken English.)

Weiss then treats us to stock footage of an airplane flying over the pyramids. Once Dan and Laura have arrived safely in Africa, they set up camp, where Dan manages to kill a mismatched stock footage tarantula just before it can bite Laura.

It's here that the film disappoints and begins to drag severely. Weiss, although much more accomplished with using appropriate stock footage, rivals Ed Wood with his overabundant use of it (there is more in this film than in Wood's *Glen or Glenda?*). The audience is made to suffer through scene after scene of people trudging through the jungle. At one point Laura exclaims, "Just one week and I feel as though I've always been here." The audience now has some idea of what's going on with Laura, but dumb Dan still can't put two and two together.

It soon comes to Dan's attention that a pair of man-eating Indian tigers is on the loose in "gorilla country." (As soon as we hear "gorilla country" we know something bad is going to happen.) Naturally Dan decides to drag his new wife out deeper into the jungle to hunt these dangerous man-eaters.

In one scene, Dan displays his uncanny fighting skills by fist-fighting a (sometimes stock footage, sometimes fake-looking) tiger. Somehow Dan manages to overcome the creature, apparently bitch slapping it to death. Later, after Laura is carried away by another gorilla, Dan will attempt to fist-fight said gorilla, but this time to no avail. Dan is knocked out cold and the gorilla carries Laura off to his lair. (Again, this scene is extremely similar to a scene in *One Million AC/DC*.) When Dan awakens, he somehow knows just where to go. When he enters the cave, he finds Laura acting like a gorilla and surrounded by two of the creatures. He once again tries to fist-fight a gorilla, but is once again knocked unconscious. Laura, now regressed into a gorilla-like human, is carried away by the prize-fight-winning gorilla.

In an abrupt and silly ending we learn that Dan left Africa without his wife and has never seen her since. Dr. Reiner again explains, "That she had been a gorilla in a past life seems rather positive."

And the film ends.

What the hell have we just seen? Did that really happen, or was this some kind of weird fever dream?

For the first ten or fifteen minutes we're led into believing that Laura and Spanky are going to have some forbidden weird-as-Wood romance, but then Spanky is killed just when the weird is getting good! That's a shame. An Ed Wood-scripted love triangle between these three characters would have been pure Edward D. Wood, Jr. gold. Instead, Wood veers off into a tepid wannabe jungle adventure/travelogue. Ah, what could have been...

Again it must be noted that while the film is boring and plodding, it is coherent in a way that most of Wood's films are not. The acting is at times a little bit leaden, but Charlotte Austin turns in a believable performance (as believable as a woman in love with a gorilla can be) as Laura Fuller. Despite the film's competency, Weiss would never direct another motion picture.

CREDITS: Producer: Adrian Weiss; Director: Adrian Weiss; Screenplay: Edward D. Wood, Jr.; Cinematographer: Roland Price; Editor: George M. Merrick.

CAST: Charlotte Austin (Laura Carson Fuller); Lance Fuller (Dan Fuller); Taro (Johnny Roth); William Justine (Dr. Carl Reiner); Gil Frye (Capt. Cameron); Jeanne Gerson (Marka); Trustin Howard (Messenger); Eva Brent (Stewardess); Bhogwan Singh (Man Killed by Tiger); Steve Calvert (Gorilla), Bobby Small (Gorilla #2).

Plan 9 from Outer Space (1959)

Everyone has heard of films labeled as being "so bad that they're good." Originally titled *Grave Robbers from Outer Space*, the 1959 sci-fi thriller *Plan 9 from Outer Space* is the granddaddy of them all. The film, which features horror movie host Maila "Vampira" Nurmi, professional wrestler Tor Johnson, the not-so-psychic Criswell, and Bela Lugosi (in what is sort of his final film role), is Ed Wood's magnum opus. He often stated that this film was his favorite, and the one he always wanted to be remembered for. Wood's wish was, of course, granted, but in true Woodian fashion, he misjudged just *how* he and his films would be regarded.

The cast, the budget, and Ed Wood himself as writer, director, and editor formed a perfect conglomeration of imperfection that critics and fans alike have hailed as an "anti-masterpiece," "the worst film ever made," "a triumph of will over talent," and "high art through sheer incompetence." We believe that this $60,000 film is truly all of those things—except the worst film ever made! There are plenty of films that deserve the moniker "worst film of all time" more than *Plan 9*. Small budgets and bad actors and poorly-written scripts don't necessarily make a film bad. One thing that does kill an audience is boredom; you can have all the talent and all the stars and all the money imaginable, and if your movie doesn't *entertain* then it will truly be bad. Put simply, we love *Plan 9 from Outer Space* because it's unpretentious, entertaining, and filled with the naivety of a man who simply couldn't or wouldn't accept his lack of talent as a roadblock to making his dreams come true.

At the beginning of the film, we see emblazoned "CRISWELL PREDICTS" so we know that the narrator on the screen is the "Amazing" Criswell, a syndicated newspaper columnist of outlandish predictions and minor Los Angeles celebrity at the time *Plan 9* was made. So, is he supposed to be *predicting* the events of the movie? Are we not supposed to guess that the onscreen Criswell is in any way related to the off-screen Criswell? And then there is Maila "Vampira" Nurmi, fresh off her stint as Vampira, a Los Angeles horror host. She attracted quite a fan following for Vampira and even received a photo spread in *Life* magazine, so she was well known and certainly her character Vampira was well known to TV viewing audiences of the day. Was Nurmi playing Vampira's zombie or another ghoul that just happened to dress exactly like the famed horror TV host?

A bizarre (and under-reported) aspect of *Plan 9* is the cast members who could actually act! Look at the talent that Ed Wood was able to round up for this mixed-up, no-budget extravaganza: Gregory Walcott, a steady character actor who would go on to appear in *Sugarland Express* for Steven Spielberg; Bela Lugosi, the man who essayed the original and best-remembered Dracula, and who, sadly enough, was at the end of his career and the end of his life, and Lyle Talbot, a star of many, many B-movies and serials in the 1930s and 1940s who simply ran out of time and luck. Even though these performers were sliding into the Hollywood abyss, there's no question that they could all still act and act well if given the proper scripts and direction.

All of the Woodian trademarks abound in this film: unconvincing, minimalist sets, inane, redundant dialogue, extremely amateurish acting, and tons of stock footage badly integrated into the body of the film. Home viewers participating in a drinking game would quickly drink themselves into a coma were they to attempt imbibing each time something goes askew on screen.

The film's most absurd moment is difficult to pinpoint. Perhaps the pilots flying in the obviously makeshift airplane cockpit (with a decidedly unneeded protractor hanging on the wall) is the film's most ridiculous moment. We can imagine Wood looking at a "set" and saying, "What this set *really* needs is more black curtains! We need them in the airplane. We need them at the police station, we need them *everywhere!*"

Or maybe it's the standoff between the aliens and the cops inside the space ship (also adorned with the same unneeded protractor), where a character responds to the alien's claim that humans are stupid brutes by promptly punching said alien in the face.

Another favorite scene takes place in the jerry-rigged cemetery, partially filmed in a small and most unglamorous cemetery in Sylmar, CA, and partially captured on a lucky sound stage. Wooden (or are they cardboard?) headstones fall over when the characters bump into them, the studio-generated "ground" wrinkles and ruffles as it's walked on, and the cemetery's sole mausoleum also appears to be constructed from particle board. Slow-moving ghouls easily elude the cops, and the dead Inspector Clay (played by the hilariously poor-acting Tor Johnson) finds difficulty in climbing out from his grave.

Neither Criswell nor John "Bunny" Breckinridge (nor Wood himself, for that matter) make even the slightest attempts to conceal the fact that they are reading their lines from notes and cue cards.

Strings are visible on the flying UFO models, which somehow look like even less than models, making way for the oft-reported rumors that they were actually hubcaps or trashcan lids.

Perhaps no element of *Plan 9* requires more suspension of disbelief than the marriage of Bela Lugosi and Vampira, who were about forty years apart in age. One might deduce that Vampira's character was only in this relationship for the old man's money, but judging from his crappy tract house (ironically, the real-life home of Tor Johnson, in San Fernando, CA), he doesn't appear to be all that rich.

Also ridiculously fun is Vampira's killing of the gravediggers. She inexplicably kills them from twenty feet away, simply by raising her arms in their general direction. It must also be pointed out that she appears in the darkness of night while it's still broad daylight (a few feet away) where the gravediggers are.

Another hilariously silly scene finds two police officers trying to overcome Inspector Clay, who is now one of the undead. When they learn that Clay is impervious to bullets, they wisely decide to sneak up on him (while he conveniently stands completely still, of course) and hit him over the head with a piece of wood. This would seem to be akin to throwing the revolver at Superman after bouncing all your bullets off his chest. But, in this case, the maneuver works! The deceased Inspector Clay immediately pitches over unconscious.

(If you're dead and being remotely controlled by a ray gun, is it even possible to be unconscious?)

The very plan around which the film is centered (Plan Nine, of course) does not hold up to any sort of logic. The plan calls for the resurrection of the recently dead to destroy humanity. Okay, well, apparently resurrecting just an old man, a fat man, and an anorexic woman is enough ghoul power to lay the human population to waste since there is never any effort to bring back more than those three dearly departed slaves.

Then there's the nutty weapon known as solarbonite (pronounced differently by everyone in the cast who says it)—an as-yet undiscovered particle that explodes sunlight and anything sunlight has touched. It is so fearsome that it could potentially destroy the entire universe and everything within it. Surely this is the craziest, most Woodian weapon ever conceived.

The dialogue is nonsensical and wooden (as are most of the actors' performances). For example, the Air Force captain says, "Visits? That would indicate visitors." This obvious observation is far from the only such comment in Wood's world. Another example of this flair for the obvious is Lieutenant Harper's observation that Clay is "dead, murdered...and somebody's responsible."

Criswell is given many of the film's most memorably inane lines in narration. He stares over the camera at his cue cards and delivers his completely incomprehensible speech in the style of a deranged newscaster with the mad zeal of a southern preacher on Sunday night. What the hell is he talking about? "Future events such as these will affect you in the future!" What? He goes on to say that the guilty should be punished and the innocent rewarded. Okay, the guilty are dead! How much more punishment do they need?

The narrator delivers another idiotic gem when he says, "Perhaps, on your way home, someone will pass you in the dark and you will never know it...for they will be from outer space!"

At one point in the film, the pilot's wife asks, "A flying saucer? You mean the kind from up there?" As if this question wasn't bizarre enough, he answers, "Yeah, either that or its counterpart." Well, what exactly is its counterpart? And why does the pilot describe the UFOs as looking like cigars when they clearly look like saucers?

When Colonel Edwards explains that the aliens once attacked a town, he pooh-poohs it by saying, "A small town, I'll admit, but nevertheless a town of people...people who died." This marginalization of the attack makes little sense. Would the deaths have been more important had they taken place in, say, New York City or Los Angeles?

Despite the ridiculous dialogue, one can't help but wonder if Wood isn't trying, in his own bizarre way, to produce a heartfelt commentary on what he saw as man's need for violence and his sad predilection for war. It certainly wouldn't be the first time Wood made a biographical statement. (Wood himself had endured the grisly realities of war as a Marine in WWII. Wood is said to have been a model soldier and a vicious fighter. He suffered several injuries in WWII, including having many of his teeth bashed out from being struck with the butt of an enemy rifle and having his leg disfigured by gunfire.)

The most important element in this madman's artistic stew and the one that is essential to understanding and loving both Ed Wood and *Plan 9 from Outer Space*—is the passion and earnestness the man felt regarding his creation. *Plan 9* wasn't just some movie he was slapping together to earn a quick buck; it was his vision and his legacy. Wood was like a nine-year-old boy making films in his backyard with his friends. The acting wasn't important. The budget wasn't important. Nothing was important but getting the vision out of his head and onto the screen for audiences to see and appreciate, quality be damned. That purity of heart and motive is apparent in every single frame of *Plan 9*.

When Wood looked at *Plan 9* he could apparently see nothing out of place. Like most madmen, he was completely blinded by his passion for the project and didn't have the capacity to look at his film objectively. Either that, or Wood could possibly have felt that the telling of this story superseded any potential flaws in the final product.

Ed Wood was undoubtedly a guerrilla filmmaker before guerrilla filmmaking was cool. Guerrilla-style filmmaking has been defined as passionate filmmaking with whatever means is at hand, and that perfectly describes *any* Wood production. One of his mantras was "Get it done!" Obviously, Wood liked "getting it done" as fast as he could complete a take. Where many films since *Plan 9* have attempted to recreate the delirious hilarity of Wood's movies by producing something intentionally campy, Wood's creations—particularly *Plan 9*—were far more than camp. Is there any doubt that Wood actually believed these were high-quality works of art? It's because he had absolutely no sense of humor regarding his films that they succeed; Wood's ignorance to their absurdity simultaneously induces both sympathy and laughter from audiences.

The few scenes in Tim Burton's biopic *Ed Wood* that duplicate scenes from *Plan 9* revel in their ludicrousness. To the uninitiated, these would seem to be the highlights of the original film's ridiculousness, but in truth Burton barely scratches the surface. The original *Plan 9 from Outer Space* features so much more silliness; it is a relentless barrage of glorious cinematic atrocities. Much of the fun of watching the film comes from the ever-present reflection on the impossibly serious motives of the filmmaker behind it. One can't help but wonder exactly what Wood was thinking when he made many of the bizarre decisions in making the film. One wonders how the screenwriter/director could have been so blind as to not see the films for what they truly were. And while we as viewers feel sorry for Wood's naivety, we also rejoice in it. What could have easily been standard, forgettable fare is here elevated to something of a schlock masterpiece.

Wood's naivety is particularly on display in his hiring of Bela Lugosi's double. After Lugosi died in 1956, Wood realized that he still had some silent footage featuring the deceased actor. Wood then conceived a "Lugosi starrer" constructed around that surviving footage. The writer/director hired a chiropractor/drinking buddy named Tom Mason to work as Lugosi's double. The only problem? Mason looked absolutely nothing like the dead icon. But Wood being Wood, he of course had a solution for this—Mason would cover his face with a cape in all of his scenes. Never mind the fact that even the top of Mason's head looks nothing like Lugosi's. In Wood's mind, it was pitch-perfect. Humorously, many viewers fail to realize that both actors are supposed to be the same character since they look so completely different.

Another behind-the-scenes story that is every bit as funny as what appears on the screen finds Wood famously convincing his landlord's church to finance *Plan 9 from Outer Space*'s seven-day shooting schedule. This, he convinced them, would make them enough money that they could then produce a series of religious films. Wood even agreed to have himself and the film's entire cast baptized in exchange for the funding.

Watching *Plan 9 from Outer Space* is a delirious viewing experience from start to finish. One can't help but be slightly embarrassed for Wood and the actors onscreen, yet morbidly fascinated by the thought of how much worse it might get as this seventy-eight-minute slow motion car wreck of a film plays out before our stunned eyes. Who could watch *Plan 9* and not find a chuckle or twelve in it? From the film's day-for-night issues to the visible boom mic in the terribly makeshift airplane cockpit, the film is, much like its creator, truly one of a kind.

CREDITS: Producers: Edward D. Wood, Jr., J. Edward Reynolds, Charles Burg, Hugh Thomas, Jr.; Director: Edward D. Wood, Jr.; Screenplay: Edward D. Wood, Jr.; Cinematographer: William C. Thompson; Editor: Edward D. Wood, Jr.

CAST: Gregory Walcott (Jeff Trent); Mona McKinnon (Paula Trent); Duke Moore (Lt. Harper); Tom Keene (Col. Edwards); Carl Anthony (Patrolman Larry); Paul Marco (Patrolman Kelton); Tor Johnson (Inspector Clay); Dudley Manlove (Eros); Joanna Lee (Tanna); John Breckinridge (Ruler); David De Mering (Danny); Norma McCarty (Edith); Bill Ash (Captain); Lynn Lemon (Reverend Lemon); Gloria Dea (Girl); Conrad Brooks (Policeman Jamie); Maila "Vampira" Nurmi (Vampire Girl); Bela Lugosi (Ghoul Man); Criswell (Narrator).

Night of the Ghouls (1959)

By the end of the 1950s, Ed Wood was starting to show signs of fatigue. The disappointments and failures were piling up and, by all accounts, excessive alcohol consumption was beginning to take its toll on him. Whereas Wood had started the decade with an exuberance for filmmaking that can be seen even in a cinematic travesty like *Glen or Glenda?* (1953), he ended it with a half-hearted effort that many consider the beginning of the end for Wood's "career." When Wood found himself unable to pay the costs of the film processing lab, he chose to walk away from the film entirely. (It would be another twenty-three years before the film would be salvaged.) Surely this is more proof of Wood's sense of defeat by this point. Considering how much we know about Wood's passion for his earlier projects, it's difficult to imagine him abandoning those.

Like the previous Wood efforts, *Night of the Ghouls* is a bad film. This one, however, is a less fun type of bad. Where Wood's love for his projects showed through even when his artistry fell short on previous projects, one clearly gets the sense that this film was more of a labor for Wood than a labor of love.

This isn't to say *Night of the Ghouls* isn't without trademark Woodian moments. The film, a sort of sequel to *Bride of the Monster* (1955) and *Plan 9 from Outer Space* (1959), once again takes place in the little shanty by the side of the lake. Of course the ramshackle house was blown to pieces at the end of *Bride of the Monster*, but this is an Edward D. Wood, Jr. production and such things as story continuity have no place here. We are told early on in the film that the house was rebuilt. Humorously, the house looks nothing like the previous house and it looks rather old. Despite this, police Lt. Bradford will later remark that he remembers the interior of the house well from the previous episode—a film his character wasn't even in! (Duke Moore appears in both films, but plays Lt. Harper in *Plan 9*.)

Gone (and sorely missed) is Bela Lugosi, but Tor Johnson's Lobo remains. And gone is the (sometimes rubber, sometimes stock footage) octopus from *Bride of the Monster*. Adding to the confusion, the body of water formerly known as Marsh Lake is now called Willows Lake. But again, this is an Ed Wood picture, so who cares?

Criswell once again returns, decked out in his finest suit and coffin, once again obviously reading from cue cards and making no attempt to hide the fact. And once again Criswell's mouth is filled with deliciously ridiculous dialogue. Interestingly, Wood recycles the nonsensical line "more than fact" from *Glen or Glenda?*. Wood would also recycle the Criswell's declaration here that these are "monsters to be pitied, monsters to be despised" in *Orgy of the Dead*. (A variation of the line also turns up in the Wood short *Final Curtain*.) It's likely that Wood believed no one would ever know considering *Night of the Ghouls* was still sitting somewhere in a film laboratory gathering dust. But like Wood's posthumous career, the film would ultimately be resurrected to enjoy a new-found glory.

Other ridiculous dialogue in the film includes the line that the events which transpire are a "nightmare of horrors," which is of course redundant. Later, when Paul Marco's returning character Kelton the Cop reports that he has seen a ghost, he is asked, "Who's been spiking your beet juice?" Bradford, played by veteran actor Moore, also has a few terrible lines. First he observes that "the ringing of the staircase is so much louder at night than the day"—a statement that makes no sense whatsoever. Then, only moments later, he will take mental inventory of the items in a storeroom, which is obviously a closet in the film studio where Wood was shooting the picture. Items in the closet include lighting equipment, props, scenery, sets, and an old organ. He then concludes, "Now what a theater group could do with these!" This is a non sequitur moment, but Wood's usage of whatever was lying around at the time is both ingenious and hilarious.

In one scene it is noted that it's rather cold in Inspector Robbins' (Johnny Carpenter) office, to which it is then observed that "maybe he's got a cold problem." What exactly does this mean? Who knows?

As stated previously, Paul Marco's character returns in this installment, and Marco gives his worst performance of the three films. Humorously, Marco's Kelton the Cop exclaims, "Monsters! Space people! Mad doctors! They didn't teach me about such things in the police academy!" Here Kelton is played for laughs much more than he is in the other films; he's apparently lost about 100 IQ points since we last saw him, and everyone on the police department seems to hate him for no discernible reason. (Maybe it was his lack of acting talent that got everyone peeved at him.)

When an elderly couple is driving down the road, there are different shades of darkness (sometimes gray, sometimes pitch black) in the same scene. Also, the old man turns his steering wheel back and forth as a child with a toy car might, but the automobile continues to drive in a straight line. They then see a woman wearing white and immediately know that she is a ghost. Since she's not floating, transparent, or making any noise whatsoever, one must wonder how exactly the couple knows this. Needless to say, the elderly couple is terrified.

Night of the Ghouls features the same harsh lighting that appears in all of Wood's films, casting looming shadows following the characters' every movement. The dialogue is frequently silly, the same old day-for-night issues pop up, and the acting performances are as poor as in any of Wood's films. However, not all of the acting here is bad. Charismatic journeyman cowboy Kenne Duncan, an actor Wood had previously collaborated with on the short films *Crossroad Avenger: The Adventures of the Tucson Kid* and *Trick Shooting with Kenne Duncan*, is actually quite good in his turn as Dr. Acula. (Get it? *Dr-acula*? Not only is this cheesy, but the film has absolutely nothing to do with vampires, so why use the name?) In fact, Duncan's performance ranks as one of the very finest to be found in Wood's body of work.

Moore's Lt. Bradford plans to go to the opera, but is instead rerouted to the old shack by the lake. So Bradford goes to investigate these presumably supernatural occurrences donning a tuxedo and tails. One might wonder why Wood chose to have the police officer performing his duties in a tux, but the answer is fairly simple; some of the footage of Moore originated in the then-unseen Wood short *Final Curtain*. (Wood biographer Rudolph Grey believes Wood also used footage from the now-lost short *Night of the Banshee* here.)

The police station is a comedy of errors. A wanted poster bearing Wood's own publicity photo hangs on the wall. It stands out because the poster looks fake and is apparently the only one hanging in the entire station. This minor detail is important to note because it would seem to be one of the only times in Wood's body of work that he didn't take himself so seriously. Then there's Inspector Robbins' name plate on the door. Except it isn't exactly a name plate—it's his name scrawled on a piece of tape. Also hilarious (and just one more indicator that Wood was really not trying his hardest with this particular film) is the fact that the inspector's office door has no doorknob. (Careful observers will also note that this same set door lacking a doorknob later appears inside the lake house.)

In one scene Duncan's character is said to be forty years old even though the actor was actually fifty-six at the time and looked every bit of it. Why Wood would include such a silly and unneeded detail makes absolutely no sense whatsoever.

The plot is a bit sketchy, as well. Upon investigating the house, Lt. Bradford stumbles across a charlatan named Dr. Acula. The con man is making a killing—no pun intended—from pretending to resurrect the deceased loved ones of rich mourners (by somehow using only candles, spices, and oils). However, this makes no sense because the old woman in the film actually sees her husband rise from his coffin (presumably the same one Criswell opened the film in). This leads to the question: if Acula is a phony, then how did he manage to produce the woman's dead hubby? Was he a doppelganger? Surely the old woman knows what her husband looks like. But I digress...

Other notable moments in the film include a scene in which the characters' movements are accidentally (one would presume this was an accident) sped up. Also, when Bradford observes a séance, Wood treats the audience to zany, madcap sound effects, which feel extremely out of place here. During this same scene, Acula produces a man in a sheet, which naturally scares everyone, despite its obviously just being a man in a sheet.

Aside from Wood's normal filmmaking ineptitude, a few familiar motifs show up here. The cemetery is filled only with fake-looking wooden crosses, just as the cemetery in *Plan 9* was. (Since this is a sequel of sorts, maybe it's the same cemetery?) Also, skulls adorn the tables and walls of Acula's shack; we will later see this in both *Orgy of the Dead* and *One Million AC/DC* (1969). Also of note are the copious hanging drapes which serve as backdrops, no doubt covering studio walls. Wood uses curtains as backdrops in other films, but utilizes them much more than usual here. Seemingly every wall inside the shack is a black curtain.

Tor Johnson shows up, once again reprising his role as Lobo. Here we learn that Lobo survived the explosion at the end of *Bride of the Monster*, but his face was hideously disfigured. The make-up here isn't great, but it's actually quite good for a Wood production. Once again Lobo is given very little to do beyond hulking around and grunting, but it's nice to see the familiar face here.

When Bradford is captured by Acula and Lobo, he is locked away in a closet. Acula plans to kill him, but naturally allows him to survive long enough to break through one of the flimsiest doors ever made.

When Acula and his gal pal, who's been pretending to be the ghost in white throughout the film, attempt to escape, they are confronted by real resurrected corpses. The dead people, led by Criswell, then whisk the two mortals off to the land of the dead. When all of the festivities are over, the dead people instantaneously turn into skeletons. Wood, it should be noted, also turns characters into skeletons in both *Plan 9 from Outer Space* and *Orgy of the Dead*.

Interestingly, Tom Mason, the dentist who stood in for Lugosi in *Plan 9*, served as a producer on this film and also appears briefly as a ghost. Paul Marco is also a producer on the picture, and Wood, Conrad Brooks, Henry Bederski, and Mona McKinnon all make uncredited appearances.

In the end, *Night of the Ghouls* falls far short of previous Wood efforts like *Bride of the Monster* and *Plan 9*, but it still offers enough bits of unexplainable strangeness to make it a must-see proposition for any serious Wood fan.

CREDITS: Producer: J.M.A.; Walter Brannon; Anthony Cardoza; Gordon Chesson; JC Foxworthy; Paul Marco; Tom Mason; Marg. Usher; Edward D. Wood, Jr.; Director: Edward D. Wood, Jr.; Screenplay: Edward D. Wood, Jr.; Cinematographer: William C. Thompson; Editor: Edward D. Wood, Jr.

CAST: Kenne Duncan (Dr. Acula); Tor Johnson (Lobo); Valda Hansen (The White Ghost); Johnny Carpenter (Inspector Robbins); Paul Marco (Patrolman Kelton); Don Nagel. (Crandel); Bud Osborne (Darmoor); Jeannie Stevens (The Black Ghost); Harvey B. Dunn (Henry); Margaret Mason (Martha), Clay Stone (Young Man); Marcelle Hemphill (Mrs. Wingate Yates Foster); Tom Mason (Foster Ghost); James La Maida (Hall); Criswell (Himself).

The Sinister Urge (1960)

The Sinister Urge was Edward D. Wood Jr.'s final "mainstream" directorial effort. It also speaks volumes about the way Wood probably saw himself in his later years of filmmaking. Basically an anti-smut PSA, *The Sinister Urge* tackles the "dangers" of viewing pornography, which Wood (earnest, as always) believed could lead to crimes such as robbery, kidnapping, and murder. Naturally we now know such a statement to be ridiculous, but Wood, just a few years away from writing and directing pornographic films (and even penning nearly one hundred lewd novels) himself, apparently believed it with all his naïve heart.

Considering Wood's obvious disdain for those who would make such films (we see it again and again throughout *The Sinister Urge*), it's difficult to imagine how he came to make such movies himself. Wood was a man who wanted nothing more than to make films for a living, and when he found his opportunities in the mainstream market to be minimal at best, he was likely fueled by the same desperation that fuels this film's porn director, Johnny Ryde (played by Carl Anthony). It is sad that Wood didn't have the courage of his convictions, even if they were somewhat wrongheaded convictions. But again, there was one bright light to be found in this portion of the Edward D. Wood Jr. story—the man got to continue making films, even if they were films he personally despised.

Back for more Woodian fun are veteran Wood actors Kenne Duncan and Duke Moore, who each had already worked with the screenwriter/director on numerous pictures. The two actors had previously worked together on *Night of the Ghouls* (1959), in which they were on opposite sides of the law. It should also be mentioned that Wood would later convince Moore to appear in a fully-clothed performance in the lost 1970 porn film *Take It Out in Trade*. In *The Sinister Urge*, Duncan and Moore yuk it up as a couple of cop buddies. Despite Wood's valiant attempts to make their characters seem like the best of pals, the two actors share absolutely no chemistry whatsoever. Despite this, Duncan is good here in his usual low-rent John Wayne sort of way. But Moore is a different story. Void of any charisma whatsoever, he once again shows us just why he would never appear in any film other than a Wood project throughout his career.

In addition to his belief that pornography leads to murder and mayhem, Wood also hints once again at some foreign conspiracy to destroy the American way of life. This was a theme that popped up in a couple of Wood projects, and it seems to be something he was quite worried about. Here they aren't necessarily portrayed as Communists, although in Wood world all foreigners may perhaps be seen as being one and the same as Commies; here many of the pornographers are depicted as swarthy, Armenian-looking fellows with ugly scars and brooding personae. Even the tried and trusted cameraman, Jaffe (Harry Keaton), turns out to be a secret foreigner. Also not surprising, this band of low-life smut peddlers are connected to the American Mafia. See, kiddies? In the paranoid world of Wood, it's another slippery slope from pornography to murder to Communism and Mafia ties. What a dangerous, dangerous thing this pornography is...

Also interesting is Wood's depiction of pornography. It is apparent that he had not seen much (or any) porn at this point in his career (which may also explain why he would prove to be rather bad at making it himself). In one scene the pornographers ask to see a starlet's leg, and nothing else. This was clearly intended to be shocking. This makes one wonder if Wood believed simply seeing a little bit of leg could be enough to send a potential killer into a killing frenzy. In the porn itself, the women wear bikinis and are whipped by one of the swarthy foreigners with a bullwhip. (Hey, what kind of porn is this, anyway?) It's ironic that the porn Wood depicts shows no nudity whatsoever, but this film itself—a "legitimate" mainstream effort—shows bare breasts at one point (but not in the "porn" scenes).

The dialogue in the film is flat and preachy, as always, but by 1960 Wood had come a long way in terms of his writing. There is none of the nonsensical repetition found in the dialogue of some earlier projects, there are no narrators (which always proved a bit problematic for Wood), and this is a coherently-constructed story with a clear opening, middle, and ending. This growth, as small as it may have been, is somewhat sad considering Wood's mainstream career was all but finished at this point; all the skills he had gained would soon be lost forever.

The film begins with footage of a woman and an obvious jump from one exterior location to another. The woman is running through the park (shot in the famed Griffith Park in Los Angeles). We then see that she is running from a man, Dirk Williams (Dino Fantini). Soon he is upon her, and he strangles and kills her. (In classic Wood fashion, the dead woman can be seen breathing.) A young couple then shows up and Dirk must flee so that he may live to strangle another day.

Wood then takes us to the obligatory expository scene in which the police are discussing the crime. Here, through characters Lt. Matt Carson (Duncan) and Sgt. Randy Stone (Moore), we learn that this is but one in a string of murders. In each of the cases, the victim was a porn actress and was killed in the park. The cops then raid a porn shoot and confiscate perhaps one hundred cans of film. As the cops talk, they continuously make such dramatic declarations as, "The smut picture racket has to be stopped!" In one humorous scene, a man opens what is visibly a prop door in the Lieutenant's office, but when he goes to shut it, it will not shut. Wood of course leaves this in. After all, why waste money on a second take?

Soon an angry taxpayer visits the police station to complain about the police wasting money on a task force to stop this "silly, dirty smut business." This provides Lt. Carson (and Wood) the opportunity to not-so-subtly lecture like-minded viewers about the dangers of pornography. In this scene, Carson delivers a long-winded soliloquy about how viewing pornography can lead to such unlawful activities as murder. Here Carson explains that smut is "worse than kidnapping or dope peddling" and can lead those who view it to only one place—the morgue. Carson and Wood have now delivered a verbal smack down on the taxpayer (and the audience), and said taxpayer goes skulking out of the office with his head down in apparent shame.

Next Wood introduces us to Gloria Henderson (Jean Fontaine), the nefarious leader of this smut ring the police are hell-bent to shut down. We also meet porn director Johnny Ryde, who serves as Gloria's right-hand man, so to speak. (One wonders if Wood could see the writing on the wall in terms of his own future here as it is frequently lamented in this film that Ryde could have been a great director had he never gotten involved with porn. Maybe Wood was on to something there; working on pornography certainly did his own career no favors.) Gloria talks openly about having had someone killed, her plans to have a second person whacked, and her ties with the Mafia.

While in Johnny Ryde's office, we see that Wood has adorned Ryde's walls with movie posters for Wood films *Jail Bait* (1954), *Bride of the Monster* (1955), and *The Violent Years* (1956). Again, this is ironic and sad since Wood would later become the real-life incarnation of this porn director character.

The next scene doesn't fit here at all, and viewers will not be surprised to learn that it was originally shot for another project (an incomplete 1956 project titled *Hellborn*) and then integrated into the film for production value. The scene depicts Wood himself and Wood favorite Conrad Brooks in a fistfight. Why does this happen? Don't ask. The explanation the film provides makes little to no sense, but it has something to do with rival factions duking it out for the right to peddle their porn in Gloria Henderson's territory. In the next scene, Wood is up to his old tricks again when he recycles an entire exchange between cops Carson and Stone from *Night of the Ghouls*.

Actor Kenne Duncan is then given the opportunity to deliver a second heavy-handed PSA-like speech to the audience on the evils of the "dirty filthy racket" known as pornography. Similar to the scenario laid out previously in *The Violent Years*, he explains how even the best of girls who are at the head of their classes can turn to crime. Wood/Duncan goes on to explain that women never perform in pornography by choice, but are always blackmailed and forced into it. (This is, of course, not true. No doubt this has happened to many a woman in real-life, but many, many young women appear in pornography by choice. This, again, is Wood hypothesizing about something he clearly knows nothing about. And if Wood was correct, then does this mean that he himself later used such tactics to lure women into his X-rated affairs? Unlikely.)

Johnny Ryde is then shown enlisting an innocent young would-be ingénue in the park. (Here's a question: why on earth would the pornographers be hanging around in the park where all the porn murders have occurred? And for that matter, how is it that Dirk has managed to lure so many porn starlets to the park after the initial murders? But then this is a Wood film, so logic plays no role here.)

The police soon come up with a most illogical plan—they will dress an undercover male cop as a woman (yes, a favorite Wood theme) and plant him in the park. Then, they hope, Dirk will attack the cop and try to kill him. There's only one problem with this plan: Dirk only kills porn starlets, so why would he attack the cop? But then maybe the cops know something I don't because Dirk soon comes out of the shadows to attack the undercover cop. How could this happen? We don't know because it's never explained. But just when it looks like the cop has the upper hand on Dirk, Johnny Ryde shows up and knocks the cop over the head. (Both the Mafia and the smut ring want Dirk alive so they can kill him themselves.) Johnny then loans Dirk an automobile. The unsuspecting Dirk doesn't realize the brakes are cut and he is nearly killed.

Dirk then goes to Johnny Ryde and threatens to kill him, but Johnny convinces him that they should get access to Gloria's contacts, bump her off, and take over the business themselves. (This makes perfect sense considering that Johnny Ryde has proven himself to be so trustworthy of an associate.) When Gloria enters, Dirk hides out on the terrace. Johnny inadvertently pisses off both Gloria and Dirk, and winds up paying the price. Dirk kills Johnny (while Gloria is absent from the room), and then Gloria shoots at "Johnny" in the dark, accidentally killing Dirk. When Gloria tells Lt. Carson that she witnessed Dirk killing Johnny, they find both bodies and pin the murder on Gloria. And once again all is well in Wood Land.

In the end, the cops once again remark, "If Johnny had stayed honest, he might have been a big man in the motion picture business." While it's clear that Wood himself would have never have been a big man in Hollywood, one has to wonder what his career might have been like had he not turned to porn. If not a *Citizen Kane* (1941) or a *Lawrence of Arabia* (1962), then perhaps Wood would have had one more *Plan 9 from Outer Space* (1959) in him. We'll never know.

It should be noted that both actor Kenne Duncan and cinematographer William C. Thompson, both of whom had worked in film since the silent film era, retired after *The Sinister Urge*. Also interesting to note is the fact that this was the first time Wood used a pseudonym (billed here as "E.D. Wood") on one of his own films.

CREDITS: Producer: Roy Reid; Director: Edward D. Wood, Jr.; Screenplay: Edward D. Wood, Jr.; Cinematographer: William C. Thompson; Editor: unknown.

CAST: Kenne Duncan (Lt. Matt Carson); Duke Moore (Sgt. Randy Stone); Jean Fontaine (Gloria Henderson); Carl Anthony (Johnny Ryde); Dino Fantini (Dirk Williams); Jeanne Willardson (Mary Smith); Harvey B. Dunn (Mr. Romaine); Reed Howes (Police Inspector); Fred Mason (Officer Kline); Vic McGee (Syndicate Man); Harry Keaton (Jaffe); Conrad Brooks (Connie).

Married Too Young (1962)

The 1962 George Moskov film *Married Too Young* had long been believed to have been either written or co written by Edward D. Wood, Jr. However, screenwriter Nathaniel Tanchuck's daughter, Heather Tanchuck, has stated that Wood had absolutely nothing to do with the film. This is the letter she wrote to an Ed Wood fan site ("Ed Wood Movies"):

> The movie, *Married Too Young*, was not partially written by Ed Wood. My father, Nathaniel Tanchuck, wrote the entire movie, and I would truly appreciate it if you would correct your site. I was a child, I have a copy of the script, I visited the movie set. Ed Wood worked at Hal Roach or some other studio at the same time as my father, but my dad, Nathaniel Tanchuck, is the only writer of *Married Too Young*.

After that letter was posted some years ago, film buffs stopped calling the film Wood's. After all, he apparently had nothing to do with it. Then Fred Olen Ray's film distribution company Retromedia obtained the rights to *Married Too Young* in 2013, and the filmmaker unearthed definitive proof that Wood did in fact rewrite the screenplay for the film. "I received a whole bunch of documents along with the film when we purchased it," Ray says. "Among these were contracts for Wood's rewrite of the film." Among the papers Ray received were court documents showing that Wood in fact sued Headliner Productions because he wasn't paid for his rewrite on the film. Imagine that—first Wood didn't get paid for his work on *Married Too Young*, and then, years later, he was falsely disassociated with the project. Talk about not getting any respect!

When watching *Married Too Young*, it's difficult to imagine anyone who had seen *The Violent Years* not knowing immediately that Wood played a major role in this script. The similarities are abundant and are less than subtle. Like *The Violent Years* (1956), this film features a judge character placing the blame on the teens' parents and delivering a heavy-handed soliloquy on proper parenting. And like the previous film, *Married Too Young* once again plays like a Wood-penned PSA—this time on the evils of, yes, marrying way too young.

When we first see the main characters, Helen (Jana Lund) and Tommy (Harold Lloyd, Jr.), it's difficult to see how they could be too young for marriage. The reason for this is, although they are playing characters who are teenagers, the actors are clearly in their upper-twenties. (This is, of course, common in Wood films, but must be noted all the same.)

At the beginning of the film, the couple make their way to lover's lane, where they almost make out. Yes, you read that correctly— they *almost* make out. This of course leads them to feel guilty and eventually they start to consider how life could be different if they were to cross the state line and get married.

So, of course, they do just that. The young couple pays $25 for a ceremony and a license. To make the less-than-subtle point that this is a huge mistake, writers Tanchuck and Wood make the ceremony as terrible as possible. The Justice of the Peace doesn't even know their names and all of it is very slapdash. He then gives them a copy of the marriage certificate. "This'll prove you have a right to keep him at home," he jokes.

Tanchuck and Wood do something interesting here. They then show us both Tommy and Helen in their natural habitats, at home with their parents, where they act very differently than we have seen them up until this point. At home, they act very juvenile and it is at once apparent that they are still way too immature to be married.

Similar to *The Violent Years*, much ado is made about the fact that their parents are too busy with their own social lives to worry about their children. Helen's mother even scolds her husband for "acting like a parent."

Finally, Tommy and Helen decide to tell their parents what they have done, but it's too late; Helen's parents find the marriage license. Again, the parents are way more worried about the effect this will have on their social standing than they are regarding their children. "I don't know if I'll ever be able to hold my head up again," Helen's mother says. "The scandal!"

When Helen's father confronts the Justice of the Peace who married them, the Justice of the Peace also delivers a patented Wood diatribe on bad parenting: "Their lives were ruined long before I set eyes on them!"

Also similar to *The Violent Years* is the ridiculous stretch from point A to point B in terms of plot; just as bad parenting ultimately led to Communism and crime in the former film, here it leads Tommy to become a part of a stolen car ring. Why does he become involved with this operation? Naturally, because he was married too young... Perhaps all of this is a slippery slope, as the screenwriters point out, but can it really be *this* ridiculously slippery?

The storyline naturally builds to Tommy taking Helen with him on a stolen car delivery. As they are driving the hot car, a police patrol car comes up behind them. Rather than stop and face the consequences, Tommy tries to outrun the cops and ultimately crashes the car off the side of a cliff. Somehow, Tommy and Helen survive.

The film concludes with a courtroom scene very similar to that of *The Violent Years*, in which a judge rails on Helen and Tommy's parents for not doing their jobs in raising their children. He then offers Tommy and Helen probation on the grounds that their parents behave properly and raise them in a manner that is more fitting.

There isn't a lot to say about this film other than the fact that Wood's contributions are rather obvious when compared to his other writings. It is also interesting to note that Wood seemed to genuinely believe that all or most of society's woes, no matter how far reaching they might be, were all a direct result of bad parenting.

CREDITS: Producer: George Moskov; Director: George Moskov; Screenplay: Nat Tanchuck; Edward D. Wood, Jr.; Cinematographer: Ernest Haller; Editor: Maurice Wright.

CAST: Harold Lloyd Jr. (Tommy Blaine); Jana Lund (Helen Newton); Anthony Dexter (Lech); Trudy Marshall (Susan Newton); Brian O'Hara (George Newton); Nita Loveless (Grace Blaine); Lincoln Demvan (George Blaine); Marianna Hill (Marla); Cedric Jordan (Mike); George Cesar (Miltie); Joel Mondeaux (Felton); David Bond (Justice of the Peace); Richard Davies (Judge); Irene Ross (Phyllis).

Shotgun Wedding (1963)

The Beverly Hillbillies first aired in 1962, becoming a smash hit, sending exploitation filmmakers scrambling to the drawing board to figure out how to make a buck off the hillbilly trend. The Robert Mitchum vehicle *Thunder Road* (1958) had already explored this world five years prior, and it had proven to be a hit, as well. In 1963, exploitation producer Pat Patterson set forth to make his own hillbilly exploitation film. He hired director Boris Petroff and screenwriter Edward D. Wood Jr. to assemble the project. That film would ultimately become *Shotgun Wedding.*

Interestingly, Patterson must have believed there was big money to be made in this budding new sub-genre, because he also hired noted exploitation filmmaker Herschell Gordon Lewis to make a second hillbilly film titled *Moonshine Mountain.* (That far superior project would be released on the heels of *Shotgun Wedding.*)

What can one say about *Shotgun Wedding*? Ed Wood used a pseudonym ("Larry Lee") on it, even though it wasn't one of his "smut" films. Think about that for a moment—the guy who proudly plastered his name all over *Glen or Glenda?* (1953) and *Plan 9 from Outer Space* (1959) used a fake name here. That should probably be enough to tell you all you need to know about the quality (or lack thereof) of the film.

Shotgun Wedding is a stinker for sure. It isn't the fun kind of bad that we associate with Wood's work; it's the boring kind of bad that makes for a tedious and forgettable viewing experience. No doubt Wood saw it as a way to make a little extra cash, and one can hardly blame the struggling filmmaker for participating in this project.

Patterson and company did manage to cast a couple of "real" actors in J. Pat O'Malley and William Schallert. Both were television character actors who made weekly notable guest appearances on such series such as *Gunsmoke* and *Leave It to Beaver*. Neither man was a huge star, but both possessed recognizable faces that would leave a film buff trying to figure out where he'd seen them before. Naturally, both actors do a fine job here. Otherwise the acting in *Shotgun Wedding* is passable at best.

Ads for the film sensationalized it, touting "The whole shocking story of child brides in the Ozarks" and "Gorgeous gals set the Ozarks on fire!" Those advertisements pretty much tell you everything you need to know about *Shotgun Wedding*: it has lots of moonshine, "authentic" hillbilly dialogue ("Tarnation!"), and a plethora of eye-pleasing, scantily-clad hillbilly babes. The only way the advertisements might have been more accurate is if they had touted, "Boring as can be! Sure to leave you fast asleep!" Okay, so *Shotgun Wedding* isn't art, and it isn't entertaining, but it's a fascinating entry in the canon of Wood films because it once again allows us to see what depths Wood would sink to for a paycheck.

The movie begins in the town of Mudcat Landing (Population: 47) with an upbeat jazz song that feels very much at odds with what we're seeing on screen. The "town" is quite obviously a movie or TV exterior set that probably, in another production, was meant to replicate the 1890s. (Everyone knows that the 1890s are most hillbillies' favorite decade, right?) Despite this aberration, the men that are seen ogling the woman we will come to know as Melanie (Valerie Allen) are all dressed in contemporary 60s clothing. Melanie's character, the jazz music, and the backdrop of Mudcat Landing make it abundantly clear that Melanie is a fish out of water Character. In the next scene we find out why.

Melanie used to be a circus shyster. Now she's shacked up with a local "river rat" named Buford who took her in and offered her sanctuary in his ramshackle houseboat after she apparently shot and killed the circus strongman. Melanie's not happy living the river-billy/hillbilly life though, and she threatens to leave. We then learn that in exchange for this sanctuary, Buford has taken the money she stole from the strongman and put it away for "safe-keeping."

Ed Wood dives right into this laughless comedy with his skewed brand of logic and dialogue such as the exchange that happens after Melanie refuses to "unload the jackass and put the vittles away."

Buford, exasperated at her lack of cooperation and enthusiasm, says "Doggone, you just can't be good to a woman!"

It turns out that the voluptuous Melanie has been wanting to get married, but the plump and homely Buford won't give in. This is, of course, Woodian logic; the sexy young woman who could get any man she set her sights on is the one who wants to get married, not the fat old man. At one point in the film Buford explains, "Nobody wants to get married unless they's trapped."

Buford reminds Melanie of all the gifts he's found for her floating down the river (including a bathtub). When Melanie tells Buford that she's carrying his child, he gives in and sends his son Chub (Peter Colt) to fetch the minister. The minister (William Schallert), a former con man and crooked three-card Monte dealer, comes to the farm and immediately begins flirting with Buford's hot young daughter, Lucy Ann (Jenny Maxwell), telling her that she looks like "an occasion of sin." He even attempts to take Buford's moonshine to "remove that temptation."

If there is one saving grace in *Shotgun Wedding* it has to be William Schallert as the huckster minister. He's believable both as the preacher/showman and as the wily grifter, and what very few laughs are to be had in this funeral of a comedy come from him. Everyone else's line readings seem like bear wrestling in comparison.

The story then takes us to Honey Bee (Nan Peterson) and her pa, Silas (Jackie Searl), who are discussing her relationship with Buford's other son, Rafe (Buzz Martin). Honey Bee is "just itchin' to get married," but Silas won't hear of it. He explains that, "Courtin' and wooin' bring dallying and doin'." He goes on to explain that "There's more to getting' married than four legs in a bed."

Rafe wants Honey Bee to run away and elope with him. He plans to steal the money Buford has stolen from Melanie to fund their trip, but Honey Bee won't hear of it.

We soon learn that Melanie is actually Tiger Rose, or "Rosie," and she was once in cahoots with Stacko Parkins, who is now pretending to be a minister. "Minister" Parkins tries to convince her to run away with him, but she isn't having it.

Parkins asks Buford if he and Melanie will be going on a honeymoon after he marries them, but Buford says, "Heck no, we done had the honeymoon. Now we wanna make it legal." Then Buford eloquently asks, "How much this here marryin' gonna cost me?" He asks Parkins to dunk Melanie in the river to baptize the unborn baby, but Parkins refuses.

Parkins then telephones Stelo the strongman, the man "Melanie" shot a few years ago. It is here that we learn that Stelo is still alive, a fact that Melanie doesn't know. Parkins offers to split the money with Stelo, but Stelo has forgiven Melanie and has no interest in finding her.

We then see Melanie in the bathtub, washing her legs sensually. (No doubt this was sexy stuff in 1963.)

Buford instructs Chub to "clean up the barn for the wedding shindig. I don't want anybody to step in anything they ought not have." At the wedding, there is an inexplicable dance number that showcases "hillbillies" who are almost certainly cut off from contemporary society dancing some very modern-looking dances. In fact, the dancing scene almost feels like it was cut in from another picture. This extended dancing scene is somewhat explained by having Parkins detained by accidentally falling into the hog pen and being stuck there for an indeterminate amount of time. Then, of course, he must marry Buford and Melanie covered in mud and feces. Presumably, that's some funny stuff. Perkins has obviously never done a wedding before and is at a loss for words. He finally manages to stammer "By reasons and, uh, authorities...," I pronounce you man and wife."

Once the marriage is over, Buford walks out of the room. Chub then starts to make out with his new stepmother—*and no one seems to notice!?* I realize that these are supposed to be stereotypically stupid hillbillies, but one would assume real hillbillies do their inbreeding behind closed doors. Surely this would have raised an eyebrow or two, but alas, here it does not.

We then go to a scene in which Honey Bee is caught sneaking into her house half-naked after a night of lovemaking with Rafe. Her father, Silas, gives her a speech about the "forbidden fruit" of premarital sex, calling her private parts "holy apples." Honey Bee naively explains, "I hate apples!" This joke is not funny, but again it's on par with the rest of the non-humor in this film.

Back at Melanie and Buford's houseboat, Melanie is tearing the place apart looking for her money that Buford has stashed away.

She plans to take the money and run. She then enlists the lovestruck Chub to help her find the cash, promising to run away with him if he locates it. Melanie and Chub kiss, and Lucy Ann sees them. She says she will be quiet and keep this secret to herself for $100. Chub reluctantly pays her.

Back at Silas' place, Silas is enlisting men for a shotgun-wielding posse to go and hunt down Rafe for having had premarital relations with his daughter, Honey Bee.

Meanwhile, Lucy Ann gives the $100 she received from Shub to Rafe so that he and Honey Bee can elope.

Chub and Melanie continue searching for the money Buford has stashed away. "If I was a drunken bum like Pa," Shub says, "where would I hide the money?" This line of thought leads him to an old moonshine jug in the barn, and Chub locates the money.

Just before Silas and his pack of rifle-toting henchmen arrive at the houseboat, Honey Bee shows up to warn Rafe. "Pa's gone plum crazy," she explains. "He's comin' to shoot y'all to kingdom come!" When Silas shows up moments later, Honey Bee says he'll have to shoot her, as well, if he plans to shoot Rafe. Silas then decides to have Honey Bee and Rafe married instead, just like that. Another non sequitur. The whole movie all Silas has obsessed about is his daughter's purity and that she marry anyone but Rafe. Now, after chasing Buford's clan around with shotguns it's perfectly acceptable that Rafe and Honey Bee are married. WTH? And now everyone are friends and all has been forgiven and forgotten. What? Oh yeah. It's a comedy...written by Ed Wood.

Stacko Parkins tells Melanie that the strongman she shot is still alive. Melanie then informs Buford that she isn't really pregnant. Stacko and Melanie run away together in a car stolen from Silas.

At the end of the film, Buford meets up with yet another hot young hillbilly woman who's new to the area, and the whole cycle presumably begins again. The film ends with Lucy Ann saying, "Aw, Pa, not again!"

With a little more sex and death and the subtraction of any hint of "comedy" (not that there's much of one anyway), *Shotgun Wedding* may have been a nice little melodrama for Ed Wood. As it is, this film reeks of Wood knocking a quick script out for a buck. We don't think anyone would accuse Wood of having a conventional sense of humor. It seems the harder he tried to be funny in a mainstream sense, the more his script(s) suffered for it (as we will see more and more as the quality of his films would decline).

Sorry Eddie, but most people would need a shotgun to put into their mouths just to attempt to make it through this tepid hillbillysploitation! *Shotgun Wedding* is a film for Ed Wood completists only. You have been warned.

CREDITS: Producer: Boris L. Petroff; Director: Boris L. Petroff; Screenplay: Edward D. Wood, Jr.; Cinematographer: Paul Ivano; Editor: Fred Feitshans.

CAST: Pat O'Malley (Buford); Jenny Maxwell (Honey Bee); Valerie Allen (Melanie); Buzz Martin (Rafe); William Schallert (Preacher); Nan Petersen (Lucy Ann); Peter Colt (Chub); Jack Searl (Silas); Jan Darrow (Mountain Gal); Art Phillips (Curley); Edward Fitz (Stelo); Jack Riggs (Henchman); Lyn Moore (Girl at Meeting).

Orgy of the Dead (1965)

Orgy of the Dead was considered a "dirty movie" at the time of its release, as it contains an abundance of female nudity. Specifically, breasts. Lots and lots of wiggling, jiggling breasts. Aside from that, a few characters allude to enjoying pain and torture, and therein you have the extent of naughtiness in this hilariously-misguided nudie film. *Orgy of the Dead* has never been (and never could be) even the tiniest bit sexy. Juvenile, definitely. Sexy? No.

Advertised as an erotic horror film, it supremely fails both promises. That's not to say it isn't fascinating, even hypnotic, in that inimitable "I can't believe what I'm seeing" Ed Wood sort of way, because it is. One just has to sit back in awe and speculate how something like this could come from the mind of a grown man, and then how exactly he convinced *anyone else* to film it. *Orgy of the Dead* is what one assumes a ten-year-old's idea of what sexy might be—a bunch of topless women parading around aimlessly, jiggling their breasts at the camera and trying to—but mostly failing at—dancing. As both writer Ed Wood and director Stephen C. Apostolof seem to have shared this ten-year-old's sensibility, it's difficult to say which of them is more to blame here.

Undoubtedly less entertaining than Wood's more famous debacles like *Plan 9 from Outer Space* (1959), *Orgy of the Dead* still has all of the dubious earmarks of an Ed Wood production. It should be noted that this was Wood's first attempt at cinematic eroticism, as well as his first collaboration with frequent partner-in-crime Apostolof. That Wood found in Apostolof a collaborator with the same artistic sensibilities is astounding. Wood was known for surrounding himself with eccentric characters, and surely Apostolof was no different.

(How else could one account for his hiring Wood to write the scripts for *eight* of his films?)

Certainly Apostolof's reasoning for collaborating with Wood is harder to understand (the cheap cost of the script—$400— probably explains Apostolof's motives) than Wood's reasons for working with Apostolof. By the mid-1960s, Wood was down on his luck and seemingly desperate to make films—*any* films—finally finding refuge in the world of adult entertainment. To understand just how low Wood had sunk here, one must look at his earlier observations regarding nudie films (collected in the posthumously published *Hollywood Rat Race*). First, Wood demonizes those (like Apostolof, for instance) who would produce such films, comparing them unfavorably to "decent" independent producers such as himself.

Sleazy producers are the scourge of all producers of films who are trying to make an interesting picture. The sleazy producer is by no means in the same category as the independent producer who, for simple economic reasons, must put his picture out on a small budget. The independent does, however, try to put out an entertaining picture on his budget, which does not venture into the obscene. He knows that today's films must have some measure of sex, but he also knows how far he can go for decency's sake. The true independent producer does believe in decency. Because of the possibility of law problems and because he has to live with himself, the indie producer feels that he is a servant of the public and must keep its respect if he is to keep his own.

Then Wood explains that these producers make films which exploit the naked body. Wood is clearly against showing breasts simply for the sake of showing breasts. If the depiction of a woman unclothed makes sense and is in service of the plot, then Wood has no problem with nudity. But Wood seems to detest what he refers to as "tittie" films.

There is little or no story line, just one weak excuse after another in incident after incident, so the girls can take their clothes off in front of the camera.

The problem here is that *Orgy of the Dead* has far less plot than it has naked breasts, making this once modest filmmaker a hypocrite. There has never been a film made with a "plot" that was more of an excuse to show naked women than this. (A good seventy minutes of the film's ninety-minute running time simply features topless women dancing around without any dialogue.) The plot finds the emperor of the dead overseeing an undead dancing festival where the evil ghouls who dance pleasingly are rewarded with some sort of semi-pleasurable eternity in the underworld. In turn, those who displease him are banished to everlasting torments.

This festival takes place under the light of a stock footage moon in a graveyard (two things Wood loved—stock footage and grave-yards). The dancing ghouls are, of course, topless women, mostly donning bad wigs and make-up that looks like it was applied by a blind man.

The cast of *Orgy of the Dead* is comprised of people who made Wood's usual actors seem highly accomplished. Even Kelton the cop is a few rungs above these poor souls. The film's heroic lead, William Bates, looks like a bloated, less-attractive Rock Hudson. To say that Bates' acting leaves much to be desired would be an under-statement. He has all of the expression of a mounted deer head and he visibly struggles just to say the lines. And that's all he's doing—saying lines. There is no hint of acting to be seen. So how did Bates, who had no prior acting experience, land the role? We cannot be completely sure, but perhaps Bates' associate producer role on the film sheds a little bit of light. Similar to the Loretta King incident on *Bride of the Monster* (1955), one might deduct that Wood and Apostolof offered Bates the role in exchange for money. But who can say for sure?

Then there is the casting of Fawn Silver as the Black Ghoul, a character made-up to look identical (save for the ridiculously tiny waist) to Maila "Vampira" Nurmi. It has been suggested that Apostolof and Wood conceived the role for Nurmi, but were then unable to convince her to appear in the film. Either way, there can be little doubt that Silver is supposed to look like her.

Also of interest, not-so-psychic Criswell returns for his third and final collaboration with Ed Wood. In this film, he actually gets to play someone other than himself. Here he plays the Emperor.

Criswell's performance is all that one might expect. He delivers each line with the gusto of a Shakespearian actor playing Hamlet while three sheets to the wind. Sure, he's terrible, but exquisitely so. Criswell is easily the best thing about *Orgy of the Dead*, even though his schtick is mostly to sit, bunch his cape about him, and give hilarious leering nods of approval.

"Eddie was the one who brought Criswell here," Apostolof would later tell *Femme Fatales* magazine. "They were friends. So finally I said, 'Okay, write his lines on cardboard,' so these two poor guys had to hold up cardboard with the lines. And Criswell, now he can't read them because he doesn't have his glasses! Then there's the fog machines, you know? And he can't read through the fog!"

Orgy of the Dead is interesting in that it plays like a less-profound nudie version of Edgar Lee Master's *Spoon River Anthology*. Each ghoul gal is introduced before her bit with a few words on why she's damned. ("One who prowls the lonely streets at night in life is bound to prowl them in eternity!"; "She loved the bull ring and the matador. She danced to their destruction. Now she dances to her own destruction"; "All others were but infinitesimal bits of fluff compared to her. This one would have died for feathers, furs, and fluff...and so she did!")

The ten dance sequences, each featuring a different motif (such as "Hawaiian Dance" and "Mexican Dance"), go on for way too long. One can go to the restroom, make a sandwich, and fix a drink without missing anything. ("She's still dancing!") These dances are painfully dull and completely devoid of any type of sensuality.

Even in crafting a nudie film, Wood and Apostolof stumble badly, breaking the most obvious rules of the genre. One of the women ("Indian Dancer") has breasts far too tiny for a burlesque show built entirely around displaying naked breasts (or, as Apostolof famously called them, "ticket sellers"). Also, the film's most attractive performer, Fawn Silver, never takes off a shred of clothing. What's up with that?

Also interesting, some of these "actresses" seem to be dancing to music that they're not actually hearing. Perhaps they were instructed to "dance like an Indian" or "dance like an ancient Egyptian" with the hopes that the filmmakers would later locate royalty-free music to semi-match their shimmying. Other dances Apostolof has them perform look rather strange and wooden. This is likely due to the fact that Apostolof fired the dance coordinator in the middle of the shoot.

The Egyptian Dancer does an awkward sideways dance that is difficult to describe, but trust us, it's silly, and the Indian Dancer has moves that look more like calisthenics than dancing. Other strange dances find a woman caressing and kissing a plastic skull, and a woman rubbing fake-looking gold coins against her skin.

Like most Wood-associated projects, *Orgy of the Dead* has day-for-night issues; in one shot it's daylight, and in the next it's pitch black. Also, one of the women dances with what are supposed to be the skeletal remains of her murdered husband. In true Wood fashion, the hook which holds up the skeleton can be seen clearly on top of the skull. In another scene, Criswell comments on it being a clear night, despite an obvious fog-maker shooting plumes of heavy smoke into nearly every shot.

Stock footage (of such things as the moon and a rattle snake) is poorly integrated into the film. Some of the stock footage even depicts events happening in daylight, despite the fact that the entire film takes place at night.

The film has very little dialogue, most of which belongs to Criswell's emperor character, and of course he visibly reads his lines from cue cards. At one point Criswell declares something to be "more than a fact." What does this even mean? How can something be more than a fact? Criswell's declaration that the attractive, nubile young women are "monsters to be pitied" and "monsters to be despised" is silly as well.

Perhaps the film's funniest, most poorly-written exchange involves the two lovebirds, Shirley and Bob. Bob is an author, and Shirley has suggested that Bob give up writing about monsters and ghouls. "My monsters have done well for me," Bob explains. "You think I'd give that up so I could write about trees or dogs or daisies? That's it!... I will write about my creatures pushing up daisies!" Shirley then kisses him. To this Bob says, "Your puritan upbringing sure doesn't hurt your art of kissing." She looks at him and says, "My kisses are alive!"

During one scene, Bob advises Shirley not to change her expression. This is humorous considering Pat Barrington, the actress playing

Shirley, never alters her expression once in the entire film. In another scene Shirley is referred to as a "panicking woman," despite the fact that she looks utterly bored and is completely devoid of any expression whatsoever.

In another scene, Bob and Shirley find themselves crouched behind bushes in the cemetery, watching the long, monotonous dance sequences. This leads to a rather obvious observation from Shirley that the dead do not generally play music. In this scene, Bob also notes that the women must be dead as "nothing alive looks like that." This is again humorous as each of the buxom women look rather attractive (save for awful wigs and questionable make-up), raising the question, what dead people has Bob seen previously that look like *this*?

Also, when the couple comes to the realization that they are watching dead people dance, why don't they leave (before ultimately being captured)? Again, character motivations play no role in Wood's (and Apostolof's) world.

Perhaps the strangest, most funny thing about the film are the cartoonish Mummy and Wolf Man characters. They appear to be horny, getting rather worked up while watching the dancers. The Mummy is so heavily made-up that his lines had to be (quite noticeably) inserted later through ADR. The Wolf Man is obviously wearing a cheap Halloween mask. One can even see the actor's neck below the bottom of the mask when he tilts his head back to howl at the moon. The mummy doesn't fare much better. His hands look like they were made out of *papier-mâché*.

In one bizarre exchange between the two characters, the Mummy discusses Cleopatra's pet snake. "Snakes," he says. "I hate snakes. I remember the one Cleopatra used. Cute little rascal! Until it flicked out that red tongue! Slimy, slinky things! When I was alive, they were the things that nightmares were made of!"

Another memorable and bizarre character is the woman who performs the "Cat Dance." She appears dressed up in a silly-looking cat costume. As one of the emperor's servants whips at the Cat Woman's feet, Criswell cries out giddily, "Torture! Torture! It pleasures me!"

Throughout the film, between almost every dance, the Black Ghoul nags at the emperor about the time. She says things like, "There is little time left for the remainder of the evening's pleasures." To this the emperor responds with some variation of "Ah, there is yet time..." So it is painfully ludicrous when he finally gets around to telling her to kill Shirley. For the moment she raises her knife to her captive, sunlight bursts over the horizon, immediately turning the emperor and his ghoul pals into skeletons (reminiscent of the fallen ghouls in *Plan 9*). Humorously, they then appear as skulls sitting atop mounds of clothing. Apparently sunlight completely destroys all the rest of the ghouls' bones except for their skulls.

How many warnings did the emperor have? Six. The Black Ghoul told him no less than six times to wrap things up, yet he did not heed her warnings. How could morning creep up so easily when you've had six warnings? (Also, the emperor could have just looked at the wristwatch he alludes to. One might ask why exactly the leader of the undead would need a wristwatch, but his losing track of time here makes such a question less necessary.) The emperor was clearly blind and depraved, most deserving of his disintegration by sunlight.

And even though the film's finale is a bit of a non-ending, it comes mercifully at a time when one can hardly endure anymore of this insidious ghoul dancing. *Orgy of the Dead* is not without its charms, but by the end of its running time those charms wear awfully thin.

It is interesting to note that Wood's thirty-eight-page script was originally titled *Night of the Ghouls*; since Wood didn't expect anyone to ever see the original 1959 film bearing that title (it was still in limbo at the film lab), he simply reused the title. (The film's working title was *Ghoulies*.) Because Wood stole budget money set aside for cast and crew food and used it to purchase alcohol, Apostolof vowed never to work with him again. Wood and Apostolof would not collaborate for another seven years after this incident.

CREDITS: Producers: Stephen C. Apostolof, William Bates, L.S. Jensen, Neil B. Stein; Director: Stephen C. Apostolof; Screenplay: Edward D. Wood, Jr. (based on his novel); Cinematographer: Robert Caramico; Editor: Donald A. Davis.

CAST: Criswell (The Emperor); Fawn Silver (The Black Ghoul); Pat Barrington (Shirley); William Bates (Bob); Mickey Jines (Hawaiian

Dance); Barbara Nordin (Skeleton Dance); Bunny Glaser (Indian Dance); Najejda Klein (Slave Dance); Coleen O'Brien (Street Walker Dance); Lorali Hart (Cat Dance); Rene De Beau (Fluff Dance); Stephanie Jones (Mexican Dance); Dene Starnes (Zombie Dance); Louis Ojena (Mummy); John Andrews (Wolf Man).

For Love and Money (1968)

By 1968, Ed Wood was churning out lurid pulp novels right and left. Most of these, with suggestive titles such as *The Gay Underworld* and *Mary-Go-Round*, were published under pseudonyms. One of these books was *The Sexecutives*, which Wood penned under the name David L. Westermier, for Private Edition. The novel, a sex-filled examination of industrial espionage, would ultimately be the first of these books to be adapted to the big screen. The resulting film, *For Love and Money*, would be directed by an old Wood associate named Don Davis. The screenplay would be adapted by James Rogers.

Although Wood didn't direct the film or write the script, *For Love and Money* remains a curiosity because it still contains a number of the elements which comprise a Woodian film. The film naturally contains Wood dialogue (straight from the novel) and familiar Wood themes such as voyeurism and heavy-handed lecturing on the American legal system. Like Wood's novel before it, the film features a handful of vignettes about a gang of female sex spies who infiltrate major corporations by bedding top executives and/or blackmailing them in the process. In the novel, this gang is known as Instant Secretaries, Inc. In the film, however, the gang goes unnamed.

The trailer for the film touted it as being "right from today's headlines," calling it "the film you'll want to see more than once!" Said trailer also boasts that *For Love and Money* is offered to audiences "in throbbing color." But the funniest claim the trailer makes is its heady claim that the film's naked body-painting scenes are some of the most dynamic ever captured on celluloid. The thing is, how many times have you ever seen naked body painting in a film, before or since? So naturally these scenes will be some of the greatest ever since they are likely some of the *only* scenes like this ever produced.

Like other Wood films, most notably *Glen or Glenda?* (1953), *For Love and Money* frames its story by having a professional sitting at a desk and explaining the back story to a seated second party. Here it is Police Chief Gardner speaking with a businessman named Don Harding. As Gardner details incident after incident involving corporate espionage, and also providing us with one of those classic Woodian diatribes about the law ("The means these criminals use are denied to us"), Harding is sitting there wondering what any of this has to do with him. It is interesting to note that there are no reaction shots of Harding; just a long scene showing the back of his head. Did Davis forget to shoot coverage here, or did the film's editor simply forget to use it? We will probably never know.

Humorously, the filmmakers apparently only had budget enough for one song, appropriately enough titled "For Love and Money," and that one song plays ad nauseum throughout the film.

Gardner tells Harding the first story, and vignette #1 begins. Here we see a successful businessman (employed by Aerospace Central) trying to lay on his charms to a supposedly unsuspecting secretary. His approach to womanizing is rather corny, and one would suspect it was equally corny in 1968. The man ends every sentence with "baby." This smooth talk works like a charm, and the man is soon involved with some heavy petting and fully-clothed moaning and sexual escapades.

Unbeknownst to the businessman, these activities are being recorded by police bugging equipment. Throughout the overly-long sex scene, Davis cuts away to show us the face of the old cop, listening intently to the groaning sounds of the two lovebirds.

When the lovemaking is concluded, the sexy secretary begins to photograph top-secret corporate documents.

Gardner then leads us to the next vignette. This one features an executive named Lorring Grant, an employee of Stallion Motors. The man pays an aspiring model named Tanya to allow his boss, CEO Floyd Shermack, to photograph her in the nude. The plan is that she will have sex with the old man, and then Grant can burst in and photograph the old man in a compromising position. He will then force Shermack to retire, allowing Grant to take his place as top dog of the company.

Humorously, the Asian actress playing Tanya is awful beyond words. Had Wood directed this picture, I think we can safely say there is no way he would have cast the woman (well, unless she gave him money to make the picture, that is). This actress, name unknown, can barely speak English, let alone act in the language. Throughout the vignette she will refer to Floyd as "Froyd." One can only wonder how this woman landed this role (although it's likely that her consenting to bare her breasts onscreen had something to do with it).

Grant drives Tanya up into the mountains to his boss' home. He introduces Froyd, er, Floyd and Tanya, and the two hit it off immediately. Floyd explains that he's a bit of a shutterbug and he enjoys taking photographs of lovely ladies. Once Grant is gone (listening through bugging equipment from his car, of course), Floyd puts the moves on her. He kisses her back. When she starts to object, he yells out, "Oh, Tanya, don't stop me! Please!" These are apparently the magic words to get into Tanya's pants, and the two are soon making out hot and heavy. "I think we should get some nice seductive poses of you in the bedroom," Floyd says. And they're off to bed...

Grant then returns, catches the old man in the act, and informs him of his plan.

This ends vignette #2, and Police Chief Gardner begins another story—one that will hit much closer to home for Don Harding.

This story involves Don Harding and a young prostitute, having sex and taking LSD (or, as Wood knowingly refers to them, "capsules"). Gardner also explains to both Harding and the audience that LSD is "another weapon in the arsenal of the espionage ring."

The chief derides Harding. "Aren't you a little old for the LSD and hippie bit?" he asks.

To this, Harding can only offer, "I knew it was wrong, but at the time it felt so right."

We then see Harding and the girl doing LSD, and the film gets a little wonky. No doubt the filmmakers were trying to capture the feeling of doing such a drug onscreen, but it doesn't work. Neither of this book's authors have ever done LSD, but both are relatively sure the experience cannot be as silly and asinine as it is presented in this film.

Harding starts to paint the girl. He asks her how she feels, and she says that she feels round. The goofily-stoned Harding tells her he knows exactly how she feels, and he begins painting circles all over her body. This scene is extremely long and is about as sensual as watching paint dry (pun intended).

Naturally, as with all of the vignettes, someone is listening in on their sexual adventures in the hopes of blackmailing Harding.

The police chief catches Harding lying, and coerces him to do the right thing and turn in the people who have blackmailed him.

And thus begins vignette #4. We see a half-naked secretary bugging the home of business executive Blake Carter. She soon begins to make out with Carter, photographing secret corporate documents in the process.

Soon, based on the assistance Harding has given them, the police burst in and arrest both the secretary and the man listening in to the bugging equipment.

The end.

At the end of the day, *For Love and Money* isn't much of a movie, even by 1968 sexploitation standards. But it remains significant because of Ed Wood's involvement in the project.

CREDITS: Producer: Donald A. Davis; Harry H. Novak; Director: Donald A. Davis; Screenplay: Edward D. Wood, Jr. (based on his book *The Sexecutives*); James Rogers; Cinematographer: Humphrey Buggit; Editor: David Leo.

CAST: Lionel Nichols (Lt. Gardner); Munroe Knight (Don Harding); Michelle Angelo (Melanie); George Cooper (Surveillance Expert); Michi Tani (Tanya); Barry Cooper (Lorne Grant); Curly Etling (Floyd Shermac); Norma Mimosa (Francie); Scott Avery (Blake Carter); Lee Morgill (Second Surveillance Man); Janice Kelly (Irene Kelly).

One Million AC/DC
(1969)

Released two years after the British film *One Million Years B.C.* (1967) bowed in the United States, this film, written by Ed Wood, is a sexploitation satire made to cash in on the success of the Raquel Welsh vehicle. Like the former, *One Million AC/DC* is ahistorical in its portrayal of humans coexisting with dinosaurs. (Hilariously, *The Thing with Two Heads*, 1972, director Lee Frost is credited as being the film's "historical consultant.") Unlike its predecessor, however, *One Million AC/DC* also features large quantities of nudity and simulated sex scenes.

One Million AC/DC shows something about Ed Wood's personality that many people who are only acquainted with his better known works like *Plan 9 from Outer Space* (1959) may not know or have guessed. That is, Wood possessed a sense of humor. Part of the charm of his earlier movies are that they're so sincere and earnest, but by the time Wood wrote this film, it's almost like he had given up on the idea of writing anything (from his point of view) artistic or biographical and just went with what he considered funny and erotic. It was a mistake. Ed Wood being dead serious is hysterical. Ed Wood trying to be funny is, unfortunately, just stupid.

Interestingly, Wood and director Gary Graver (as "Ed De Priest") superimpose the hippie lifestyle onto these prehistoric cave dwellers. Life in the cave is communal, sexual freedom is encouraged, and the cavemen make peace signs with their hands and even say the word "peace." The hairstyles and sideburns of the cave dwellers are contemporary, as is profane English like "fuck" and "bitch." The women wear make-up, and at least one of them has visible fillings in her teeth. The cavemen drink from coffee mugs and eat from bowls. There is also an asinine *Wizard of Oz* (1939) reference in which a caveman declares, "I'm off to see the lizard."

The nonsensical film begins with a virgin "sacrifice" in which a woman is pleasured by several people and a phallic tool of some sort with a point at its end. Just to ensure that the scene remains free of any expected sexiness, the camera constantly cuts away to a leering caveman recording the event on a stone tablet and on the cave walls.

The cave's fat chieftain provides us with some broad and very short narration similar to that which Criswell (sorely missed here) provided in earlier Wood outings. When one of the women is whisked away and raped by a man in an obvious ape suit, the chieftain says, "Tragedy is happening." Later he will inform us that "tragedy is done." After being raped and then being given the opportunity to escape, the woman will repeatedly return to the ape's lair for another go-around, suggesting that she enjoys the rape (or just loves having sex with an ape). This theme repeats itself throughout the film—men routinely take sex by force, and the women are depicted as enjoying the act. This is, of course, the male fantasy and rationalization of someone with juvenile views and attitudes toward sex and just what constitutes eroticism. In this case, those adolescent attitudes seem to belong to Wood himself as he wrote the screenplay.

It is interesting to note that Wood frequently used the device of the bizarre quasi-omnipotent authority figure as narrator in many of his films. In *Glen or Glenda?* (1953) it was "the scientist"; in *Plan 9 from Outer Space* it was "Criswell the psychic"; in *Orgy of the Dead* it was the Emperor of the Dead. In this film, we have the chieftain who magically knows that "tragedy" has begun and when it ends, and we have the voyeuristic artist that ogles his cave mates having sex and paints representations of it on the walls, on stones and parchment (also anachronistic). Wood seemed preoccupied with the idea that someone was always watching, always recording, and always "pulling the strings" of the characters inhabiting his stories.

It's also strange to note that Wood apparently had some sort of weird ape/homo sapien woman romance fetish as this theme appears in both *One Million AC/DC* and *The Bride and the Beast* (1958).

The interior of the cave is rather phony-looking (just as one expects in a Wood film), and is adorned with skulls à la the cemetery in *Orgy of the Dead* (1965). *One Million AC/DC* suffers from about every shortcoming imaginable, but mostly it is the absence of Woodian dialogue that makes this film difficult to stomach. Hard to imagine an Ed Wood film without that insipid, stilted, and stream-of-consciousness dialogue we all know and love, but it's true. Here the characters mostly just grunt and groan. We are provided a few instances where dialogue is spoken for no reason. We keep expecting it to develop into a plot point, or at least have some sort of a point, but it doesn't The case in point involves the cave leader telling his underlings repeatedly not to let anyone close to the opening of the cave because of the huge plastic dinosaur head outside. Of course, cave people come and go for the duration of this epic and supposedly the underling dutifully jots their names down. What is being done with this information? We never find out. We're just told he has some names. Were those people to be punished? Perhaps the leader wanted to make examples out of their disobedience by making them watch this film over and over again.

There is some small degree of ridiculous dialogue, but these few gems are more juvenile exchanges than the typically inane Wood dialogue.

"Do you have any filthy pictures of your sister?" asks one caveman. He then says, "Wanna see some?" In another such exchange, a caveman says to a female, "That's a terrific outfit you have on. What is it, fox?" And the woman of course answers, "Beaver."

Even the simulated sex scenes are Woodian here. Aside from simply being monotonous, uninspired and poorly acted, these scenes contain such strange absurd sensual acts as sharing chewed-up chicken from one another's mouths. Equally wince-inducing is the silly and juvenile "rhinoceros-style" sex, which is, of course, what is now known as doggie style. Another example of Woodian weirdness is the cave's leader, who enjoys the grapes he eats during intercourse far more than the act itself. When the ruler is called away from sex to a fight to the death, he says only, "Save me some grapes."

At several points in the movie we are treated to integrated footage from other films. Some of these include Ray Harryhausen-like stop motion dinosaurs, as well as footage of two lizards fighting from

Robot Monster (1953). Other footage is from *The Mighty Gorga* (1969). At one point Graver utilizes a fake-looking dinosaur head, which comically peeks over the top of the mountain. He then cuts back and forth between this head and a plastic dinosaur toy. Also of interest, the dinosaur changes colors (the miniature is red, the prop head is green) from shot to shot. One of the film's most Woodian moments comes when the toy dinosaur "eats" a cavewoman; here we see only the feet and legs of what looks like a Barbie doll protruding from the dinosaur's mouth. It's also quite humorous to see the dinosaur tear a woman's clothing off for no other reason than to provide more nudity.

Color is used in an interesting way in *One Million AC/DC.* Several colors of tint are used (green, yellow, and red) in the film, most likely in an attempt to obscure the integrated footage. Also of interest is the top-notch camerawork, provided by Graver, who also worked as a cameraman with the likes of Orson Welles, John Cassavetes, Ron Howard, and, of lesser note, schlockmeister Al Adamson. One scene in particular stands out as being a particularly impressive piece of camerawork; an overly-long scene in which a man chases a woman through the woods looks far better than any scene in such a film as this deserves to look.

And speaking of the woods, *One Million AC/DC* was obviously shot in a variety of locales, such as the desert, the woods, and a waterfall, despite its story all taking place in one location.

In one humorous scene, a caveman chooses to woo a cavewoman the leader has his eye on. This leads to the caveman getting knocked to the ground and speared through the stomach with a magic spear that allows the leader to stab away and never get a drop of blood on the spearhead even though it renders the victim's body a complete mess.

Wood and Graver's caveman opus also depicts the creation of the bow and arrow, which are humorously named backwards (the bow is the arrow, the arrow is the bow). When the cavemen are about to kill the toy dinosaur with the bow and arrow, they sing. The banal song they sing is set to the tune of "For He's a Jolly Good Fellow" and goes as follows: "The spear goes into the monster, the spear goes into the monster, the spear goes into the monster, the monster loses his mind."

One Million AC/DC feels like several different movies in one. Unfortunately, they're all bad movies. First, it's a soft-core porno film (yawn). This may just be the most amazing use of libido-wrecking, snooze-inducing sex ever crafted in the Ed Wood pantheon (and that's saying something). Then, it's a historical adventure with no accurate historical elements and no real adventure. It's also a comedy without laughs. Despite these many shortcomings, followers of Edward D. Wood, Jr.'s work are sure to find this a fascinating example of the impact Wood's dialogue (and the lack thereof) makes in his films.

It should also be noted that while much has been made of the pseudonym Akdon Telmig (a slight reworking of "vodka gimlet"), the pseudonym was used by Graver, not Wood as has been previously reported. Graver rewrote much of the screenplay adding in jokes pulled directly from back issues of *Playboy.* He then credited this pseudonym rather than himself or Wood. "Gary used to get so mad because everyone thought the Akdon Telmig thing was Ed Wood, but it was him," Graver's friend and collaborator Fred Olen Ray says. "But you know, people think they know everything."

CREDITS: Producer: Gary Graver; Director: Gary Graver; Screenplay: Edward D. Wood, Jr.; Cinematographer: Gary Graver; Sound: Mike Strange; Sam Kopetzky.

CAST: Susan Berkely; Billy Wolf; Sharon Wells; Natasha; Nancy McGavin; Todd Badker; Tony Brooks; Pam English; Shari Stevens; John Lee; Bonnie Walker; Harry Stone; Mary Doyle; Gail Lavon; Greg Mathis; Larry Vincente; April O'Connor; Lesley Conners; Jacqueline Fox; Gary Kent; Jack King; Maria Lease; Antoinette Maynard; Alain Patrick; Walt Phillips.

Love Feast (1969)

As ridiculous as *One Million AC/DC* (1969) was, *Love Feast* (also known as *Pretty Models All in a Row* and *The Photographer*), written by Wood and directed by Joseph F. Robertson, somehow managed to lower Ed Wood further down into the depths of the porn abyss into which he had been sinking for some time. Although it is not one of Wood's hardcore efforts, we believe it represents a low-water mark in the canon of his films. Why? Because Wood appears in the lead role of this film (as Mr. Murphy) and engages in a number of embarrassing acts. One must wonder if Wood was as uncomfortable performing these strange acts as his fans are seeing him doing them.

By 1969, the skinny, dapper good-looking Edward D. Wood, Jr. of the 1950s was a thing of the past. After decades of alcoholism, Wood looked terrible here. No Dentures. His disheveled hair was now shoulder length, and he had gained a bit of weight; he wasn't obese, but he was considerably heavier than he had been when audiences had last seen him. He just looks beat down here, as though time and countless failures had begun to take a significant toll on his body.

Wood spends a great deal of this picture in baggy, ill fitting underwear, crawling around on all fours and acting silly. When he isn't doing that, he's dressing like a woman (natch!) and/or licking someone's boots clean. Whether Wood himself was embarrassed by this, we will never know, but we can conclude that this wasn't the type of thing Wood initially got into film making to do. Clearly his idol Orson Welles, who sank as low as to do beer and wine commercials, would never have made a film in which he wore only underwear and licked people's dirty footwear.

Wood manages to cram so much of his own personal brand of weirdness (as well as his own fetishes) into this film that one must wonder if this was a case like *Glen or Glenda?* (1953), where the producers asked for one thing and Wood delivered something else entirely. We can easily envision the film's financiers asking Wood to script an orgy film. We find it somewhat more difficult to envision them asking him to write in scenes in which he dresses like a woman and licks boots. In terms of pornography, a simple orgy is quite vanilla (especially as it is shown here); however, much of the strangeness Wood brings to the film is less than mainstream in terms of fetishes and accepted sexuality. In many ways this, like *Glen or Glenda?*, is clearly Wood's own fantasies coming to life before our eyes. The fact that he managed to find someone to finance the filming of these fantasies is really quite remarkable.

As the opening song (the aptly-titled "Love Feast") plays over the soundtrack, the film's opening credit sequence provides us with a pretty good idea of what this film is all about; we see an abundance of hairy vaginas flashing across the screen, and the names of the actors and crew members are painted on the bodies of naked women. While this may have been hot fare in the time in which it was produced, the film's stark lighting and ridiculously-hairy vaginas now make the film sort of repellent (at least in our humble opinions).

Wood's character, Mr. Murphy, dressed in a cheap off-the-rack suit, informs us that he loves all types of girls but that there isn't enough time for all of them. Murphy then shows us his sleazy technique in bedding women. He pretends to be a photographer and telephones numerous modeling agencies, asking to have female models sent to his home.

When the first model arrives at Murphy's home, he tells her that he wants to photograph her wearing a new line of see-through garments and that he must photograph her nude in order to size her up for the clothing. The model, who only moments before said she would not allow herself to be photographed nude, falls for this ploy and begins stripping down. When Murphy assists her in getting undressed, she apparently sees nothing out of the ordinary in this.

Murphy salivates over her. "Yes, I think you will do nicely." He then tells us that his motto is "a model is a model is a model." When

Murphy starts to make out with the prudish model who only moments before said she would never take off her clothing, she goes along with it and even spurs Wood on. This is, of course, Woodian logic. After all, what beautiful young model wouldn't immediately respond to a wet slobbery kiss by becoming a lust-inflamed sexpot for Wood's pervy old fat photographer?

But just as they start to make out heavily, the doorbell rings and Murphy must go and answer the door. When he does, he finds another model standing there waiting. She then calls Murphy a "big beautiful gorgeous hunk of man." Murphy then exclaims that "a photographer's life is a tough one." This second model doesn't even pretend she's there for anything beyond sex, and Murphy doesn't bother to mention the photography. He just pushes her into the bedroom with the first model and then all three of them begin to make out. The two beautiful women are completely naked while Wood's Murphy resumes crawling around amongst them wearing only unappealing baggy underwear.

When the doorbell rings again, we the audience understand that this is supposed to be one of the running gags through the film and that presumably we're supposed to find this repetition funny. Not so much. Fifteen minutes in we realize that *Love Feast* is going to be tediously repetitive and the jokes are going to make us pine for the deathly-serious efforts Wood made a decade earlier. "Playtime's over again," Murphy says, putting his clothes back on. When he leaves to answer the door, the two models left on the bed begin to kiss each other passionately in an overly-long scene that reminded us of a mother bird trying to feed her hungry chick.

Murphy, who still hasn't had any sex yet, is already so exhausted that he doesn't want to answer the door. This is played for laughs, but such scenes are only (inadvertently) funny in this film because of their sheer ridiculousness and utter ineptitude. When Murphy finally answers the door, he, of course, finds a third model awaiting him. He looks her over and then says, "I thought I was worn out, but after looking at you I feel like a new man!" Murphy then plays some "undressing music" on the phonograph player and the model strips with absolutely no prompting whatsoever. Murphy then snaps a couple of photos of her and says, "You photograph wonderfully!" He then delivers some deliciously cheesy Woodian dialogue—

"from the top of your head to your toes, toes, toes, you make me want to go, go, go!"

Predictably, all four of them end up in bed, rolling around (again, all the women are nude and Murphy wears only his briefs. Why doesn't Wood fully undress? We can't say for sure, but it doesn't make us sad that he doesn't). And, even more predictably, the doorbell rings again. Murphy screams angrily, but then gets up. (The thought of not answering the door never occurs to him.) This time it's not a model but a male cabbie who has gone to the wrong address. Murphy then invites him to join the orgy and more sex ensues.

Murphy, now even more worn out, leaves the cabbie and the three models to have sex in his bedroom. He goes outside for relaxation. He sits down and fixes himself a drink. The film then cuts back and forth between Murphy, enjoying his drink, and the orgy inside. (The orgy as it is depicted in this film is much less than arousing; all of its participants are just rolling around and giggling nude in a giant wad of humanity, and the camera seems to linger on hairy, writhing buttholes, both male and female.)

A fourth model then shows up. Murphy tells her to join the fray. He himself is about to rejoin the orgy when the doorbell rings again. By this point in the film, ringing doorbells and needless scenes showing Ed Wood stripping and then redressing have become more than a little bit tedious. When Wood answers the door, guess who's there? Yes, of course, it's model number five. "Come in and have a ball," Murphy says, "or two!" He then laughs maniacally.

The doorbell rings again. Murphy gets up but doesn't answer it. "I need a coffee break!" he exclaims. He then returns to his drink in the backyard. "Peace and quiet at last!" It is never made clear why exactly Murphy is always tired despite the fact that he has had absolutely no sex. And if he didn't want all of these women here, then why did he invite them? Of course this is a Wood script, so such questions will never be adequately answered.

Model number six continues to ring the doorbell, but no one answers.

"My god," Murphy says. "Don't they ever stop?"

This sixth model opens the door and just goes in and joins the orgy with no prompting. (Man, models must really be easy!) Murphy soon rejoins the group. "Well, here we go again!" But just as Murphy climbs into the bed and buries himself in a sea of naked bodies, a car pulls up out front and the driver starts honking the horn. The exhausted Murphy crawls, his shirt half off and backwards, to the front door, where he finds four models.

Meanwhile, back at the orgy, a pair of male plumbers show up out of nowhere. Where the hell did they come from? We have no clue. One of the plumbers is carrying a huge wrench and the other a toilet plunger. The one with the wrench starts attempting to stick the wrench into bad places on the men and women in the orgy, and the other plumber begins plumbing people's butts with the toilet plunger. If all of this sounds hilarious, it is, but not in the way Wood intended; this scene is surely Exhibit A in the How Not to Make a Porno tutorial. It's just terrible, even by the exceedingly low standards of pornography.

Back in the front room, the four beautiful models who have just shown up fasten a dog collar around Murphy's neck. These models apparently showed up for no other reason than to have sex with Murphy. In what is clearly a Wood fantasy, the four beautiful women force him to dress in women's garments and high heels. Then, in what must be seen as the lowest ebb of Wood's career, he is forced to lick one of the women's boots clean as one of the women rubs his dirty underwear all over his body.

At the end of the film, Murphy promises that he will continue to call modeling agencies in the future.

Love Feast is ridiculous yet fascinating for many reasons, and all of them have to do with Wood's view of what people consider erotic and scintillating. Porn "logic" is skewed at best; after all, porn is a world where plumbers and pizza delivery men routinely plumb and deliver more than toilets and pizzas. Despite the accepted level of absurdity found in such films, they still manage to be more logical than the "logic" employed by Wood here. It's almost as if he sat down with a child on the verge of adolescence and asked him what a porno was and then went on to ask the child to describe what he/she imagined that would look like and then sat down to write his script.

There is nudity aplenty in *Love Feast*, and arguably sex too, but it's all as flaccidly depicted as Mr. Murphy's baggy underwear. There's not one ounce of eroticism, no fire whatsoever to be found within this film. It's amazing to us that anyone who has ever had sex could conceive of such a bland, monotonous movie. It's like the cross dressing *is* Wood's sex; the fetish of wearing women's clothing is the whole of the act. Everything else, like the actual sex, is just extraneous material thrown in to pad the running time. If old-fashioned tried-and-true intercourse is boring to Wood imagine the disconnect most of the audience will feel.

One person present for a screening of this film commented, "I don't watch porn films, but I find it interesting that there clearly is a way to make them ineptly, and Wood found it."

Despite its many shortcomings, *Love Feast* remains a curiosity for Wood enthusiasts. While it's painful to see the depths to which Wood sunk here, the film contains enough unintentional humor to make viewing it a worthwhile experience.

CREDITS: Producer: Joseph F. Robertson; Director: Joseph F. Robertson; Screenplay: Joseph F. Robertson; Edward D. Wood, Jr.; Cinematographer: Hal Guthu; Editor: Harry Kaye.

CAST: Edward D. Wood, Jr. (Mr. Murphy); Mia Coco (Black Model); Linda Colpin (Linda); Casey Lorrain (See-Through Clothing Model); Cynthia Denny (Dolly); Neola Graef (Girl in Red Miniskirt); Lynn Harris (Credits Girl); Heather Starr (Susan).

Take It Out in Trade
(1970)

Down on his luck and hard up for money (as was the usual), Edward D. Wood, Jr. turned to hardcore pornography to make a quick buck. Despite its dubious nature, *Take It Out in Trade* would be Wood's first film as a director in a decade.

In casting the film, Wood selected frequent collaborator and longtime drinking buddy Duke Moore to appear in the film as a wealthy socialite. He then asked his old pal Kenne Duncan's girlfriend, burlesque dancer Nona Carver, to appear in the film. She agreed, and they were on their way.

As the story goes, Wood met a man in a bar who said he wanted to get hold of some pornographic films. Wood then convinced the man to allow him to make a porno film specially for him. "[He said] if you got a couple thousand dollars, you can make some money, and I'll make two versions," Carver later told Wood biographer Rudolph Grey (in *Nightmare of Ecstasy*). "One you can sell to the distributors, perfectly legit. And we'll get some scenes in there that you can cut out for your private collection."

Sadly, the original film is lost today. Rudolph Grey claims to have seen the film, so one must believe a copy of it exists *somewhere*. But it is not currently available to the masses. Interestingly, a sixty-nine-minute-long collection of outtakes exists, giving us some idea of what the film would have looked like.

Take It Out in Trade was to be a detective story about a private eye named Mac McGregor (Michael Donovan O'Donnell), who interviews a lot of people in the film and also has sex with many different women. Unlike Wood's previous films, this picture was to rely on a number of sight gags. Also of interest, almost everything in the film is red; carpets and drapes and stairs, etc.

When watching the *Take It Out in Trade* outtakes, one thing stands out regarding Wood's filmmaking—he frequently used multiple takes, dispelling the theory that he only ever used a single take and then moved on.

It should also be noted that Wood himself appears in an extended scene in the film as "Alecia," a drag queen wearing an angora sweater.

Based on the outtakes, the film doesn't look to be much; the world did not lose another *Casablanca* (1942) when it lost *Take It Out in Trade*. However, the film remains significant as it was one of the few features actually directed by Wood himself, and it also marked his first foray into hardcore pornography. Perhaps one day the copy Rudolph Grey saw will see the light of day. Until then, we can only watch the outtake reel and speculate on what might have been.

CREDITS: Producer: Richard Gonzales; Edward Ashdown; Director: Edward D. Wood, Jr.; Screenplay: Edward D. Wood, Jr.; Cinematographer: Hal Guthu; Editor: Michael J. Sheridan; Edward D. Wood, Jr.

CAST: Donna Stanley (Shirley Riley); Michael Donovan O'Donnell (Mac McGregor); Duke Moore (Frank Riley); Edward D. Wood, Jr. (Alecia); Nona Carver (Sleazy Maisie Rumpledinck); Casey Lorrain; Linda Colpin; Monica Gayle; Emilie Gray; Donna Young; Lynn Harris; Andrea Rabins; James Kitchens; Hugh Talbert; Judith Koch.

Venus Flytrap (1970)

In the midst of his ongoing adventures in the world of pornography, Ed Wood returned to his science-fiction/horror roots with the Japanese-produced *Venus Flytrap*. The film, which stars James Craig as a scientist gone crazy, was also released under the alternate titles *The Devil Garden, The Double Garden* (likely just a poor Japanese translation of the former title), and most interestingly *The Revenge of Doctor X*, which has nothing whatsoever to do with the film's storyline. (One might guess it was intended to fool viewers into believing it was a sequel to *Doctor X* and/or *The Return of Doctor X*, which again bear no relation to this film.) For many years Wood's involvement in the project was unknown; however, it appears on a resume Wood himself provided for filmmaker Fred Olen Ray in the mid-1980s. Interestingly, it is unknown whether this film ever played in the United States.

Despite its being directed by Kenneth G. Crane, *Venus Flytrap* contains all the classic tried-and-true elements of vintage 1950s-era Wood projects. The film is of course a science fiction film featuring a mad scientist, is as melodramatic as the day is long, is deathly serious, contains its fair share of stock footage, non sequiturs, forgotten plot threads, stiff acting, flat dialogue, and a story steeped in the sort of logic only Ed Wood could bring to a project.

As with every film written by Wood but directed by another helmer, it's fascinating to see how someone else approaches the material. In most cases, the spirit and absurdity of Wood's contributions shines through despite the film's having numerous fingerprints on it, so to speak.

As is the case with many of Wood's classic films, *Venus Flytrap* opens on a man sitting stationary behind a desk. In this case the man is

Dr. Bragan (Craig), a National Aeronautics and Space Administration (NASA) scientist awaiting the launch of a rocket he has toiled on for the past five years. At first it appears that weather conditions will delay the rocket's launch, but in the end it is launched on schedule. However, after a few moments of stilted dialogue, Dr. Bragan's team rushes in to explain that there may have been a grave mistake in calculations. Bragan reacts by shouting that there's no margin for error and "those are the facts!" (Wood certainly loved to make his characters soliloquize on the "facts." We're not counting but it seems to happen in nearly every one of his horror/sci-fi efforts.) Bragan collapses under the strain of all this hard work, and it is suggested that he take a lengthy vacation. Bragan explains in Woodian fashion that his fatigue is largely caused by mathematics, which are "more complicated now than in any other time of history."Humorously, a miniature American flag adorns Bragan's desk to let us know that this scene is supposed to take place in the United States (it was actually filmed in Japan).

When deciding where to go for his hiatus, Bragan's superior, Dr. Nakamura (James Yagi) suggests his homeland of Japan. He then arranges for Bragan to be escorted by his cousin, who will assist him during his stay in Tokyo.

En route to the airport, Bragan's car breaks down. (Luckily this happens right smack dab in front of a gas station that proudly sports a wooden sign advertising gas *and* snakes.) When he gets out of his car, Bragan cannot find anyone at the station. He then walks around the building and opens the door of a garage labeled "Snake House." There he finds a man who doubles as a snake handler and mechanic. The man giggles maniacally while holding two snakes, which he has named Ernie and Gordon. He explains that his garage is filled with snakes, and urges Bragan to go inside and look at them. "Snakes have never been of interest to me," Bragan says, but the man insists; he says he will look at the broken-down automobile while Bragan takes a look at the snakes.

Inside the garage, Bragan finds a Venus Flytrap—a carnivorous plant that feeds on unsuspecting flies. When the snakehandler/mechanic returns, Bragan asks if he can purchase the plant. The man tells him no, but tells him that he can locate many of them in the swamp which happens to be located right behind the filling station.

(In Wood Land, there always seems to be a swamp on hand. Cemeteries are another classic Wood staple, although there is not one to be found in this particular scene.) In classic Wood fashion, Bragan is immediately confronted in the swamp by a large rubber snake that is coiled into a sinister nap position. The snake does absolutely nothing and Bragan heroically scoops it up with his shovel and hurls the vile creature away (after all, you never know when a rubber snake may spring to life) and goes about his business searching for a Venus Flytrap. He eventually locates one and takes it with him.

Next we are treated to stock footage of a passenger plane flying. Bragan is onboard, and when he takes out his Venus Flytrap during the flight, a stewardess marvels at it. She says thankfully it's a small plant as "a big one could take your arm off." After landing, Bragan is met at the airport by Dr. Nakamura's cousin, Noriko, who turns out to be a lovely young woman. After a quick refreshment— "refreshment" being Wood code for alcoholic beverages—Bragan and Noriko head for an old abandoned hotel which is owned by her father. During the drive, the two are nearly killed by a stock footage landslide. Bragan gets out of the automobile and within thirty seconds—off-screen—manages somehow to move the large boulders out of their path. Then a stock footage volcano erupts, threatening to harm them. (These are apparently rough lands, where one could be killed by a stock footage disaster at any given moment.) Once they arrive at the hotel, the stock footage volcano erupts again, and with a little cinema magic by way of a shaken camera, the ground shakes them violently. Then, about a minute later, everyone seems to have completely forgotten and/or simply stopped caring about the dangerous eruptions.

At the hotel, Bragan and Noriko are met by the caretaker, who has a visible Quasimodo hunchback (in one of many nods to classic Universal horror films) and loves to play foreboding music on the pipe organ. The caretaker will soon become a second assistant to Dr. Bragan, who is then shown to his greenhouse laboratory; this is surely the crappiest cinematic mad scientist laboratory this side of *Bride of the Monster* (1955), showcasing little more than dirt clods and tangled plastic vines. Bragan immediately sets out to string up some electrical wires to his laboratory in a severe windstorm in which we can hear the wind howling and yet nothing is disturbed in the slightest.

We are never told why this is, but the once-likeable Dr. Bragan soon begins to experience severe mood swings. (Perhaps this was Wood's way of telling us that Bragan was turning into a mad scientist.) When Noriko tries to tell him about an impregnated dog that lives on the premises, Bragan rudely informs her that he has more important things on his mind. Later, when Noriko touches the box containing the Venus Flytrap, Bragan once again loses his cool. "That box is not to be disturbed!"

Later Bragan changes his mind and asks Noriko to be his assistant on his little science project. He shows her the Venus Flytrap, saying, "It's an interesting plant, our little cannibal." After showing her that the plant can reason, passing on an insect it deems too small for appropriate nourishment, Bragan explains that he believes mankind evolved from plant life. "This plant can think," he says. "Why can't it be human?" This of course makes no sense, but that's part of the fun of this Ed Wood-penned screenplay.

In the next scene Bragan sits in his room obsessing on his Venus Flytrap while somewhere else in the hotel the caretaker pounds a dirge on the pipe organ. Just in case someone somewhere missed the fact that ominous things are afoot we are treated to a rumbling thunderstorm. Bragan decides he can't sit in his room any longer. He grabs his lab coat and goes sneaking across a cemetery located behind the hotel. (See, we told you.) This has nothing to do with anything, but nevertheless the cemetery is there. Also, we're curious why Bragan would sneak to his lab when he would have every right to go there whenever he chooses. Hmm.

Soon Bragan begins speaking to the Venus Flytrap as though it were human. "Like all humans, you're weak," he says. He then declares that it's his mission to make the plant "the most powerful thing in the universe." When lightning strikes outside, he screams giddily, "Perhaps lightning will become your father!" At this point we have no clue what exactly this means (other than it's an obvious nod to *Son of Frankenstein*, 1939), but who cares? This is all deliciously-good Woodian fun.

Bragan comes up with a new theory; he plans to graft together a Venus Flytrap and a Venus Vesticulosa—a plant found on the bottom of the ocean that eats fish—to create an all new species of carnivorous plant. He then goes to the beach and dives into the water in search of the plant. When he is unable to locate it, he goes berserk and begins tearing random plants from the bottom of the ocean. "I tried to tear up the whole ocean bottom with my bear hands," he later explains. Noriko proves to be an able assistant, introducing Bragan to a group of bare-breasted native women. (They use snorkels and masks but apparently know nothing about clothing to cover their breasts.) Bragan shows the women a photograph of the Venus Vesticulosa in a book he just happens to be carrying around with him, and they point him in the right direction.

Bragan then locates the plant, digs it up from the ocean bottom, and takes it with him. He explains to Noriko that he plans to create a "plant as human as the human element itself."

Despite his new find, Bragan is soon up to his old tricks, lashing out at Noriko. "The success of my creation is all that matters to me!" As the experimentation continues, he becomes meaner and meaner.

After Bragan grafts the two plants together and we're given an ultra cheap rehash of Frankenstein hoisting his creation into the raining night sky to make contact with lightning. He unveils it. It now looks like a monster (read: man in a ridiculous rubber suit) with a sweet onion head, stiff stringy roots for hair, eyes and human appendages, as well as Venus Flytraps for hands and feet. It is as wacky and silly as anything in this film. Eyeballing his new creation, Bragan does what any self-respecting mad scientist would do—he throws his head back and cackles maniacally. Within the next day, Bragan realizes that the plant is dying. Noriko urges him to bury the plant and forget about it, but the doctor has other plans. He attempts to feed puppies to the plant, but Noriko manages to stop him. "I wish that thing had died!" she exclaims, running out of the room. We have now journeyed into an epically inferior riff on *Little Shop of Horrors* (1960).

As if the puppies weren't enough, Bragan vows to feed the plant human blood, thus making it more human. Rather than taking a sample of his own blood—that would be far too easy—Bragan breaks into a nearby sanitarium and steals a needle full of blood from a patient. He then injects the blood into the plant creature. "By morning we should have proof positive," he says.

Only moments later, the plant grabs the hunchback servant's head and tries to eat him, but the man gets away.

"You are no longer Dr. Bragan, scientist," Noriko screams. "You are becoming Dr. Bragan, madman!" When the doctor and Noriko are away, the mother dog is killed by the plant. Noriko doubts that the creature can move from place to place on its own volition, but Bragan sets out to prove it can walk. He tells Noriko that the two of them will sit and watch the plant until it moves. This, however, fails to work as the plant sees them and sprays some sort of knockout gas into their faces, rendering them unconscious. It gets loose and leaves the hotel and laboratory and begins killing unsuspecting villagers.

When Bragan awakes, he screams, "My creation! It's gone!" He then sets out to find the stray plant, discovering that the villagers have already assembled in Frankenstein fashion with lit torches in tow.

"Unless I miss my guess," Bragan says, "my creation is so powerful now it can devour anything."

He promises to go and kill the plant, urging Noriko to stay. He explains that it's his creation, and thus his responsibility. He goes into the mountains in search of the plant monster, carrying a lamb to lure it. Once he's away from Noriko, he explains his true motives—he plans to save the plant monster and continue his experimentation. "We'll fool 'em, you and I," he says. "We'll escape, you and I."

Suddenly Bragan is enveloped in a thick layer of fog-machine-made fog. After all, this is high drama; you've gotta have some fog...

The plant approaches Bragan. He holds out the lamb, and the monster reaches its leafy arms for him, inadvertently knocking them both into a fiery death inside a stock footage volcano.

And the film is over.

Venus Flytrap is Wood's own concoction containing equal parts *Frankenstein* (1931) and *Little Shop of Horrors* with a little *Day of the Triffids* (1963) thrown in for good measure. Despite the best efforts of those involved, the film really doesn't work at any single point during its entire ninety-four-minute running time. And while the film contains its fair share of classic Woodian elements, one can't help but think it would have been a better film had Wood been given the opportunity to direct it himself. Kenneth G. Crane does an adequate job in terms of el cheapo Z-grade movies, but *Venus Flytrap* lacks the underlying passion that typifies Wood's own directorial efforts.

Another problem with the film is that the music playing on the soundtrack is frequently at odds with what's going on onscreen. An even bigger complaint concerning the music is that it feels like a disjointed mishmash, a very jarring and irritating mishmash as though it were a collection of songs from different movie soundtracks randomly selected with absolutely zero thought in placement. Some of the tunes are bouncy and light while others are dark, menacing organ compositions. Then there's the odd appearance of Bach's "Toccata in d minor." Our best guess is that, in true Wood fashion, the soundtrack was made up of royalty-free public domain music in an effort to save producers a few dollars.

Humorously, the credits that appear on the movie as it now exists are actually from another film, Eddie Romero's *Mad Doctor on Blood Island* (1968). These credits have nothing to do with this film, but apparently ended up tacked onto the film when the two movies were going to be released in theaters together.

Unlike most of his projects from the 1970s, *Venus Flytrap* is a must-see proposition for Wood fans. While the rest of them were depressing sex pictures lacking the spunk (no pun intended) of Wood's previous work, this one contains enough wacky Woodian moments to make for a memorable viewing. It's not quite *Plan 9 from Outer Space* (1959), but then what is?

CREDITS: Director: Kenneth G. Crane; Screenplay: Edward D. Wood, Jr.

CAST: James Craig (Dr. Bragan); James Yagi (Dr. Paul Nakamura); Lawrence O'Neill (American at Airport); Al Ricketts (Gas Station Owner); Atsuko Rome (Noriko Hanamura); Edward M. Shannon (Dr. Shannon); John Stanley (Dr. Stanley); Tota Kondo (Customs Officer).

Necromania: A Tale of Strange Love (1971)

Very little is known about Ed Wood's very first hardcore porn effort, *The Only House* (1970), as it remains lost today. We do know that Wood climbed back on that same horse only months later to craft a second hardcore feature, based on the same Wood novel, titled *Necromania: A Tale of Strange Love*. The film, which was released in two versions—a fifty-one-minute "R" rated movie and a fifty-four-minute "X" rated movie—is not very good to say the least; not even by Wood standards. This film, which Wood wrote and directed under the pseudonym Don Miller, is as repulsive and repellent as anything ever produced, even by typical 1970s porn standards. Perhaps this is the reason why the film tells us its cast "wishes to remain anonymous."

Interestingly, Wood had to utilize two cameramen—Ted Gorley and Hal Guthu—on the film because one of them refused to shoot the hardcore scenes.

The film, which would be Wood's first team up with porn starlet Rene Bond, fixates on many of Wood's old obsessions—primarily death and mortality. If these sound like strange themes for a porno movie, you're absolutely correct. So what's wrong with it, speaking strictly in standard porn standards? The women have sagging breasts and hairy, pimply asses, and the men have ugly uncircumcised penises that never seem to be hard. Also, the women's vaginas are so grotesquely hairy that they look like they've got bear heads in leg locks. The vaginas in this film don't even look like vaginas, but rather some hideously repulsive thing you'd never want to see again as long as you live!

And the film's plot? What plot? Even by the standards of other Wood films and typical porno films of the era, the plot is less than thin. Anyone watching *Necromania* strictly for classic Woodian moments are bound to be disappointed.

The film opens with a young couple arriving at the sex-filled lair of Madame Heles, a "necromancer"—don't bother looking up the word, Wood has his own definition—who uses black magic to enhance the sexual prowess of her guests. The young couple are pretending to be married, and they have a discussion about keeping this information from their hostess.

Soon after their arrival, the young couple meet Madame Heles' assistant, Tanya, who informs them that her boss doesn't receive visitors until the hour of midnight. In the meanwhile, however, she hands them a dildo "to service you." She also instructs them to "squeeze this little dong for attention."

Once Tanya is gone, the woman insults her boyfriend's manhood and reminds him that they are here because he cannot satisfy her. She says this is his last chance to learn to satisfy her, or she's going to dissolve the relationship.

Meanwhile, behind closed doors, Tanya informs her boss, Madame Heles, that the couple is "as you suspected—not married." To this Madame Heles says they are "ripe for our purposes." Tanya then goes to the room of "quickie artist" Carl, who wants to have sex with her. "Haste makes waste," she reminds him. He then performs cunnilingus on her for what feels like half the running time of the entire movie. She then reciprocates as Madame Heles observes their actions through eye-holes in a painting.

Humorously, both of them have dirty blackened feet, making their lovemaking somewhat less than appealing.

Next up is a lengthy lesbian twist between the young woman and an "inmate" of Madame Heles' sex compound. As the two women go at it, each of them looking disinterested, we are exposed to what have to be the hairiest pubic patches ever captured on celluloid. And guess what? The two lesbians also have black feet. One might guess the black feet represented something deep and profound—either that or the house where Wood was shooting had extremely filthy carpet. (We'll go with that one.) Because one of the women spends ten minutes licking the other woman's pubic hair rather than actually performing cunnilingus, one would guess the actress had reservations about doing what Wood's script called for. Perhaps she was a method actress, and was questioning her character's motivations... But more than likely she just didn't want to commit to the act.

After having sex with Tanya, Carl attempts to put his pajama pants on, but finds difficulty in doing so. The actor even laughs at this, and guess what? Wood leaves all of this in the film. Tanya then moves on to the other guy (we have no idea what his name is) who arrived with the other woman (ditto) and seduces him. She plays around with his uncircumcised johnson for a while, and says, "This could prove to be very interesting." He responds with the inspired line, "This is all very confusing," to which she says, "Soon you will be confused no more!" (What is he confused about? Probably the plot, which makes zero sense; either that or why we haven't heard his name mentioned yet.) Tanya explains to the young man that she and Madame Heles work to "scare devils and inhibitions from the mortal soul." This is, of course, gibberish. She also says that "not all react to the treatment successfully," pointing out that those who fail are doomed to have wild orgy sex for all of eternity.

Soon both couples converge at an altar that is adorned with an inverted cross, skulls, chalices, and a variety of candles. As part of the ritual, the two women caress each others' flabby breasts, then breaking into full-fledged half-hearted sex. We then hear moaning from inside the coffin (which was reportedly the same coffin Criswell used in the early Wood films), and Madame Heles sits up inside the coffin.

It is now time for Madame Heles' "personal sex teachings." The man is then forced into the coffin, where he and Madame Heles have wild sex, occasionally bumping its lid open.

The end.

Interestingly, the role of Madame Heles was initially offered to Maila "Vampira" Nurmi, who promptly said hell no, calling it "professional suicide." Also of note, Wood supposedly directed *Necromania* while wearing pink women's clothing. Is this fact or just more made-up lore? Sadly, we'll probably never know.

But we shouldn't be surprised at the low quality of the film, which is clearly Wood's worst as director, considering it was shot from a scant twenty-page script on a meager budget of $7,000. The career decline of Wood, who once believed his *The Sinister Urge* (1960) was a "racy picture," is very much evident here. While he doesn't lick anyone's dirty shoes here like he did in *The Love Feast* (1969), this must surely have been an embarrassing moment in Wood's career. *Necromania* may not have been the lowest point of Wood's entire career, but it is certainly the lowest point of his directorial filmography.

CREDITS: Producer: Edward D. Wood, Jr.; Director: Edward D. Wood, Jr.; Screenplay: Edward D. Wood, Jr. (based on the novel *The Only House* by Ed Wood); Cinematographer: Hal Guthu; Ted Gorley; Editor: Edward D. Wood, Jr.

CAST: Maria Aronoff (Madame Heles); Rene Bond (Shirley); Rick Lutze (Danny).

The Undergraduate (1971)

At the outset of hardcore pornography, adult film producers often made their smut under the guise of being sexual education documentaries. *The Undergraduate*, written by Edward D. Wood, Jr., is one of these pseudo-sex-education films. During this period, there were numerous exploitation films that made their money from footage of babies being born. (Imagine masturbating to that!) *The Undergraduate*, thankfully, does not feature such footage. However, the footage that it does feature isn't much better...

This is a film for completists only. (We will say this numerous times in this volume in regards to Wood's smut output, considering so much of it wasn't very good—even by porn standards.) *The Undergraduate* is the worst of the worst in the Wood canon of pornography. It has no plot, features no Woodian dialogue, and isn't even remotely sensual.

For example, this "educational film" features such (sarcasm here) erotic scenes as an extreme close-up shot of a vaginal suppository being inserted into a vagina. While such a scene might have been considered sexy (doubtful) in a time when vaginas simply weren't shown onscreen, it certainly isn't sexy now.

But if you are 12-years-old and want to know about the basics of sex, this is your movie. In *The Undergraduate* viewers learn about the origins of masturbation, how to put on a condom, and what exactly a dildo is ("the replacement for a male penis"). However, if you are over the age of 12 or know anything at all about sex, this film is likely to be of little interest.

One of the film's most (only?) interesting scenes features a narrator quoting from the Bible as a man's testicles are massaged on screen.

This is surreal as all hell; it's not exactly entertaining, but it's one of those things only Ed Wood could have dreamed up.

The Undergraduate was lost for many years until Alpha Blue Archives dug it up and released it to DVD in 2014. While it's interesting in that it helps to fill in the holes in Wood's filmography, it isn't interesting for much of anything else.

CREDITS: Producer: Jacques Descent, John Flanders; Director: John Flanders (as Ron Black); Screenplay: Edward D. Wood, Jr.; Cinematographer: Howard Schwartz; Editor: Unknown.

CAST: Suzanne Fields, Tina Russell, Cindy West, Eve Orlon, Edward D. Wood, Jr.

The Young Marrieds
(1971)

The Young Marrieds is another pseudo-documentary presented with the intentions of improving viewers' marital relationships. It was written and directed by Edward D. Wood, Jr., whom uses the pseudonym "Richard Trent" here.

The film follows Ben (Louis Wolf), a man who is obsessed with strippers and magazine smut models. He cannot gather much interest for his frigid wife, Ginny (Alice Friedland), as she does not fit into his view of what a sensual woman should be. He longs for the pin-up girl, the stripper, who will fulfill his sexual desires.

As Ben searches for personal fulfillment, Wood takes a moment to incongruously vent about homosexuals—a theme that will recur in several of the screenwriter's films. Through the Ben character, Wood explains his views that homosexuality is "weird" and "not right." He goes on to say, "I don't like fags and queers," and proclaims that gays are "lousy weirdo freaks." As we will discuss time and time again in this book, it's fascinating that Wood, who longed for people to understand his own sexual appetites, seemed to have absolutely no tolerance for homosexuality. This theme is particularly nasty and biting in this instance as it has absolutely nothing to do with the story he is telling; it is completely non-sequitur and unneeded.

Making matters worse, Wood apparently wants us to feel sympathy for Ben, a cheater, a louse, and a homophobe. Wood's and Ben's conclusion is that all of Ben's problems can be solved if the frigid wifey character succumbs to all of Ben's desires. But Wood (and Ben) completely disregard her wants, needs, and desires. Next to no thought is given to the female perspective. Instead, Ginny is treated like an irritating bitch when she wants to be wanted for her own merits and not as some generic sex-toy model for Ben to desire.

This, like the other smut films Wood himself directed, isn't particularly good, even in terms of 1970s pornography. When studied closely, *The Young Marrieds* gives us one of the clearest looks at Wood, the man, and what we see isn't particularly likeable.

This film was lost for many years until Alpha Blue found it, restored it, and released it on DVD in 2014. Perhaps this one should have remained lost.

CREDITS: Producer: Edward D. Wood, Jr.; Director: Edward D. Wood, Jr.; Screenplay: Edward D. Wood, Jr.; Cinematographer: Unknown; Editor: Unknown.

CAST: Louis Wolf (Ben), Alice Friedland (Ginny), George Blac (Friend), Cynthia Walker (The Girl).

The Nympho Cycler (1972)

This Ed Wood-directed sex picture was lost until 2013. In fact, it was basically unknown until that time, as it is not listed in any previous book or article on Wood. Unfortunately for some of us, this film resurfaced. With *Nympho Cycler*, Wood obviously sought to cash in on the biker movie trend that was popular at the time. Perhaps in his haste to serve movie audiences with a topic in vogue, or perhaps in a dash to pay the rent, Wood forgot to include a coherent (even by his standards) script or plot; the only thing that mattered was that there was sex and motorcycles in it.

The film features actress Casey Larrain, who had made a small appearance previously in *Love Feast* (1969). According to Larrain, Wood cast her because she could ride a motorcycle. But Larrain shows a capability of doing much more than simply riding a motorcycle in this film, as her acting is as good as anything that appears in any of Wood's films. On the flip side of that coin, Wood himself plays her transvestite (naturally) hubby, and his acting is about as bad here as it is any of the Wood canon. Interestingly, Wood yells most of his lines.

The film begins with our protagonist, Misty (Larrain), asking, "Have you met any nymphomaniacs lately?" She then goes on to tell us that she is a nymphomaniac and that she loves sex and motorcycles.

We then meet Francis (Wood), her husband, and the two engage in a long kissing scene in a hot tub. It is soon revealed that the two have an open relationship, and that Francis pimps her out to friends and business acquaintances. He also makes her pose for nude photographs that he then sells. "These pictures mean an awful lot of money to me," explains Francis. Misty then explains that Francis is a terrible photographer, and that only one out of 100 of his photographs turn out well.

Just before having sex with a John, Misty says, "I'm in show business alright—I'm about to show my business!" (Groan.)

We then see Misty riding her motorcycle, and she explains that this is the only place she finds peace. "The wind seems to blow away my cruddy sham of a marriage," she explains. However, her peace is about to come to an abrupt ending as her motorcycle breaks down on the side of the road.

Lucky for Misty, two hot lesbians drive by, spotting her on the side of the road. In a scene that is pure Ed Wood in terms of direction, their conversation is filmed entirely from the backseat, so only the backs of their heads are visible. They then drive through a long tunnel, and the screen becomes so black that hardly anything is visible.

The lesbians circle back and pick up Misty, fondling her as they drive. "I know they're lesbians," Misty says in voice-over. "It's not my bag, but as I often say, what the hell?"

The lesbians then take Misty back to their house, where they ply her with a joint. This of course leads to the inevitable lesbian three-some. The scene is ugly and red, and it is difficult to ascertain whether or not it was intentionally filmed that way or if the redness is just a by-product of the print's aging. It's hard to say which is worse—the boring stuff before the sex or the sex itself.

The lesbians then drop Misty back off on the highway and wave goodbye. She soon meets up with a biker named Carl, and she rides off with him. The two of them naturally go to a secluded area and have sex on a blanket. The sound on the only known existing print is rather bad here, so it's difficult to make out anything.

We learn that Carl is part of a biker gang. This gang engages in such exciting activities as driving in circles for several minutes at a time. Once night falls, the gang then partake in an orgy, which is standard practice after all of that furious driving in circles. However, before the orgy can truly get underway, we must endure the non-excitement of watching said gang gyrate about in the nude. It's probably one of the most unarousing scenes we've witnessed in an Ed Wood skin flick. There is also a long montage of sex with no sound, only musical accompaniment. As a testament to the film's low production values, many scenes in the film were apparently shot without sound. Some of them even feature unheard dialogue.

Once Misty and Carl are alone again, three men—paid by Misty's husband—show up and beat the living hell out of Carl with chains. They then tie Misty up and rape her. In the voice-over, Misty calls one of the guys a "fruit," which seems like one of Wood's own patented lines of homophobia.

In the film's closing scene, Misty and Carl go to Union Station, where Carl climbs aboard a train headed for San Diego. We are not told why Carl is going or why he's not taking her with him.

The train pulls away, and Misty turns and walks away. This scene feels like Wood believed he was making a serious film here, which is laughable considering this is a biker-exploitation porno.

All jabs aside, after being lost for so many years, it's good to see *The Nympho Cycler* found and released (by Alpha Blue Archives) for mass consumption. It doesn't shed much new light on Wood's career, but it's important because it features Wood as an actor, and also because it shows that Wood was still struggling to achieve some minor level of artistry even while working in pornography. Unfortunately, the film doesn't really succeed in being sexy or artistic, and its plot is so muddled and ham-fisted that it makes for a difficult viewing.

CREDITS: Producer: Edward D. Wood, Jr.; Director: Edward D. Wood, Jr.; Screenplay: Edward D. Wood, Jr.; Cinematographer: Unknown; Editor: Unknown.

CAST: Casey Larrain (Misty), Edward D. Wood, Jr. (Francis), Stud Stetson (Carl), Sherry Duz, Lotti Moore, Betty Boobs, Mary Wood.

Drop-Out Wife (1972)

True to his word, Stephen C. Apostolof refused to work with Ed Wood again for seven years. Their time apart had been fruitful for Apostolof, who directed seven sex pictures during that period. In 1972, Wood and Apostolof buried the proverbial hatchet and reunited for their second collaboration, *Drop-Out Wife*. This flash-back-heavy film can be seen as Wood's own perverted version of Bergman's *Scenes from a Marriage* (1973).

When watching *Drop-Out Wife* after *Necromania: A Tale of Weird Love* (1971), it is painfully obvious that Apostolof was far better at helming adult films than Wood. The difference is day and night, the difference between a fifty-watt light bulb and the sun. This is not say that Apostolof was some sort of porno Kubrick, but he was at least adequately proficient in a way Wood was not. Apostolof's films are standard fare of their time, whereas *Necromania* was somewhat of an (unwanted) oddity.

The film, which features budding porn starlet Angela Carnon, can also be seen as Wood's take on women's liberation. Just as the screenwriter had been afraid of the evils of Communism previously, he now seemed equally paranoid regarding women's lib. As the film's tagline says, women's lib may be nothing more than "women's fib." Wood seems to believe that a woman in search of empowerment might very well decide to leave her husband and children behind in search of sexual fulfillment. But then Wood was always a little bit distrusting of women; just as the girlfriend in *Necromania* promises to leave her boyfriend if he cannot fulfill her sexually, Peggy, the wife in this film, does likewise. If Wood really did wear his loyalties and beliefs on his angora sleeve as it appears, then his distrust of women and perhaps his own sexual inefficiencies are as on display here as his personal fetishes were in previous films.

Meanwhile, Apostolof is busy in this film attempting to make artistic porn by using a bright and diverse color palette, and frequently blurring images as though this were a Fellini film. He also uses a kaleidoscope effect in *Drop-Out Wife* similar to that Wood used in *Necromania*. Although this effect works a little better here, it still looks somewhat amateur and out of place. It must also be pointed out that the acting is better in the Apostolof-helmed films than in Wood's, and here the actors actually look engaged during sex scenes, whereas the performers in *Necromania* looked bored beyond belief (and their limp penises seem to attest to this).

The film opens with Janet having sex with her boyfriend. As she pleasures him orally, the audience is treated to the best Woodian dialogue in the film—"You suck a good cock. Remind me to buy you that horse!" During this little bout of lovemaking, the doorbell rings. When Janet goes to the door, she finds her friend Peggy in tears. Peggy, it seems, has left her husband and children behind. "I had to get out of the whole mess," she explains. She offers up another bit of Woodian incoherence when she observes, "It's hard for me to realize that things are real anymore."

The film then takes us via flashback to Peggy and her hubby, Jim's, honeymoon night in a motel room. They kiss for what seems like forever. Apparently it seems like forever to Jim, as well, as he starts to get handsy. "Don't be so impatient," she says. "We've got the rest of our lives." When Peggy goes to the bathroom to undress, Jim watches her through the crack in door. Peggy, having no idea she's being watched, gently caresses her body in the mirror. Moments later Jim enters the bathroom and the two kiss naked, eventually working up to passionate sex.

But things will not be this good for long. The film flashes forward to a sexual encounter between the two in which Peggy is displeased. During sex she says, "I don't want to have any more kids, Jim." This of course being excellent pillow talk, the mood is ruined for Jim. However, he doesn't give up. After admitting that their lovemaking is "old hat," he convinces her to make love to him in the rain, where she enjoys three orgasms.

The film then goes back to Peggy and Janet playing cards. These liberated women are, of course, men-haters in Wood's limited vision, and the dialogue he gives them only serves to prove this further. "Men are the most disgusting creatures God ever put on this earth," Janet says.

Wood and Apostolof then flashback to the turning point in Jim and Peggy's relationship. Peggy is pregnant with the couple's third child. Jim angrily says things like, "There was a time when you didn't look like this," and berates her for not doing housecleaning. She gets pissed and responds, "It was your cock that got us into this!" Despite the absurdity of her statement, Jim is enraged by it and slaps her face, causing her to miscarry the baby.

Having heard about this for the first time, Janet says, "That goddamn bastard!" Peggy then tells her friend about she and Jim's trying to have sex, but finding it boring. "What the hell has happened to us?" Jim asks. He then mentions that Clyde Allen, a work buddy, says his marriage was saved by joining a wife-swapping club. Jim convinces Peggy to join with him in an attempt to save their own marriage. We then see a scene at the wife-swapping club meeting, where five couples have sex in all different positions. This seems to go on forever... Of course audiences at the time were there to see more sex and less dialogue, whereas audiences today are looking for the exact opposite.

"I've come back to life!" Peggy exclaims after having had sex with multiple partners. But does she feel any closer to her husband, or does she just feel sexually liberated by the experience?

We are soon shown another scene involving Jim and Peggy, in which she tells her poor hubby, "Every time you touch me it makes me sick!" Jim tells her he knows she's been cheating on him with other men and women, saying he's the only person she doesn't want to have sex with. He accuses her of being a lesbian, which makes her angry. "I even lost a baby for you!" she says.

And this ends the relationship, bringing us up to date.

"Let's start living again!" Janet encourages. She then sets up her friend on blind dates that naturally end in sex. One of the dates is with a pilot. "I'm the original jet set pilot," the man says, delivering one of the film's most Woodian lines. After sex, Peggy passes out, and the pilot invites his buddy to join in. When Peggy wakes up, however, she is not displeased; instead she goes along with it, having sex with both men.

The next morning she looks in the mirror and smokes a cigarette. (We know her life is going downhill because she's now smoking...) "You look like hell," she tells herself. "You've aged ten years in a month." She then looks at photographs of her children and finally decides to pick up a telephone and call them. Jim won't let her talk to them. He tells her that she's both a bitch and an unfit mother and informs her that he's filing for custody.

Being the swell friend she is, Janet convinces Peggy that she needs to continue this hedonistic lifestyle. This leads to them having sex with a couple of random guys they meet at the bar, who then encourage them to have sex with one another. This act of lesbianism, which we are told is not her first, angers Peggy. "I don't make it with girls!" she screams. Of course we know this isn't true, but whatever... Peggy leaves in tears and Janet goes ahead and has sex with both men by herself. (What a great friend, right?)

The film ends with Peggy watching her children on the playground. She decides to go back to Jim. "Maybe we'll make it work this time," she says. "I just know we will."

And, curtains... The end.

Drop-Out Wife is rather forgettable, but it represents a return to a higher standard of pornography in the career of Edward D. Wood, Jr. That might sound like a rather dubious distinction, but it was a huge step up for Wood at a time in his life where he had no other options.

CREDITS: Producer: Stephen C. Apostolof; Director: Stephen C. Apostolof; Screenplay: Stephen C. Apostolof; Edward D. Wood, Jr.; Cinematographer: R.C. Ruben.

CAST: Angela Carnon (Peggy); Fred Geoffries (Jim); Terry Johnson (Janet); Forman Shane; Lynn Harris; Douglas Fray; Jean Louise; Corey Brandon; Sandy Dempsey; Duane Paulson.

The Class Reunion (1972)

In 1972, after a seven-year-hiatus from working with one another, screenwriter Edward D. Wood, Jr. and writer/director Stephen C. Apostolof would churn out three sex pictures—*The Drop-Out Wife, The Class Reunion,* and *The Snow Bunnies. The Class Reunion,* which would mark the second collaboration between Wood, Apostolof, and budding sex star Rene Bond, features very little plot, even by normal porn standards of the time. So what is this film? Imagine *The Big Chill* (1983) without the groovy soundtrack or the life-reaffirming conversation, and with everyone having lots and lots of sex, and you will have a pretty good idea of what this picture is.

The film's advertising trailer titillated audiences with the promise of "wild uninhibited frolicking," explaining that this class reunion was one "where biology is studied outside the classroom." The ad goes on to say that "the sexual revolution is foremost in everyone's mind," giving us some idea of the themes Wood and Apostolof will attempt to shoehorn into this sex flick in an attempt to be timely.

Like many an Apostolof epic, *The Class Reunion* wastes no time as the first thing we see is set of giant breasts being washed and caressed in the shower. We soon find out that the breasts belong to Rosie, who immediately remarks, "I wonder what this day holds in store for me." She then receives a letter informing her that her college class—the "Class of '69"—is having a reunion. (While the "69" is a rather unfunny joke making reference to reciprocal oral sex, it makes little sense when taken literally; is this to be the class-mates' three year anniversary? Then why do they all look like they're in their thirties?) "It could turn out to be a very fun weekend,"

Rosie says. It's humorous to note that in the very first scene of the old group getting back together one of the characters muses, "Everyone looks so mature..."

An anti-war protest in the street outside the reunion spurs an argument about the differences between the two generations. (Rather than using obvious stock footage as Wood would have done, Apostolof seems to have actually shot some second unit footage of a real protest.) The conversation ultimately leads to the screening of a home video featuring all of the classmates dancing (badly) in the nude similar to *Orgy of the Dead* (1965) and eventually having lots of sex. Curiously, nobody at this private little screening thinks that the film is even the slightest bit awkward or embarrassing given that at least a handful of years have passed and old acquaintances have seemingly drifted apart into separate lives.

"I'm just trying to show you that kids today are no different than we were," explains one of the classmates. (In this film, their names don't really matter as there is zero character development. These aren't characters, but rather a handful of woefully bland and inter-changeable sex partners.) He then concludes, "I think we're capable of doing now what we did then." This leads to an overly-long sex scene (again in which no one seems even the slightest bit inhibited after the passage of time) which is observed by a closeted homosexual classmate. The inclusion of this character seems to have been for two primary reasons—to have a voyeuristic character, as we have at some point in almost all Wood-penned sex films, and to poke fun at homosexuals. Again, it should be noted that Wood, who longed for the public to accept his own sexual condition as a transvestite, frequently showed homosexuals in a negative and/or comedic light.

In one scene, Rosie attempts to bed the bellboy by saying, "Let's take it out in trade" (which is, of course, also the title of another Wood skin flick). When he refuses to have sex with her, she berates him, calling him a "faggot" and a "queer," highlighting more of Wood's blatant homophobia. Another scene featuring two homosexual characters ultimately winds up being nothing more than an excuse for Wood to make fun of the women's liberation movement, which he was clearly very distrusting of.

As there is very little plot in this film, which is basically just scene after scene of sexual escapades, there is very little to report here. Wood's involvement is irrelevant as there is only so much the writer can offer in a film crammed with sex scenes and featuring very little dialogue; his job as screenwriter is simply to put characters in a room together where they can have lots and lots of boring but competently shot sex.

In his book *Ed Wood: Mad Genius*, author Rob Craig asserts that *The Class Reunion* was perhaps Wood's "last great screenplay." The author goes on to point out that Wood tackles the subjects of feminism, the sexual revolution, and the countercultural movement. "Within all the deadening sex and pointless plot twists lies the true soul of the poet-philosopher, featuring contradictory yet fascinating observations on sexual mores, socio-political phenomena, and the deathless existential riddles shared by the human race," writes Craig. With all due respect, we disagree with this assessment. Sometimes a cigar is just a cigar, and sometimes a porno film is just a (painfully and poorly made) porno film. While it's true that Wood does touch on many of the aforementioned themes, he does so in a slapdash way that seems more about simply including them in the film than actually examining them.

Given the film's lack of plot, the fact that it was shot in the same hotel as many scenes in *The Drop-Out Wife*, and that it features several of the same performers as the latter, it would seem that very little thought was given to *The Class Reunion*. It's likely it was just a quickie two-day shoot (shot back-to-back with *The Drop-Out Wife*) to get another film in the can and make a little easy cash.

CREDITS: Producer: Stephen C. Apostolof; Director: Stephen C. Apostolof; Screenplay: Stephen C. Apostolof; Edward D. Wood, Jr.; Cinematographer: R.C. Ruben.

CAST: Marsha Jordan (Jane); Rene Bond (Thelma); Sandy Carey (Fluff), Starline Comb (Rosie), Terry Johnson (Liza); Forman Shane (Charlie); Flora Weisel (Henrietta); Fred Geoffries (Wimpy); Rick Lutze (Harry); Con Covert (Bruce); Ron Darby (Tom); Mark Nelson (Bellboy).

The Snow Bunnies (1972)

The Snow Bunnies is yet another Ed Wood/Stephen C. Apostolof "classic." *Ed Wood: Look Back in Angora* (1994) director Ted Newsom calls it yet another product of the "collective genius of Wood and Apostolof." If you've seen one 1970s soft-core porno, you've seen them all; the same can be said of the Wood/Apostolof collaborations.

Most of this film is supposed to take place in Canada. However, aside from a few mismatched stock footage shots, most of it was obviously filmed in Los Angeles' Griffith Park (where you might remember some scenes from *The Sinister Urge*, 1960, were filmed, as well). Naturally the mismatched stock shots and scenes filmed in Los Angeles look messy, and never once are we even remotely close to being convinced that this is actually Canada.

The Snow Bunnies opens exactly the same way *The Class Reunion* (1972) opened—with an ample-bosomed woman taking a shower and spending way too much time washing and lathering up her breasts. Although one wouldn't expect much in the way of creativity in films like these, you might expect to not experience the *exact same opening* in two of them in a row. Perhaps Wood and Apostolof thought, if it ain't broke don't fix it; apparently the opening of *The Class Reunion* played so well they decided to basically reuse it. Or maybe they were just lazy. Who knows? But one thing is certain— this shower scene goes on for so long that one almost hopes to see Anthony Perkins standing outside the tub with a knife in his hand.

After five minutes of showering, Joan's (Marsha Jordan) private time is interrupted by a ringing telephone. She goes and answers it, still wet, and finds that the head nurse has requested that she come in to work at the hospital on her vacation. "Go to hell!" she says. "Take that!" She then finds a brochure for a Canadian ski lodge lying next to her telephone. (How did she not know that was there? Where did it come from?) So, of course, she decides to go to Canada for a ski and sex extravaganza.

Joan then telephones her friends to ask them to go along with her. (Their names aren't important as they're basically interchangeable dummies who are good at little beyond sex.) The first friend explains that she can't go because they "need" her to model for the cover of *Teen* magazine. It is here that we realize these women, all of whom are at least thirty-years-old if they are a day, are supposed to be teenagers. Joan looks like she's at least forty-five or fifty! These are easily the oldest teeny-boppers ever captured on celluloid. Finally Joan convinces this "teen model" to skip the shoot and come with her to Canada. (Oh, yeah, and did we mention that there is a man licking her breasts throughout this entire conversation?)

Joan next telephones everyone's favorite gap-toothed porn starlet Rene Bond. Here Bond plays a school teacher grading papers. She quickly agrees to go to Canada.

Next up is a friend who just broke up with Herbie, her married boyfriend. "I've been drowning my sorrows ever since I broke up with Herbie last night," she explains. Joan easily convinces her that this trip will be an opportunity to forget her woes and maybe even have sex with a stranger or two.

Once they arrive at the stock footage ski resort, one of the women—does it matter which one?—hooks up with James (Apostolof favorite Forman Shane), a "college student" who looks like he's at least forty-years-old. (Obviously they will make a splendid pair of "young people" since each of them are approximately the same age.) "Who's got time for wars and drafts?" asks the idealistic James. He then lays it on thick, hitting on her with such winning lines as, "Life is very short. We should take advantage of every minute."

Here this magnum opus provides us with sequence after sequence of the girls being picked up in bars, on the slopes, and in the ski shop.

All of the men in this film are absolute heathens, and one can't say much better about the women who gladly jump into bed with them at every turn. We are also treated to one of Wood's favorite sexploitation sayings, that "sex is the universal language"; this line appears in no less than three of Wood's scripts. Characters in *The Snow Bunnies* say things like "far out" and mention (in passing, of course) things like the sexual revolution and the war in Vietnam in what are likely Wood and Apostolof's attempts at creating something timely.

At one point, another woman is introduced inexplicably. She is a prostitute who works at the lodge. After she is beaten by a john, she winds up having sex with Joan. How does she know Joan? We have absolutely no idea. She just shows up and they happily begin licking each others' breasts. In another scene that makes absolutely no sense and feels like it was added to pad out the running time, Rene Bond does a striptease in the ski lodge bar. This scene goes on for what seems like two days shy of forever...

The sad fact of the Wood/Apostolof collaborations is that Apostolof was just mediocre enough as a screenwriter to cancel out Wood's contributions and craft something bland. Had Wood been given the opportunity to write these films himself, we have no doubt they would have at least amounted to something memorable. As it stands now, most of these pictures run together in a blur of simulated sex, pointless plots, and mundane scenarios.

CREDITS: Producer: Stephen C. Apostolof; Director: Stephen C. Apostolof; Screenplay: Stephen C. Apostolof; Edward D. Wood, Jr.; Cinematographer: Allen Stone.

CAST: Marsha Jordan (Joan); Rene Bond (Madie); Terri Johnson (Brenda); Sandy Carrey (Tammy); Starline Comb (Carral); Forman Shane (James); Christopher Geoffries (Chris); Marc Desmond (Bartender); Ric Lutze (Paul); Ron Darby (Fred).

The Cocktail Hostesses (1973)

The tagline for this fifth Stephen C. Apostolof/Edward D. Wood, Jr. collaboration, *The Cocktail Hostesses,* exclaims, "They're here to please you!" Other ads boasted, "You pay for the drinks... They do the rest!" By this time, Apostolof and Wood had somewhat of an acting troupe with the likes of starlet Rene Bond, Ric Lutze, and Forman Shane. Having already knocked out three soft-core sex pictures the previous year, the filmmaking team no doubt had little trouble producing yet another standard sex film.

As with the best of Apostolof's efforts, *The Cocktail Hostesses* opens right in the middle of the action; here we begin with a scene between secretary Toni Rice (Bond) and her boss. As the boss is paying attention to Toni's bottom line, the young secretary is fixated on the literal bottom line. She realizes she is still making a mere $86 per week despite her going above and beyond to service her boss. So when a friend informs her that she makes nearly that much each and every day as a cocktail waitress (hooking on the side), she naturally decides to leave her job and go to work in a cocktail lounge.

When Toni goes to apply, the boss asks her to show him her wares. She then undresses, with his help, and the two of them engage in some good old-fashioned simulated sex.

Naturally one doesn't look to pornography to find progressive stances on women's rights, but Wood and Apostolof's views on the subject are consistently bothersome; not only are all of the women in their works more than happy to sell their bodies for money, but they are almost all bimbos who seem to live only for sex. This is, of course, a stereotypical male fantasy, and is as naïve a position as anything found in Wood's novels and films. Again, Wood constantly seems to be observing the idea of women's liberation from a viewpoint of contempt and distrust. It would seem that as long as Wood is able to keep women in their long-accepted place—in either positions of subservience or as empty-headed whores—then all is right in the world. It is only when women attempt to rise above their societal positions (see *The Drop-Out Wife*, 1972) that the American way of life crumbles.

Equally alarming is Wood and Apostolof's take on rape. *The Cocktail Waitresses* features a long and uncomfortable rape sequence—likely nothing more than an attempt to cash in on the then-emerging rape exploitation market. The rapist in the film is never apprehended, no one ever bothers to raise a finger to help, and Larry the bartender, a supposed friend of the raped waitress, dismisses the whole thing, saying, "What's a little screw to her?" The entire thing is handled very callously, and is dismissed in a very male "whores-get-what-they-deserve" manner. Later, the rape will be revisited only as a plot device to get the raped waitress to have lesbian sex with a coworker.

In another startling sequence, a male character becomes somewhat violent after demanding that he be spanked. In this scene, he calls the woman a bitch and forces her to engage in anal sex against her will. In the typical male fantasy/juvenile way such things are handled in the Apostolof/Wood films, she then decides she enjoys it and is once again happy.

Like all of the Apostolof/Wood efforts, the film is filled with naked, writhing bodies, squirming uncomfortably on camera. There are threesomes and group sex and lesbian encounters, none of which are even the least bit sexy. It is interesting that in Apostolof, Wood found a collaborator that was almost equally as inept. While Apostolof was a better technical director than Wood, he lacked the passion and drive that fueled Wood's own works, and as a result, his films come up flat and hollow.

The Cocktail Hostesses is significant because it's extremely difficult to locate; it's about one step away from being one of the "lost" films except that it does exist. Should you be lucky enough to locate a copy, don't expect to find lost treasure, though. The film is as lame as anything Apostolof and Wood ever created, and is notable if only because of the duo's handling of rape and sexual aggression.

CREDITS: Producer: Stephen C. Apostolof; Director: Stephen C. Apostolof; Screenplay: Stephen C. Apostolof; Edward D. Wood, Jr.; Cinematographer: R.C. Reuben; Editor: Unknown.

CAST: Rene Bond (Toni); Rick Cassidy; Starline Comb; Sandy Dempsey; Douglas Frey; Susan Gale; Lynn Harris; Kathy Hilton; Terri Johnson; Jimmy Longdale; Ric Lutze; Duane Paulsen; Candy Samples; Forman Shane.

Fugitive Girls (1974)

Sure, you've seen movies like *The Shawshank Redemption* (1994) and *Escape from Alcatraz* (1979), but you've never seen a prison-break flick quite like this one. Known also as *Five Loose Women*, this Wood/Apostolof effort is way better than it has any right to be. With far less sex than their previous collaborations (the sex is held to about the same amount we might see in an American International Pictures film of the same era), this one actually has a plot. *Fugitive Girls* is quite similar in theme to films like *The Big Doll House* (1971) and *The Big Bird Cage* (1972) (only without a director so talented as Jack Hill at the reigns) with a little bit of *The Violent Years* (1960) thrown in for good measure. It's not the best film you'll ever see—it's not really very good at all—but it's clearly the best of Wood/Apostolof collaborations.

The film begins with a slow tracking shot across stripped clothing strewn about on the floor, leading up to a couple having sex on the bed. (As usual, Apostolof wastes no time getting to the sex.) When the couple finishes their sexual encounter, they decide they need more alcohol. The woman, Dee (Margie Lanier), offers the $20 she has in her purse, but her boyfriend insists on going to a liquor store across town where he says he can get free booze. Once they are across town at said liquor store, the boyfriend robs the place and shoots the cashier (he doesn't even get the booze he supposedly came for—or the cash. He just pockets the gun and runs). Dee is understandably upset. When she starts to scream, her boyfriend pushes her out of the driver's side of the car. Dee hits the pavement with her shoulder after falling something like 4 inches to the ground and is of course immediately rendered unconscious by the impact. Everyone quickly gathers around her and deduces that she's responsible for the shooting as indicated by no weapon being on her and being completely unconscious when the police arrive.

In the next scene, we see Dee being escorted to a place labeled "Correctional Facility for Women." This so-called scary prison appears to be nothing more than a summer camp with no security whatsoever. So cheap is this movie that no prison guards are ever seen, and the only prisoners we ever see are the five who will ultimately break out. Dee is told early on that tough lesbian Kat runs the place and that she should do absolutely nothing to cross her. The four girls Dee will ultimately team up with are all caricatures—the white trash redneck girl, the tough lesbian, the tough black girl, and the total bitch.

Dee doesn't exactly hit it off with the other girls and does her best to mind her own business, but they inexplicably begin speaking about their impending prison break right in front of her. Kat turns to Dee and says, "If you repeat one word I'll cut your tits off." That night Dee is crying in her bunk, distraught at being imprisoned in a place that seemingly doesn't allow you to do anything but play cards and make escape plans. It doesn't take long (as one would expect in a picture like this) before Dee is "comforted" by Kat, who threatens to take her lesbian virginity by force if she has to. They then wind up having sex, most of which consists of Dee receiving a breast massage and in turns enjoying it and being revolted by it. Everything else happens off camera. It's humorous as the lesbian love scene plays out to notice how the walls in the "prison" are dotted with All-Star wrestling posters! (According to actress Brenda Fogarty, the prison was actually a Boy Scout camp, which explains a lot.)

The next day, a guard named "Old Hazel" (who is never seen) agrees to assist in the break-out as long as Toni promises to pay her some of the loot she's got squirreled away from before her incarceration. Kat forces Dee to go with them so she won't tell anyone that they've escaped. All of this leads to the single most boring prison escape sequence in the history of film. First the girls climb under an average chain-link fence (in broad daylight) before they take off running for what seems like an eternity. After running through the woods and eluding the tracking dogs, the girls decide to rest—right next to a swamp. (Has there ever been an Ed Wood movie that didn't take place next to a swamp?)

The group eventually stumbles into a hippie camp where a fine, topless time is being had by all. There's food and music and boobs aplenty! The hippies know right away that the five strangers are fugitives but are gracious and accepting. That is, until for no comprehensible reason, the prison ladies inform the hippies that they smell bad and ask if they ever take baths. The hippie leader informs them that "water is for growin' things." The hippies then give the five girls clothes, and the escapees naturally strip down naked right there in front of them. When the girls figure out that the hippies have designs on raping them, they fight them off. "Good Christ, a lesbian!" exclaims one of the hippies in the film's funniest moment. Finally the hippies let the girls leave in peace after the prison girls put a quick smack down on them. "They got nothin' we want, and trouble we don't need!" one of them says.

Paula and Toni, the white trash girl and the tough black girl, argue throughout the film. Here we get such wonderful dialogue as, "You'd screw a cockroach if it turned you on!" To this, Toni says she would not screw a cockroach because cockroaches are black and she will not go black.

In a strange scene, the sheriff (played by Ed Wood) telephones the caretaker of a nearby airstrip (also played by Wood) and tells him to keep an eye out for the escapees. We then see the caretaker fighting off a biker gang. As the caretaker, Wood is easily the worst actor in what is otherwise a competently-acted sexploitation picture.

The girls soon attempt to hitchhike from Apostolof favorite Forman Shane, who quickly becomes the victim of a women-on-man gang rape similar to that found in *The Violent Years*. Once the girls are finished with their captive, they leave him tied up on the side of the road and take off in his car. "You sure took that white boy like a sex-starved pussycat!" Paula tells Toni.

The girls find that their newly-acquired automobile is about out of gas, so they pull into the airstrip (where Wood's caretaker works) and ask to purchase gas. In a ridiculous scene, the caretaker attempts to call the sheriff (again, also played by Wood) on a telephone that is only a few feet away from where the girls are. As if the caretaker's plans aren't obvious enough, he begins begging the sheriff (fairly loudly) to answer the phone as the fugitives are at his airstrip. Kat snatches the telephone and beats the caretaker over the head, knocking him unconscious.

Soon a fight breaks out between the girls and the male biker gang we saw earlier in the film. The fight becomes intense and weapons like chains and nunchucks are used. In the end, the girls come out on top.

The fugitive girls then stage a home invasion, taking over the home of a young couple. The husband, a Vietnam vet, is in a wheelchair and finds himself unable to do much to stop the prison gals. When shouts of "Get out of my house!" and "Leave her alone!" get on the prisoners' nerves they simply kick over his wheelchair and continue to rape his wife in front of him. The scene is then somewhat softened by Dee getting hold of a rifle and shooting Kat for what we assume was crossing some line of criminal conduct. Kat dies instantly. Paula and Toni escape, leaving the others to fend for themselves.

The sheriff (Wood) arrives soon after and informs Dee that her boyfriend has confessed and that she will likely be freed soon (even if she has killed Kat, which we're told was self-defense even though what we saw moments earlier doesn't quite jive with that).

Paula and Toni show up at a dilapidated farmhouse to retrieve Dee's "well-hidden" money (which just sits in a briefcase under the edge of the house, leaving it susceptible to rain, snow, animals, etc.). The cops show up immediately after, following them. The two remaining girls and the cops all end up at a gravel pit showdown, where Dee double-crosses Toni, eventually killing her. Toni tries to run, but falls down for no reason, drops the money, and is captured by the police.

Sadly for Wood fans, this nudie update of *The Violent Years* does not end with a Wood-penned PSA on the evils of bad parenting or Communism or marrying too young (or whatever said culprit of the moment might be).

Fugitive Girls' biggest sin is that it's a rather bland exploitation film. It doesn't deliver on the promised titillation. It's almost as if Wood thought the very idea of a lesbian would be more than enough to excite the audience. Oh, and if that doesn't do it let's just throw in lots and lots of boobs. Again, Ed Wood's juvenile sense of "exploitation" is really on display here. Also, this is an escape movie but it plays like five people poking along in the desert, going idly from one scene to another. There is no real tension. They might as well have been looking for Sunday afternoon picnic spots. *Fugitive Girls* isn't on par with the better pre-Apostolof Wood films but it is clearly the best of their wonky collaborations—a dubious distinction to be sure.

CREDITS: Producer: Stephen C. Apostolof; S.B. Cooper; Director: Stephen C. Apostolof; Screenplay: Stephen C. Apostolof; Edward D. Wood, Jr.; Cinematographer: Robert Birchall; Editor: Luigi Rogatoni.

CAST: Jabie Abercrombe (Paula); Rene Bond (Toni); Tallie Cochrane (Kat); Donna Young (Sheila); Margie Lanier (Dee); Forman Shane (Cadillac Driver); Niccolle Riddell (Phil's Wife); Douglas Frey (Presser); Eve Orlon (Tears); Gary Schneider (Bat); Maria Arnold (Carrie); Armando Federico (Biker); Janet Newell (Calico); Con Covert (Sunshine); Edward D. Wood, Jr. (Pop/Sheriff/Liquor Store Witness).

The Beach Bunnies (1976)

The Beach Bunnies would be Edward D. Wood Jr. and Stephen C. Apostolof's seventh collaboration. (They would later collaborate on an eighth film, *Hot Ice*, 1978, with Wood only participating as an actor and not a screenwriter.) This would be the last film made during Wood's life that was based upon one of his screenplays. As one may have come to expect by this point, the film isn't particularly good aside from the occasional funny line of dialogue (such as "I've got to know if Rock Sanders has a cock!").

The film's plot is as thin as the paper it was written on, but it provides Wood and Apostolof with more than enough opportunities to show lots of naked breasts and scenes of simulated sex.

The film's flimsy plot deals with a magazine's attempts to get a scoop regarding a popular movie star named Rock Sanders (Marland Proctor). Thus far, the magazine's reporters have only managed to provide rehashes of already-known stories. However, there's a juicy bit of gossip going around the water cooler that says Sanders had a sex change and has fallen in love with his male manager. The magazine's editor, Elaine Street (Brenda Fogarty), wants definitive proof as to whether or not Rock Sanders is a man or a woman. Feeling that she cannot trust such an undertaking to her reporters, she takes on the task herself of finding out if Rock Sanders has a cock.

Elaine knows that Sanders is staying at a beach-side resort known as the Silver Cove Lodge. So she decides to go to the lodge and try to get a glimpse of Rock Sanders' penis (but not before first performing oral sex on her publisher). To aid her in her investigation, she takes along three attractive gal pals, Sheila, Lorrie, and Bonnie.

After a long montage of footage featuring an automobile driving along various highways, the women arrive at the beach resort. Once they are inside their room they complain about their hot and sweaty clothing. This of course leads them all to take off their clothes and stand around naked.

After the other women leave for the beach, Elaine attempts to seduce a bellboy in exchange for Rock Sanders' room number. The bellboy giggles through the entire thing, continuously repeating that he cannot give out that information. After a long struggle, the bellboy eventually relents and gives up the goods (as does Elaine, although in entirely different ways). "I can pump information out of anybody," she later brags.

Apostolof then takes us out to the beach, where (during Woodian day-for-night issues) the other three women sit and watch men surf awkwardly. (Apparently this production couldn't afford surfers who could actually surf well.) One of the surfers asks Sheila out on a date, and she accepts.

Back inside the hotel, Elaine telephones Rock Sanders' room. Instead of reaching Sanders, however, she reaches his flamboyantly gay agent Bruce Collins, who denies her access to the star. Undaunted, Elaine cooks up a new scheme. She pays a maid for her uniform and goes to Rock Sanders' room, pretending she's there to clean up. Sanders lets her into the room just as he goes into the bathroom to take a shower. Elaine cracks the bathroom door and attempts to get a peek at Rock's goods, but is immediately caught by Collins and tossed out of the room.

A couple of goofy-looking guys (one played by Apostolof regular Forman Shane) corner Bonnie and Lorrie in the bar and begin hitting on them. When one of them says he's a pilot, Lorrie boasts, "Well, you just met the best landing strip around."

Meanwhile, Elaine is just getting started in her attempts to find out if Rock Sanders has a penis. When she sees him sitting on the beach alone, she goes out in front of him and pretends she's being attacked by a shark. This, she hopes, will get Sanders into the water in an attempt to save her so she can grab his package. Sanders, however, doesn't bite; he just watches her thrashing around in the water and screaming, "Help! Shark!" When a Japanese man finally rushes into the water to aid her, Elaine pushes him away. All of this is to no avail, however, as Sanders doesn't budge.

We then cut to Sheila walking along the beach later that evening. She encounters three creepy guys camping out on the shore. One of them chases her, catches her, and rapes her. In yet another bothersome instance in Wood and Apostolof's work, the rape is depicted in terms of male fantasy and rape justification. While being raped, Sheila (naturally) decides she enjoys being raped. Soon the other two guys join in and Sheila willingly has sex with all of them. Going further down this road of rape justification, Wood and Apostolof will later have Sheila tell the others she was raped, thus giving credence to the caveman-like belief that women who cry rape actually enjoy the act itself. Again, no one looks for particularly enlightening or progressive ideals in pornography, but Wood and Apostolof's irresponsible portrayal of rape in multiple (otherwise vanilla) films goes a step further towards illuminating a perhaps less-than-pleasant viewpoint of women and their rights in the minds of the filmmakers. So at this point it should come as no surprise that this rape incident leaves Sheila feeling enlightened, having had some sort of sexual awakening. She then vows to have sex with every man she can find, and once again the filmmakers have managed to be completely dismissive of rape.

Never one to give up, Elaine yells "fire!" outside Rock Sanders' room. Her plan is to grab his crotch when he runs out of the room. However, this plan also ends badly as she winds up with a handful of Bruce Collins' manhood rather than Rock Sanders'.

Things all work out for the best in the end, however, as Elaine is approached by Rock Sanders at a beach party. The two wind up having sex and Elaine learns the truth about Sanders' penis the old fashioned way. The audience is never told in definitive terms that Rock Sanders is indeed a man, but we assume this to be the case as "he" and Elaine apparently have sex.

It's sort of sad to think that Wood came bursting onto the scene back in 1953 with a movie as daring and absurd as *Glen or Glenda?* but then finished with somewhat of a whimper rather than a bang with the largely-generic soft-core porn *Beach Bunnies.* However, when one considers that *The Beach Bunnies*, like *Glen or Glenda?*, deals with a potential sex change, it may be seen as a fitting bookend to a rather fascinating career.

CREDITS: Producer: Stephen C. Apostolof; S.B. Cooper; Director: Stephen C. Apostolof; Screenplay: Stephen C. Apostolof; Edward D. Wood, Jr.; Cinematographer: R.C. Reuben.

CAST: Brenda Fogarty (Elaine Street); Mariwin Roberts (Lorrie); Linda Gildersleeve (Sheila); Wendy Cavanaugh (Bonnie); Forman Shane (Chris); Johnny Fain (Dennis); Rick Cassidy (Dave); Con Covert (Bruce Collins); Cory Brandon (J.B.); Robert Bullock (Bellboy); Marland Proctor (Rock Sanders); Stephen C. Apostolof (Piano Player).

I Woke Up Early the Day I Died (1998)

In the final years of Wood's life, he continued writing screenplays and pulp novels, still hoping that he might find just the project that would make him a star. There was one screenplay in particular that Wood believed he could accomplish this feat with—an avant-garde project he had started on way back in 1960. Through the years its title changed from *Silent Night* to *Night of Silence to I Awoke Early the Day I Died*. Wood tinkered with this script on and off for many years. This, he believed, would be his masterpiece. He envisioned the project as a film with absolutely no dialogue, but with screams, music, and sound effects à la Charles Chaplin's *City Lights* (1931). Wood even managed to convince a couple of former marquee stars to sign on in Aldo Ray and John Carradine. Unfortunately, however, Wood still couldn't find financing for the project.

According to Richard Crouse's book *Son of the 100 Best Movies You've Never Seen*, Wood was once evicted from a house and given only minutes to clear the premises. Crouse quotes Wood's wife, Kathy, as saying that the filmmaker took only two belongings with him—the script for *I Awoke Early the Day I Died* and an angora sweater (no joke) that he loved.

In 1978, Edward D. Wood passed away at the age of fifty-three, leaving the script still unfilmed. The project was now the property of Kathy Wood, and she refused to allow anyone to film the screenplay unless they were going to do it exactly the way Wood had wanted it made. She didn't want the film to be made as one last joke poking fun at her dead husband, either; she wanted someone to make the film with the reverence it deserved.

Then she met a would-be Italian director named Aris Iliopulos, who believed he could make the film Wood had always envisioned. So he went to work, lining up an incredible cast that included such names as Billy Zane, Karen Black, Tippi Hedren, Ron Perlman, Tara Reid, Nicollette Sheridan, Eartha Kitt, Rick Schroder, Andrew McCarthy, Steven Weber, John Ritter, Bud Cort, Taylor Negron, Will Patton, Christina Ricci, Leif Garrett, Jonathan Taylor Thomas, Sandra Bernhard, Max Perlich, Mark Boone, Jr., and even Kathy Wood, Vampira, and Conrad Brooks.

Iliopulos' film, retitled *I Woke Up Early the Day I Died,* would be met with the same critical contempt that Wood's films had faced. The *New York Times* reported that the film was "sad and misguided and boring. Pretending to make a pathetically amateurish movie isn't nearly as effective as accidentally making one because you don't know any better." James Berardinelli of *Reel Views* said, "It's probably not possible to make a *good* film based on an Ed Wood script. Despite being enthusiastic, Wood had no discernible talent when it came to making movies....Aris Iliopulos must be a brave man with cajones the size of melons. He may also never direct again."

Iliopulos never did direct another feature—at least he hasn't made one in the past 15 years since *I Woke Up Early the Day I Died* was completed—but that doesn't make this a bad movie. It simply makes Iliopulos the victim of (we believe) critical misjudgment. Not helping matters, most people have never seen it because of a legal brouhaha that left the film without a proper release anywhere but in Germany.

The authors of this book believe the film is a masterpiece of avant-garde camp comedy and deserves to be seen by the masses. It features some incredible performances, and what is probably the finest turn in lead actor Billy Zane's career. In this film, Zane seems to channel the likes of Keaton and Chaplin, delivering a performance that comes across like a deranged version of Chaplin's tramp character.

Sure, it's easy for critics to dismiss the film because it was written by Wood. And yes, it's easy to label the film as something of a gimmick because it's a silent film in an era when silent films simply aren't made anymore. But those simple labels are just that—simple. To prejudge this film based on those things does a massive disservice to a truly remarkable little film. As for *The New York Times* saying that Iliopulos pretends to have no talent, and thus, as it is implied, to make a film the way Wood would have made it, simply isn't true. Intentional camp rarely works, but it does work here. But pretending that he is anything less than a virtuoso filmmaker is something Ilipulos does not do here.

The direction of the film is ridiculously stylish. If it's guilty of anything, it may be that it's over-stylized. But let's not mince words here—*I Woke Up Early the Day I Died* is a masterpiece that deserves a second look (and in many cases a first look). This is the masterpiece that Wood always envisioned, the film that he (regrettably) lacked the directorial talent to make himself. This is in no way intended as a slam to Wood, but he wasn't half the director Iliopulos proves himself to be with this film. Where the best of Wood was often workmanlike, the self-assured Iliopulos makes it all look easy.

One of the knocks against the film is that it's goofy. Yes, it is that, and intentionally so. But that doesn't mean it lacks style or is artless. Its goofiness is the sort of goofiness that Harold Lloyd and Charles Chaplin films possessed. It is now in vogue to fall all over oneself calling those films art, just as it is in fashion to label Ed Wood's films trash. But what such critics fail to grasp is that *I Woke Up Early the Day I Died* is the heir to those classic films. It's not *City Lights*, but it doesn't have to be. But it does contain a certain beauty and elegance that the best of the silent comedies possessed. It's slapstick without being ridiculous. There are the normal Woodian plot holes and failures in logic, but Iliopulos was aware of those things. This is the theater of the absurd, and Iliopulos and Wood reign supreme here.

"Stylistically, Iliopulos steers the film into ground somewhere between an Ed Wood picture and the kitschy surrealist philosophy of John Waters," Richard Crouse writes. "He plays up the laughs more than Wood would have—one of the joys of Wood's work is its deadpan seriousness—but he is faithful to the spirit of the script."

Like many of Wood's films, *I Woke Up Early the Day I Died* features many of Wood's favorite obsessions, from cemeteries and death to transvestism and the burlesque. There are also some truly bizarre moments in the film that are clearly the work of Wood.

Another aspect of the film that works like gangbusters is the wall-to-wall musical soundtrack Iliopulos employs here. The film uses everything from mariachi music to hard rock to Italian opera. One particular song resonates the most—rocker Darcy Clay's hilarious "Jesus I Was Evil." The aural assault of the film's uniquely eclectic soundtrack is extremely effective.

The film begins with The Thief (again, similar in name to "The Tramp") in a sanitarium, dressed as a female nurse, killing someone with a syringe filled with god knows what. He then flees the building and changes clothes on the run. In a true Woodian bizarro moment, a clothing store worker picks up The Thief's freshly-discarded high-heel shoes and sniffs them. This has nothing to do with the film's plot; it's just one of the strangely surreal moments in this film.

We soon learn that The Thief damaged his ears as a child. He now hears loud sounds inside his head that drive him to acts of insanity and murder. Loud external sounds only seem to make things worse. At different points in the film he will attempt to cover his ears with such strange items as rocks and leaves to try and stop the ruckus.

The Thief next goes to a street corner hotdog vendor and orders a hotdog. Said hotdog is only 45 cents—the first clue that this surreal little film operates in its own time frame. When Wood wrote the script back in the late 60s and mid-70s, hotdogs may have cost 45 cents, but they certainly did not at the time the film was made. The Thief then flees the scene, kills a man, and steals a car. As he is driving, he comes across an armored car, complete with guards transporting large sums of money into a quick loan shop. The Thief then waits for the guards to leave and robs the place. When the loan officer attempts to shoot him, The Thief is forced to kill him.

In another bizarro Wood moment, a female loan officer begins to kiss the mouth of the dead loan officer. Why does this happen? Well, why not? This is all the logic Wood needed, and it is good enough for us.

In a surrealistic dream sequence somewhat reminiscent of those found in *Glen or Glenda?*, The Thief dreams about various people who have screamed at him during his lifetime. After he wakes, The Thief attends the funeral of the loan officer, and watches the affair from behind a nearby tree. After the funeral, as the caretaker

(Perlman) is getting drunk in his own personal pyramid—yes, you read that correctly. Why? Again, who knows?—The Thief peers into the casket of the dead loan officer, but discovers that the body is missing. In its place is a skeleton wearing what is described as the garb of a cult member. When the caretaker starts to play the bagpipes (again for reasons unknown), The Thief grabs at his ears and has another episode in which he goes crazy. He runs away screaming, accidentally dropping the money he stole into the casket. Still running and screaming (wouldn't the screaming hurt his ears, as well?), The Thief falls into an open grave and is knocked unconscious. He has another surrealistic dream sequence before waking up.

Once he is awake and out of the grave, The Thief goes hunting for the money he lost. When he does not find it, he believes the caretaker took it. He goes to the caretaker and winds up killing him. After he does, he discovers a letter explaining that the cemetery is being closed and the bodies and caskets are being exhumed and moved to the mortuary.

Naturally he then goes to the mortuary and locates the coffin. When he opens it, however, the money is gone. He screams (again, his head?) loudly and accidentally knocks the coffin over. The Thief quickly dips out of sight, and the cult members who operate the mortuary (what?) show up to investigate matters. While this is happening, The Thief goes into the front office and locates a list of "professional mourners" from the funeral. Obviously something is amiss here, but The Thief doesn't care; he doesn't investigate matters and Wood doesn't spell it out for us. Why? Because it doesn't matter; that isn't the story that's being told. What matters here is that The Thief locate his missing cash. He then begins paying visits to everyone on the list of mourners.

The first place The Thief goes hunting is a burlesque show, where one of the mourners, Sandy Sands (Bernhard), dances erotically. When The Thief does not find the money in Sands' dressing room, he kills her and moves on to the next name on the list. The next name on the list is Tom Harris (Michael Greene). The Thief finds him drunk and passed out in a bar. He takes the drunk back home to a ramshackle shack. When he cannot find the money, he sets the place on fire and kills the drunkard.

It is interesting to note here that after each of The Thief's misdeeds, his crimes make the front page of the Los Angeles newspaper just the way they wood in one of Wood's own films. One would think that in a city the size of Los Angeles there would sometimes be stories that are more important than these. But this does not appear to be the case, at least not in Wood Land.

Broke and down on his luck, The Thief steals a woman's angora (of course) purse and runs away. Much to his chagrin, there is only five bucks in the purse. The Thief is then pursued by a police officer who is just about to shoot him when a car accident with four fatalities intervenes. This particular scene is handled quite well, as the music that accompanies the aftermath of the accident is pitch-perfect here, once again lending the scene a surreal feel.

Next up is Maylinda Austed (Hedren), a deaf woman who lives in house connected to a lighthouse. Why does she live there? Because Iliopulos wants to reference actress Hedren's affiliation with Alfred Hitchcock; when The Thief ultimately kills her, he strangles her, tossing her from atop the lighthouse as music from *Vertigo* (1958) plays. Just before this payoff, a nod to *The Birds* (1963) is also made through the appearance of a plastic bird inside the woman's home.

The Thief wanders aimlessly through the city before spotting a sign reading "ROOMS FOR RENT." He obtains a room for a mere seventy-five cents—again, this is a deal only found in Wood Land—similar to the forty-five cent hotdog. The hotel manager sends a teenage hooker (Ricci) up to The Thief's room. The two embrace at once and begin to dance. The Thief then realizes the hooker has picked his pockets, and he sends her on her way.

The last name on The Thief's list is Robert Forrest (John Ritter). Forrest, a well-known television and movie villain, is inside a bar. The Thief then gets into a massive brawl and delivers a Bruce Lee-esque Kung Fu beat down on several people before a loud noise sets him off again. He then follows Forrest to a circus, where the star is performing. The Thief sneaks his way inside, but before he can confront Forrest, he is attacked by a band of midgets and circus performers.

The Thief runs for his life, steals a cab, and returns to the cemetery. There he (we're not sure why) steals the caretaker's body from inside his pyramid (yes, we know). He also steals the bagpipes. When he hears the sound of the bagpipes, The Thief goes crazy and throws the instrument. The bag to the instrument breaks open and the money comes fluttering out all over the cemetery. As The Thief attempts to round up all the money, he falls into a grave and breaks his neck.

Did what we just witnessed actually happen? Or was it the mad ravings of a lunatic? A hallucination? A dream? A bad trip? The audience is left to wonder.

It's ironic that Ed Wood's best developed character never utters a single word and yet he comes across as better realized than every one of Wood's other characters combined. Yes, we know the thief is batshit insane, and we can't exactly comprehend his madness, but we can understand hunger, and misery, and fright, and pain, and loneliness, and desperation—all of which Billy Zane makes the audience feel in spades. Nobody likes to be trapped or on the run. We get a character here that the audience can identify with to some degree. There are no lessons to be learned with this film, no leaden performers spouting pretentious sermons in monotone. To the extent of the script, the thief feels like a living, breathing human being. We even see (through flashbacks) some of the bad things that may have tipped this character's mental stability. Wow! No other Wood character besides maybe Dr. Vornoff in *Bride of the Monster* (1955) ever seemed to have a preexistence; they were seemingly created to spout a few lines of dialogue as needed and then exit stage right.

This film also goes a great length in displaying how much Ed Wood's material improves when more talented actors and crew members are involved. It's utterly amazing that Wood accomplished what he did with the money, time, actors, and equipment he had. Yes, the plot of this film is absurd. Iliopulos knew the plot was absurd when he signed on to direct this film. But here, unlike with Wood's more earnest films, this absurdity meshes with the plot, the soundtrack, the actors, the direction, and becomes part of a larger picture. It becomes a work of art, a sort of living, breathing Salvador Dalí painting.

This is Edward D. Wood, Jr.'s greatest film. Period. It's too bad he wasn't around to see it. We believe it proves, unequivocally, what we've been saying throughout this entire book: Ed Wood was a man of peculiar genius. It was often ignored, dismissed, derided, and buried under bad circumstance and bad decisions, but it was there for all to see, if only in rare but brilliant flashes.

CREDITS: Producer: Dody Dorn; Jordan Gertner; Oscar Gubernati; Chris Hanley; Anne McCarthy; Jennifer Peckham; Don Sales; Mary Vernieu; Billy Zane; Director: Aris Iliopulos; Screenplay: Edward D. Wood, Jr.; Cinematographer: Michael F. Barrow; Editor: Dody Dorn.

CAST: Billy Zane (The Thief); Tippi Hedren (Maylinda Austed); Ron Perlman (Cemetery Caretaker); Michael Greene (Tom Harris); Christina Ricci (Teenage Hooker); Roberta Hanley (Housewife); Andrew McCarthy (Cemetery Cop); Ann Magnuson (Loan Secretary); Robert Musselman (Eartha Kitt's Escort); Marvin Lorence (Piano Player); Bud Cort (Shopkeeper); Taylor Negron (Loan Office Cop); Megan Odebash (Wardrobe Mistress); Carel Struycken (Undertaker); Max Perlich (Assistant Undertaker).

Devil Girls (1999)

Director Andre Perkowski was a big fan of Ed Wood's films and novels. After reading Wood's 1967 magnum opus *Devil Girls*, notable for featuring the first appearance of recurring character Sheriff Buck Rhodes, Perkowski set out to make his own cinematic adaptation. Despite the best of intentions, the resulting film, reportedly shot for a meager $500, is a mixed bag that mostly leans towards the bad. This is one of those films where you have to really work to find anything good to write about—and this is coming from the authors of a book on Ed Wood's films, no less.

The biggest problem is that *Devil Girls* looks like it was shot on an iPhone. It's heavily pixilated and looks like it's been blown up many times larger than its shooting format intended. But then this just may be early digital video and only looks like something that was filmed with a cell phone. Ed Wood was a man who used whatever low-budget equipment he had at his disposal to make his films, so he would no doubt have used digital cameras and maybe even cell phone cameras himself had they been available to him. But this does not excuse the film's poor picture quality. Perkowski and crew have tried to make the picture look like an old weather-beaten print circa-1955, but mostly it just looks amateurish.

But then almost everything about this film reeks of amateurism. We really hate to knock Perkowski's film as it tries so, so hard to be funny and to be Woodian. But that's part of the problem—it just tries too hard. Where Wood's films were made in earnest with accidental flaws abounding, Perkowski's film was made to intentionally look like one of Wood's films. Perkowski tries to emulate flawed techniques utilized by Wood, such as visible cameramen on screen, visible boom mics, stock footage, etc., but the end result is a failure because camp is difficult—in fact, damn near impossible—to produce intentionally. Very, very few films that attempt this succeed.

Devil Girls is the story of a group of female juvenile delinquents, similar to those of *The Violent Years* (1956). The girls get into all kinds of mischief, including murder, vandalism, drug smuggling, and frequent marijuana usage. In the end, however, their biggest crime is horrendously bad acting. And they're not the only ones; all of the acting in the film is poor. We may joke and poke fun at the wooden acting in Wood's films, but again, it was done in earnest. *Devil Girls* fails because it has bad actors trying their hardest to be even worse actors. The harsh truth is that Wood would never have used any of the actors in this film. Some are passable, but most are terrible, leading us to believe they were given very little or no direction from Perkowski. To be honest, one of the biggest problems is that Perkowski chose to cast many "actors" who are just downright annoying to spend time with. In Wood's films, the bad performers at least looked like real actors, but in this film a fair number of the actors look like they were rounded up at the nearest Starbucks.

Characters show up with no explanation as to who they are, and the plot, basic as it may be, is difficult to make heads or tails of. The film just sort of meanders along. Every scene featuring the preacher character attempts to intercut halves of conversations obviously shot at different times and locations. Orson Welles is said to have pulled this trick off more than once in his unfinished film *The Other Side of the Wind*, but most directors lack the talent of Welles and fail miserably when attempting this. Perkowski is no exception. Also, most of the silly dialogue comes directly from Wood's own prose, but its effect is lost when coming out of the mouths of these amateurs with bad video sound, to boot.

Credit the director for trying hard to give the film a Woodian feel. The soundtrack consists of library music found in other Wood films, more than a few lines of dialogue were aped from other Wood films (mostly *Orgy of the Dead*, 1965), and events are said to happen down by the old cabin on Marsh Lake. Criswell and Lobo even make appearances here. Lobo looks like a pretty good facsimile of Tor Johnson, but Criswell looks like he's being played by a 19-year-old wearing a strange little hairpiece, and that's rather distracting.

While it's nice to see characters that are familiar, both Criswell and Lobo seem to have been shoe-horned into the film simply for the sake of having them there.

Other nods to Wood include characters reading the Wood novels *Let Me Die in Drag* and *Security Risk*, the same commandments appear on the blackboard as those which appeared in *The Violent Years,* stock footage of an atomic bomb is used, much of the film features the sheriff sitting at his desk talking as we've seen in so many Wood films, a photo of Wood appears in one scene, and the sheriff's office is rather minimal just like in all the other Wood films (this one even features a folding aluminum chair behind the sheriff's desk). We'll say this for Perkowski, he's done his homework.

The truth is that most micro-films are bad. They almost all suffer from the same problems *Devil Girls* does in that they look and feel amateurish, so they must be graded on somewhat of a curve. However, if you make a micro-film with Ed Wood's name on it you'd better be prepared to have your film compared to other films in the Wood canon.

We appreciate what Perkowski tried to do here and we feel that he had only the best of intentions when he crafted this movie, but you know what they say about the road to hell being paved with good intentions.

CREDITS: Producer: Andre Perkowski; Christine Malcom; Director: Andre Perkowski.; Screenplay: Andre Perkowski (based on the novel by Ed Wood); Cinematographer: Dick Trent; Editor: Ontor Pertawst.

CAST: John Badalamenti (Deputy Klein); Stefanie Caterer (Babs); Arlene Cooney (Miss Kathy O'Hara); Mike Cooney (Lark); Sandra Delgado (Lila); Katie Dugan (Rhoda); Rob Gorden (Criswell); Victor Granata (Lonnie); David C. Hayes (Reverend Steel); Paul Hoffman (Buck Rhodes); Lobo (Himself); Jody Ann-Martin (Dee); Kristin Palker (Vixen/Good Girl); Andy Wibbels (Principal Carter).

The Vampire's Tomb (2013)

Ed Wood originally wrote *The Vampire's Tomb* as a vehicle for Bela Lugosi. However, life (and Lugosi's death) got in the way of his plans, and Wood never got around to making the film. Instead it became one of a dozen or more Wood scripts to sit around gathering dust.

But imagine Wood had actually made *The Vampire's Tomb* during his heyday and no one had known it existed. Imagine that film finally turned up nearly forty years after Wood's death and it contained nearly every one of the Wood trademarks. Imagine it also starred Lugosi, Tor Johnson, Criswell, and Vampira. What a find that would be!

Well, as we all know, that didn't happen. But imagine instead the project was filmed in the late 90s by a young up-and-coming filmmaker named Andre Perkowski. Imagine it still had all the trademarks of Wood's finest work, and it starred Lugosi, Tor Johnson, and Vampira "lookalikes," as well as featuring audio by Criswell himself.

Perkowski's *The Vampire's Tomb* isn't a verbatim telling of Wood's screenplay, but rather a pastiche of Wood's writing from various short stories, essays, and novels, shoehorned into the screenplay in the attempt to make the ultimate Woodian tribute.

The trailer for the film raves, "Available at last, the forgotten horror classic from beyond the grave, from beyond space and time, beyond anything your mind can conceive. From the muddled mind of Edward D. Wood Jr. comes a tale to torment you." The trailer also refers to *The Vampire's Tomb* as "an orgy of madness" and "a maze of howling terror." "This film is devoted to that hour of the morning when nightmare and reality merge into one, when the monsters and illusions of darkness remain lodged within the horrified skull; when the howl of the wolf chills the body into spasms of terror and ultimate dread. It is the hour of the nightmare." The trailer goes on to boast, "This film is not a record of mere death and unheard of sexual atrocity but a vision into the twilight of sanity where nothing exists within the frame of human reason."

With all of these things going for it, how could *The Vampire's Tomb* possibly go wrong? Surely this film will stand as the end-all-be-all tribute to Wood's talents and lack thereof. Sadly, however, this is not the case.

The Vampire's Tomb should be a blast to watch, especially for fans of Wood's absurd dialogue and unique sense of illogical logic. But, again, if all of this seemed to good to be true, it is for a reason.

The biggest problem with the film is that it is incoherent in a way that none of Wood's actual films were. For better or worse, each of Wood's projects had a clear beginning, middle, and end. His plots were often childishly simple, but you could understand what was happening onscreen. It saddens me to say that after three viewings of *The Vampire's Tomb*, we still can't tell you exactly what it's about. It's a mishmash of ghosts, vampires, and some sort of fiendish plot to murder a relative in order to secure the family inheritance, or something of that nature. It's really very difficult to say exactly what the plot of the film is as it's as muddled as Wood's mind was said to be.

The biggest reason for this is Perkowski's abundant love for the most convoluted of Wood's prose. The screenwriter/director apparently had such an affinity for this particular brand of Woodian dialogue that he crammed the screenplay full of it. As a result, the dialogue is difficult to make heads or tails of at times, doing absolutely no favors for an already incoherent plotline. And you would think that, despite its weaknesses, *The Vampire's Tomb* would be brimming with endlessly quotable Wood dialogue. And maybe it is. The problem here seems to be that the actors' deliveries are so bad that the occasional funny line becomes lost in translation. (One character's dialogue is inexplicably unintelligible throughout most of the film.) Another problem is that there are so many of these lines present that they get lost in a blur of repetitive sameness.

Another major problem with the film is that Perkowski chose to frame most of the film with random Criswell observations (taken from the album *Criswell Predicts*) that have absolutely nothing to do with what is happening onscreen. So while it is at first a welcome discovery to hear Criswell speaking over the soundtrack, it is a gimmick that wears thin within the first minute or so of the film.

A lot of work obviously went into this project (it spent nearly fifteen years in postproduction), and *The Vampire's Tomb* was clearly a labor of love for its director. However, it's just too amateurish a production to leave any kind of positive lasting impression. It was a neat concept, but it fails in just about every way conceivable.

At one point a character concludes, "Vampires exist only in the minds of transvestite writers." This is a somewhat funny line, but it feels like Perkowski and company are trying way too hard. Seemingly every Woodian reference imaginable is thrown in for good measure, but it just feels false and hollow. Again, Perkowski's love for his subject is obvious and does manage to show through, but it just isn't enough to save this problematic project.

And the acting is terrible. It isn't just hammy, it's downright bad. But the one thing that makes the least sense is a character who seems to be wearing a fat suit and delivers all of his lines like he has muscular dystrophy. It's difficult to say if the actor had some sort of real life affliction or if this was simply a strange and unexplainable decision on the part of the actor and Perkowski, but virtually all of this character's dialogue is unintelligible.

All of the standard Wood problems are here, from visible boom mics, to obvious ADR dialogue, to actors clearly reading from the script, to day-for-night issues, but again it all seems too much like someone *trying* to make a bad film. The spontaneity and child-like naivety of Wood's finest (and worst) films is absent here.

If *I Woke Up Early the Day I Died* (1998) represents the finest film in the Wood canon, then *The Vampire's Tomb* surely represents the worst of it (not counting Wood's pornography, of course).

CREDITS: Producer: Andre Perkowski; Director: Andre Perkowski; Screenplay: Andre Perkowski; Edward D. Wood, Jr.; Cinematographer: Andre Perkowski; Editor: Andre Perkowski.

CAST: Criswell (Narrator); Katie Dugan (Barbara); Keith Heimpel (Judson); Paul Hofman (Lake/Buck Rhodes); Andy Wibbels (Butler).

The Short Films

RANGE REVENGE (1948)

Very little is known about this project other than it is a western that stars acting brothers Conrad Brooks, Henry Bederski, and Ted Brooks. It is believed to have been Wood's first film. Supposedly the three brothers also funded the now-lost film. Wood apparently directed this while working simultaneously on his stage play *The Casual Company.* According to Brooks, the brothers were not happy with the western film as Wood did not employ any authentic western locations, but instead shot in Griffith Park. The film was never completed.

CREDITS: Producer: Edward D. Wood, Jr.; Director: Edward D. Wood, Jr.; Screenplay: Edward D. Wood, Jr.; Cinematographer: Edward D. Wood, Jr.; Editor: Edward D Wood, Jr.

CAST: Conrad Brooks, Henry Bederski, Ted Brooks.

THE STREETS OF LAREDO (1948)

This thirty-minute western short was never completed. It was shot silent, but its soundtrack was never added.

CREDITS: Producer: Tony Lawrence; Joan Crawford Thomas; Director: Edward D. Wood, Jr.; Screenplay: Edward D. Wood, Jr.; Cinematographer: Ray Flin; Edward D. Wood, Jr.; Editor: Edward D. Wood, Jr.

CAST: Duke Moore (Lem); Ruth McCabe (Barbara); Don Nagel (Tex); Chuck LaBerge (Sheriff); John Crawford Thomas (Deputy); Edward D. Wood, Jr. (Cowboy); Bill Ames (Bartender).

THE SUN WAS SETTING (1951)

This was Wood's first paying job as director. He wrote, produced, and directed this competently-made thirteen minute melodrama featuring Phyllis Coates of *Superman* fame. Its story is a rather simple one about a dying woman who is locked away in her apartment. She begs her would-be boyfriend to take her out to the nightclub for one last hurrah, knowing her heart would not be able to stand the excitement. Finally she convinces him to take her out for one last night, but she dies in his arms before they leave the apartment. "We almost made it, didn't we?" she says.

Wood expert Ted Newsom observes, "What's interesting about [*The Sun was Setting*] is its very uninterestingness."

Shot at KTTV Studios the week of Dec. 17, 1951, the short is also known as *The Sun Also Sets*.

CREDITS: Producer: Edward D. Wood, Jr.; Director: Edward D. Wood, Jr.; Screenplay: Edward D. Wood, Jr.; Ben Brody; Cinematographer: Ray Flin.

CAST: Angela Stevens (June); Tom Keene (Paul); Phyllis Coates (Rene).

CROSSROAD AVENGER: THE ADVENTURES OF THE TUCSON KID (1953)

Unsold television pilot for a western TV series starring Tom Keene as the Tucson Kid. The twenty-five minute short also featured Lyle Talbot and Kenne Duncan, as well as an uncredited appearance by Wood riding a horse.

CREDITS: Producer: Lew Dubin; John E. Clarke; Director: Edward D. Wood, Jr.; Screenplay: Edward D. Wood, Jr.; Cinematographer: Ray Flin; Film Editor: Lou Guinn.

CAST: Tom Keene (The Tucson Kid)

BOOTS (1953)

A "lost" film, this short was reportedly a second episode of Wood's proposed series *Crossroad Avenger: The Adventures of the Tucson Kid*. Also known as *Crossroad Avenger Returns*. According to Wood biographer Rudolph Grey, the two episodes of *Crossroad Avenger* were combined into a fifty-minute film titled *The Adventures of the Tucson Kid* and screened for potential buyers. However, it did not sell.

CREDITS: Producer: Lew Dubin; John E. Clarke; Director: Edward D. Wood, Jr.; Screenplay: Edward D. Wood, Jr.; Cinematographer: Ray Flin; Film Editor: Lou Guinn.

CAST: Tom Keene (The Tucson Kid)

TRICK SHOOTING WITH KENNE DUNCAN (1953)

Another paying gig for Wood, this nine-minute short features "movie and tele-villain" Kenne Duncan, "The Face That Is Known to Millions of TV and Western Movie Fans," performing trick shots with a variety of Remington rifles. Duncan shoots nickels, wafers, candles, and balloons, all while wearing a gaudy cowboy shirt with a huge Indian headdress on the back.

CREDITS: Producer: Edward D. Wood, Jr.; Director: Edward D. Wood, Jr.; Screenplay: Edward D. Wood, Jr.

CAST: Kenne Duncan (Himself).

FINAL CURTAIN (1957)

Two years before *The Twilight Zone* had its debut, Wood conceived a similar horror series entitled *Portraits in Terror.* Each episode would have been written and directed by Wood. Wood filmed this, the pilot episode, *Final Curtain.* The episode features a silent performance by the always-flat Duke Moore. Interestingly, the part was written for Bela Lugosi, who was reportedly reading this script when he died.

Final Curtain was lost for many years. After years of searching for it, actor Paul Marco's nephew located the film.

In the film Wood makes the most out of what little he had to work with. In this story of spirits haunting a theater late at night, Wood attempts to make frights out of such benign happenings as a light being turned off. Nothing much happens during the film's twenty-two-minute running time, but it is fascinating to be sure. Certainly it's no *Twilight Zone*, but it is an interesting viewing and it's one of the more competently-made Wood productions.

Humorously, Wood announces that the pilot was written, produced, and directed by himself not just once, but two times in the opening credits. Also of note, the short once again features one of Wood's apparent favorite lines—"creatures to be pitied, creatures to be despised." Later Wood integrated some footage from this pilot into the film *Night of the Ghouls* (1959).

CREDITS: Producer: Edward D. Wood, Jr.; Ernest S. Moore; Anthony Cardoza; Thomas Mason; Walter Brannon; Director: Edward D. Wood, Jr.; Screenplay: Edward D. Wood, Jr.; Cinematographer: William C. Thompson; Editor: Edward D. Wood, Jr.

CAST: Duke Moore (The Actor); Dudley Manlove (Narrator); Jenny Stevens (The Vampire).

THE NIGHT THE BANSHEE CRIED (1957)

This was apparently a second episode of Wood's proposed horror series *Portraits in Terror.* Wood later integrated some elements of the episode's storyline into his novelization of *Orgy of the Dead* (1965). As of now, this is a lost film. Wood's biographer, Rudolph Grey, believes some of *The Night the Banshee Cried* appears in *Night of the Ghouls*.

CREDITS: Producer: Edward D. Wood, Jr.; Director: Edward D. Wood, Jr.; Screenplay: Edward D. Wood, Jr.

BEACH BLANKET BLOODBATH (1985)

In 1978, director Fred Olen Ray commissioned Wood to write a screenplay entitled *Beach Blanket Bloodbath*. However, Wood died before completing the script. Years later, Ray decided to shoot one of the only scenes Wood completed and release it as a short. Its running time is just over three minutes.

CREDITS: Director: Fred Olen Ray; Screenplay: Edward D. Wood, Jr.

CAST: Forrest J. Ackerman; Bobbie Bresee; Martin Nicholas; David O'Hara; Susan Stokey; Dawn Wildsmith.

TO KILL A SATURDAY NIGHT (2007)

Short film black-and-white 16mm short based on Wood's story of the same title from his *Tales for a Sexy Night, Volume Two* paperback. The film features Conrad Brooks and *Astro-Zombies* (1968) director Ted V. Mikels as a couple of down-on-their-luck winos chugging booze and philosophically considering murdering a prostitute.

CREDITS: Producer: Andre Perkowski; Director: Andre Perkowski; Screenplay: Andre Perkowski (based on a short story by Edward D. Wood, Jr.); Cinematographer: Andre Perkowski; Editor: Andre Perkowski.

CAST: Ted V. Mikels; Conrad Brooks.

The Lost Films

Each of the following films is currently lost or no longer in circulation. As stated previously in this volume, *Take It Out in Trade* (1970) supposedly exists, as Wood biographer Rudolph Grey reports having seen it, but it is not available to the general public at this time. However, a compilation of outtakes from the film exist and are readily available.

OPERATION REDLIGHT (1969)

CREDITS: Producer: Jacques Descent; Director: Don Doyle; Screenplay: Edward D. Wood, Jr.

CAST: Edward D. Wood, Jr.

GUN RUNNERS (1969)

CREDITS: Producer: Donald A. Davis; Director: Donald A. Davis; Screenplay: Edward D. Wood, Jr.

CAST: Unknown.

THE ONLY HOUSE IN TOWN (1970)

CREDITS: Producer: Edward D. Wood, Jr.; Director: Edward D. Wood, Jr.; Screenplay: Edward D. Wood, Jr. (adapted from his novel *The Only House*); Cinematographer: Ted Gorley.

CAST: Unknown.

TAKE IT OUT IN TRADE (1970)

CREDITS: Producer: Richard Gonzales; Edward Ashdown; Director: Edward D. Wood, Jr.; Screenplay: Edward D. Wood, Jr.; Cinematographer: Hal Guthu; Editor: Michael J. Sheridan; Edward D. Wood, Jr.

CAST: Donna Stanley (Shirley Riley); Michael Donovan O'Donnell (Mac McGregor); Duke Moore (Frank Riley); Edward D. Wood, Jr. (Alecia); Nona Carver (Sleazy Maisie Rumpledinck); Casey Lorrain; Linda Colpin; Monica Gayle; Emilie Gray; Donna Young; Lynn Harris; Andrea Rabins; James Kitchens; Hugh Talbert; Judith Koch.

Photo Gallery

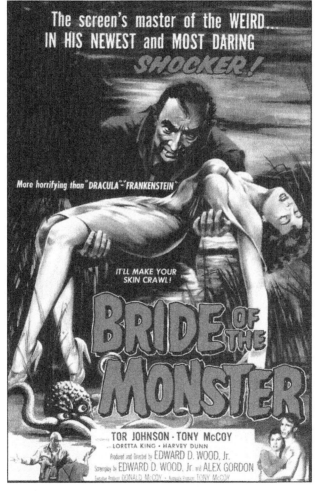

This one-sheet for Wood's *Bride of the Monster* is visually stunning, more of an advertisement for the film Wood envisioned than the one he made.

Advertising poster for the Ed Wood/A.C. Stephen (Stephen Apostolof) nudie collaboration *The Cocktail Hostesses*.

This poster for Wood's debut film, *Glen or Glenda?*, is almost as fascinating as the film itself.

Bela Lugosi
Edward D. Wood Jr
Dolores Fuller

in the Edward D. Wood Production
GLEN OR GLENDA ?
(aka I CHANGED MY SEX)
Copyright 1994 Wade Williams Productions

A still featuring the great Bela Lugosi from the film *Glen or Glenda?*

Dolores Fuller
Lyle Talbot
Steve Reeves

in the Edward D. Wood Production
JAIL BAIT
Copyright 1995 Wade Williams Productions

The big plot twist scene is depicted in this still from the film *Jail Bait*.

PLAN 9 FROM OUTER SPACE

STARRING PAUL MARCO "KELTON THE COP"

THE VERSATILE actor **Paul Marco** is best know for his role as **"Kelton the Cop"** - and who is **"Kelton the Cop"**? Well, it's certain that millions of film fans would know the answer to that one!

Paul had the good fortune to team up with legendary cult director **Edward D. Wood Jr.** for a trilogy of films that are now an integral part of popular film culture.

Paul introduced the fun character, *Kelton*, in the 1954 production, **"BRIDE OF THE MONSTER"** starring Bela Lugosi. The gosh, bumbling, fumbling cop was **Marco's** conception. How *Kelton* ever got on the police force is anyone's guess, but he made his second appearance in the cult film classic, **"PLAN 9 FROM OUTER SPACE"**.

PAUL MARCO

Perhaps **Marco's** best role can be seen in the final part of the **"Kelton Trilogy**, **"NIGHT OF THE GHOULS"**. This became a huge hit on video when released in 1980.

With the release of the three **Wood** films starring **"Kelton the Cop"**, **Paul** achieved cult status.

Paul had the rare opportunity to work in the Buena Vista film **"ED WOOD"** directed by Tim Burton, starring Johnny Depp as Ed Wood along with Martin Landau, who won an *Academy Award* for portraying **Bela Lugosi**. **Paul Marco** was played by **Max Casella** the star of the hit TV show **"DOOGIE HOWSER"**.

In working with **Ed Wood**, **Paul** was considered to be a *"good luck charm"* by the infamous director. **"PLAN 9"** now has the

great distinction of being honored by winning the *Golden Turkey Award* for the worst movie ever made, **Ed Wood**, also won for worst director of all time.

Today millions of people including the famous director **Joe Dante** director of **"GREMLINS"** calls it **"The Greatest Worst Movie Ever Made."**

Paul has been honored by the **Academy of Science Fiction Fantasy and Horror Films** with the *Golden Scroll Award of Merit for Outstanding Achievement*. He is also an active member of the *Academy of Television Arts & Sciences* for over 35 years.

Paul is currently developing a TV show called *"I Love Kelton The Cop"*, a comedy/mystery/horror show. *"Ed Wood "Kelton the Cop" Explores The Plan 9 Files"* for video. For Film: *"The Dead Never Die"*, a Hollywood story. *"Someone Walked Over My Grave"* about San Francisco.

A special offer to all fans of

PLAN 9 FROM OUTER SPACE

and the films of ED WOOD

FRONT COVER
BACK COVER

FOR A LIMITED TIME, we have a special product for fans of the classic movie PLAN 9 FROM OUTER SPACE and the films of ED WOOD (as depicted in the 1994 Buena Vista Film release, now available on video).

PAUL MARCO (KELTON THE COP) went into the music studio recently and recorded a spooky comedy record, HOME ON THE STRANGE. Paul Marco is now offering to all his fans of classic cult cinema the chance to purchase a special *collector's item*. This 45 rpm record is now available to *you* for a *limited time only!*

HOME ON THE STRANGE (4:30) on color vinyl as recorded by PAUL MARCO (KELTON THE COP). This hit tune is backed with CRISWELL (the psychic who could tell your future), he was in Ed Wood's "Plan 9" and "Night of

the Ghouls". CRISWELL is featured on the flip side with the eerie, first time release *"Someone walked over my Grave"*. He will personally sign the picture sleeve with a *special message for you*.

April 30, 1999. Paul was given the Southern California Motion Picture Council Special Merit Award and the Jeanie Emerald Angel Award for his contributions to the entertainment industry and the performing arts.

Horror/Cult Video Review Show, one-on-one cable show now in release. A new film, *"The Sci-Fi Project"* will be released soon.

"GOOD LUCK FOREVER"

Your Pal, Kelton

Paul Marco of "Kelton the Cop" fame established his own short-lived fan club. This is a flyer from that endeavor.

A film program from a German screening of Wood's *Plan 9 from Outer Space*.

The advertising poster for Wood's magnum opus, *Plan 9 from Outer Space*.

A still from *Plan 9 from Outer Space* featuring Tor Johnson and Maila "Vampira" Nurmi.

A surrealistic portrait of Ed Wood himself from *Glen or Glenda?*

A sexy shot of Wood collaborator Maila "Vampira" Nurmi.

This Japanese poster for Wood's posthumous film *I Woke Up Early the Day I Died* manages to capture the absurdity of the film.

No. 85 • September 1992 • Monthly newsletter of Kitchen Sink Press, Inc. • 2 Swamp Rd., • Princeton, WI 54968

Much MORE inside:
Briggs' FLASH GORDON
BETTY by OLIVIA sign
CRUMB'S "LET'S EAT" sign
ORIGIN SPIRIT #3
HOLLYWOOD CARDS relist
SAUCER PEOPLE relist

Ed was "The World's Worst Director"–Time Magazine

Drew Friedman presents:
Ed Wood, Jr. Players card set!

Coming in **September**, it's our newest trading card set, written and drawn by **Drew Friedman**. It's the *Ed Wood, Jr. Players Trading Card Set*, and nobody but Friedman, creator of *Warts and All*, could do it justice!

Friedman has long held **Ed Wood, Jr.**, the eccentric (to say the least) movie director, and his films dear. The actors who appeared in Wood's films–*Glen or Glenda*, *Plan 9 From Outer Space*, *Jailbait*, and others–have been seen in many of Friedman's previous works. **Tor Johnson, Vampira, Bela Lugosi, Criswell**–they've all appeared in Friedman's lovingly detailed, pointilistic studies. And they're all in the card set.

Now Friedman brings his knowledge and enthusiasm for Wood and his players to the *Ed Wood, Jr. Players Trading Card Set*, which will be printed in four separate colors on heavy card stock and come in a full color box. The **36-card set** is for all ages and retails for $10.95. Friedman has also written the card backs.

Ed Wood, Jr. became famous in cult film circles several years after his death in 1978. *Plan 9 From Outer Space* was named the "Worst Film of All Time" and Wood was named the "Worst Director of All Time" by the *Golden Turkey Awards* in 1980. From there, interest in Wood and his creations has increased dramatically, to the point that *Time Magazine*, in its June 1, 1992 issue, just featured Wood in a full page review of a new book about him, *Nightmare of Ecstasy*.

The sources of Wood's renaissance are his bizarre lifestyle and his weird films. A transvestite, Wood was a Marine in World War II and claimed that he wore women's lingerie under his uniform when he took part in the invasion of Iwo Jima. He later worked in a carnival as a "half man, half woman" before breaching Hollywood with *Glen or Glenda*, in which he starred–as a man who wants to be a woman. His subsequent films set records for cheapness, brief production times, and surrealism. *Plan 9* is an anti-atomic warfare film featuring ghouls and alien invaders, notable as Lugosi's last film and for the use of automobile hubcaps as flying saucers. Wood's films were made quickly and ineptly, but they were never boring. Today, **Ed Wood, Jr.** film festivals are common, and he is more highly regarded than most traditional Hollywood directors.

Drew Friedman has long carried Wood's banner; Friedman is one of the people who has made the director famous. In the *Ed Wood, Jr. Players Trading Card Set*, the artist pays homage to this fascinating fringe character. Be sure to have enough of this set on hand this September.

A set of 36 color trading cards celebrating the actors who appeared in "The World's Worst Director's" cult films, by one of the top artists working today!

A flyer advertising trading cards featuring the likenesses of Ed Wood and many of his crazy cohorts, including Criswell, Bela Lugosi, Vampira, and Tor Johnson.

Interview: Rob Craig

Rob Craig has been writing about cult film since the early 1980s, at the moment when the theatrical film landscape began to morph into the corporate-dominated horror show it has now become. To Craig, pretty much any film made pre-1984 is worth cherishing and writing about—especially the low-budget and obscure. Craig has penned books on cult film legends Larry Buchanan (*The Films of Larry Buchanan: A Critical Examination*), Edward D. Wood, Jr. (*Ed Wood: Mad Genius, A Critical Study of the Films*), and Andy Milligan (*Gutter Auteur: The Films of Andy Milligan*). He is currently working on two projects: the films of Jerry Warren and the history of American International Television.

ANDREW RAUSCH: *When did you first become aware of Ed Wood, and what were your initial thoughts of his work?*

ROB CRAIG: I first became aware of the weird and wonderful world of Ed wood in a most circuitous way, which I now think, upon reflection, was the best way to discover this bizarre and most unusual filmmaker. I grew up in New Jersey and like any self-respecting baby boomer I was completely enamored of monster movies. There were many television programs broadcast from New York City, which showcased horror and science fiction films. All of the independent stations—Channel 5, Channel 9, and Channel 11—had their own horror movie show. Channel 11,

WPIX-TV, had a Saturday night program called *Chiller Theater*, which has since become iconic and, in fact, I believe, was the inspiration for the long-running Chiller Conventions in New York and New Jersey. In the early 1960s, when I first started watching this program, the opening sequence was a montage of short clips from various films which I assume were all in Channel 11's film library, with a creepy bit of library music accompanying. This was a very exciting, evocative opening which really set the mood for the films that they showed. If memory serves correctly, amongst the movies that were sampled in the opening were Bert I. Gordon's *The Cyclops* (1957), the Peter Graves film *Killers From Space* (1954), the completely bizarre creature from *The Crawling Eye* (1958), a ridiculous scene of an ape "going ape" from *Bride of the Gorilla* (1951) (or possibly *White Pongo*, 1945), and the magnificent Allison Hayes busting out of a balsa wood house in *Attack of the 50 Foot Woman* (1958).

However, the one clip which really resonated with me—and which I would not identify for many years—was a very strange scene showing a sexy young woman with a tight black dress, long black hair, heavy makeup, and long dark fingernails. This sexy/creepy monster woman was walking towards the camera in a menacing way, with a deranged grimace on her face. Now, to an eight-year-old monster movie buff—it may sound funny to say now—but I found that clip extremely creepy. The woman's grimace indicated some sort of madness or evil which really unnerved me. It was an interesting combination, I think, of sex and horror. However I was processing that subconsciously who knows, but neither I nor my immediate circle of friends had any idea what movie this strange scene was from—we just loved it.

This menacing "vampire girl" was an indelible image in my mind for many years. Fast forward to the mid-1970s, while in college, I started attending movie conventions and *Star Trek* conventions, and at one of them, a dealer was selling 16mm prints of the *Chiller Theater* opening! (Needless to say, this is an artifact I dearly wish I still had today, but of course it is long gone). According to the dealer, who worked part-time at a local film laboratory (it may have been DuArt), before video tape was readily available to local TV stations, they actually made 16mm prints of various opening and closing segments, and spliced them onto the beginning of every movie they showed. TV stations thus ordered these short films by the hundreds, and some ended up being tossed out. Of course being the quintessential movie nerd, I already owned a used 16mm projector, and had some films I had purchased from the used film marketplace. I spliced the *Chiller Theater* film onto the head of one of the few feature films I had at the time—I think it was *Untamed Women* (1953)—and my friends and I had a little *Chiller Theater* revival. Running the film again, it was so good to see that crazy sexy vampire girl. At this time, I still did not know who she was.

Circa 1978, the "bad movie" revival began in earnest. I think the first book out was *The Fifty Worst Films of All Time*, by one of the Medveds, and in it *Plan 9 from Outer Space* (1959) and Ed Wood were featured prominently. The authors gushed on about how horrible Wood's movies were, how pathetic and amateur, how they should have never been shown on the big screen, etc. Flying saucers out of paper plates, cardboard tombstones, and all that legacy. But one of the images showed Vampira walking through a makeshift graveyard set—I had found my dream woman! Needless to say, boy did

I wanna see that movie! *Plan 9 from Outer Space* sounded right up my alley because, even as a small child, when watching monster movies, I tended to gravitate towards—I didn't know why then, I have all kinds of reasons for gravitating towards these films now—but at the time I had nothing but the fact that I was a weird kid and I liked weird movies—the weirder the better in fact.

Anyway, I was very intrigued by the revelations in the book and pretty much wanted to see every movie that was discussed. Shortly, other books came out—*The Golden Turkey Awards*, the Danny Peary *Cult Movies* book, and all of these championed the "good-badness" of Ed Wood, making him an even more intriguing figure to me. Somewhere in the early 1980s, I read in the newspaper that they were having a theatrical showing of *Plan 9 from Outer Space*—the one and only—hosted by the Medved brothers at a revival theater in Manhattan. (I can't recall if it was the Bleeker Street or the Thalia or the 57th Street Playhouse or one of the several other revival houses in NYC at that time—there were so many revival houses in New York at that time which was of course a lovely thing which is completely gone now, but that was then.) So of course I make haste to this rare screening, at some large auditorium somewhere, so I don't think it was one of the major revival houses. The room had horrible, horrible sound. I basically could not hear a word of the dialogue. Also, they appeared to be showing a 16mm dupe of the film, so the picture was very murky, as well. Of course, everyone in the audience—which was packed—was dutifully howling at every frame of the film like it was the most ridiculous and pathetic thing they had ever seen. I agreed in principle—some of the acting and the set designs were borderline amateur—but to me *Plan*

9 from Outer Space was a revelation; a bizarre, dreamy, weird, enigmatic experience. It had a true artist's signature to it, an aesthetic and thematic style which its maker could not articulate by any stretch of the imagination, but it was there nonetheless.

The histrionic acting of *Plan 9*, the gloomy ambiance, it was all rather breathtaking to me. It looked in some ways like Wood was trying to recreate a poverty-row horror melodrama from the early 1940s, transplanted into the science-obsessed 1950s, a conceit which made for a truly disorienting experience. Also the jarring aesthetic and structural anomalies of the film: the grainy home movie footage of Bela Lugosi against studio footage of an obvious stand-in; glaring day-for-night discrepancies, Tor Johnson trying to crawl out of a giant hole, the spacemen with their strictly earthbound costume and furnishing. The film seemed almost to dare you to take it seriously.

The special effects in *Plan 9*, although primitive certainly, were fantastic to me, and a key element in my instant love for the film. Of course, the flying saucers I immediately saw were not paper plates or hubcaps or trash can lids or whatever else the Medveds claimed they were, and this may be where I first started a break with the "bad film" crowd, who wanted nothing more than to mock strange films, even if they had to misread them, or outright lie to do it. It was fairly obvious to me that the flying saucers were some kind of toys or models, and fairly accomplished at that. Of course, they are filmed badly: they are much too shiny, you can see the strings they hang by, they wobble, etc. It was a very primitive attempt at miniatures effects, and all the more dear to me for that. And the graveyard set was so theatrical, so arty in a way, with fake tombstones and gnarly limbs just tossed about pretty much anywhere, and that wonderful black nothing of a backdrop, and the fog... Watching these scenes made me wonder what the film must have looked like on the big screen in its initial theatrical release. I think it must have been a severe shock to the senses, a real trip to another world.

Looking back now, I can see why I immediately fell in love with *Plan 9* and Ed Wood. I always gravitated towards the weird, primitive, and low-budget, and that of course very often segues into the so-called "so bad it's good" category, because one of the criteria most people have for judging a film is how "professional" it looks—how expensive it looks, how many people were involved in its making, how realistic the special effects are, how competent the acting, all that stuff in a certain way picking up from the mythos of the "golden age of Hollywood" as the only true litmus test of a film's quality. A "good" film should have a certain look and polish, and ideally it should show no rough edges whatsoever. In contrast, I liked seeing films which almost looked like I could picture making it myself. I don't know what that is—it might be in something problematic in my own nature—but that's how I felt then, and largely still do.

Anyway, after the movie ended I realized I had found a new culture hero. This was actually several years before home video, and there was precious little to find on anything cult film related, on TV, in the theaters, anywhere. (The 1980s was, to me, a bleak, bleak decade for film in general.) However, luckily this same group of people sponsored another Ed Wood Festival in Manhattan soon afterward—a double feature of *Jail Bait* (1954), and *The Sinister Urge* (1960). Now what was exciting about these two films was that although they didn't have the runaway science fiction and horror elements of *Plan 9*, what made these two films all the more dear to me was that here were a crime melodrama and a light sexploitation film and they had the same basic lunacy, the same haphazard avant-garde style of *Plan 9*. They were, like *Plan 9*, very nicely filmed with professional black-and-white cinematography (usually by Bill Thompson). They kind of visually aped the classic Hollywood look, ostensibly at least, but within that the sets were off, the actors were off, the screenplay was nuts, and the dialogue was way out. Everything about *Jail Bait* and *The Sinister Urge* was just "off," and to me this made them beautiful and dear. Again, most in the audience howled at the films' narrative and aesthetic excesses and flaws, which were many, and most obviously found them hilariously bad. That's fine, by the way; I enjoy this aspect of this type of film as much as any other fan. But I also was aware that I just saw more rare texts from a really interesting filmmaker.

The rest, as they say, is history. Around '82 or '83 Paramount tried to mount a revival release of *Glen or Glenda?* (1953), but for some reason I was unable to locate a screening of that, and never saw it on the big screen. But one of the first video tapes I bought around 1985, when VCRs became really affordable, was Wood's *Bride of The Monster* (1955), on Star Classics, in really crappy LP Mode. This was my first viewing of this glorious, baffling film, and to me the first viewing of a film is sacred thing—what I call the "virgin viewing"—preferably without any foreknowledge whatsoever about the film or its history. In this first viewing, if one pays attention, one can easily discern the spirit if you will, of its maker, and the effect is often electric. At any rate, this was true for *Bride of the Monster*, which washed over me in a way I can still vividly recall. Here Wood seemed to be attempting to make a "quote-unquote" traditional horror film, which looked like a rabid, deranged alcoholic bum was trying to remake a PRC Sam Neufield movie from the early 1940s, like *The Ape Man* (1943) or *The Corpse Vanishes* (1942). Wood of course augmented this time-worn template with wild excesses of dialogue, plot, acting, and an extraordinary ability to rent asunder the accepted tropes of narrative cinema, only to bring them all back in the end to tie everything up neatly.

By the early 1990s, of course, there was the Rudolph Grey book, which was a revelation to many Ed Wood fans, finding out about our hero, what a desperate and sad and pathetic life he had. His truly heartbreaking life story added yet another dimension to Wood's films—they made him not only a tragic figure, but a larger-than-life one, and made the films, therefore, precious documents from a tortured artist. Wood's wonderfully weird films are made with some excruciating handicaps (alcoholism, poverty, probably mental illness), but look at what he did with all that emotional and existential baggage. I still consider Wood an artist, and when people laugh at the thought, I tell them, "Look what Wood did with a couple hundred bucks, a few thousand bucks, and some close friends—he made films that almost everybody knows about, that have endured, that are still loved by many." I consider this a great feat, actually.

So, to summarize my initial thoughts on Ed Wood, he was obviously a outlaw, a renegade filmmaker, what might be called an independent filmmaker. That is, before the term lost all meaning—when you have $20,000,000 movies being called "independent film," that isn't independent, that's just low-budget corporate—but here was somebody who threw these movies together with spit and polish and Wood's films didn't have a few rough edges: they were all rough edges. If you like a certain type of film, you like to see what might be called "the hand of the artist," you know like in a painting you like to see the brush-strokes, the texture, the lines of the piece, the artist's process at work. It's not slick and airbrushed and perfect and all signs of humanity have been "brushed" out of it—take any Steven Spielberg film, for example. Ed Wood's films seem like what primitive, raw, independent film was originally intended to be. It has that quality the artist being visible in the work. To a lot of people that's bad. But there are a small minority of film buffs, I think, who really appreciate the aesthetic qualities of the true outsider filmmaker. Now I am not implying that Wood was a conscious genius, who put all this stuff in deliberately. Film and other art forms are a creative process which is largely unconscious; you just throw these elements together and see what sticks. I don't think even the most arrogant artist in the world would claim that he designed every single aspect of the finished product. He would honestly have to say that a lot was left to chance, and film—because it is such a complex medium—has so many steps that it would be impossible to predict exactly how the finished product will turn out.

So, when that finished product turns out to be *Night of the Ghouls* (1959) or *Glen or Glenda?* or *Plan 9*, something that is just so structurally, aesthetically, and thematically bizarre and convoluted and rich—so unique—to me this is a cause for celebration. As I have mentioned elsewhere—and I still stand by the statement—Ed Wood at his best came very close to the cinematic experimentation that was going on at the time in the underground film movement of the day. I have no pretense that he was doing it consciously, but a lot of his films are nonlinear and structurally complex. Even though there is a narrative, the films do not follow logical (or traditional) expositional templates, and in addition there is so much of symbol, theater, and ritual in them that they often come remarkably close to the work of avant-garde filmmakers like Kenneth Anger, Curtis Herrington, or Man Ray, and others working during that time period. To me its uncanny how much a film like *Night of the Ghouls* looks like an underground art film. Wood's films, although they borrow ostensibly from the look of a traditional Hollywood mythos, they do not work well as typical narrative film, yet one might say they do work quite well as a art film, which is very interesting if you think about it. I think a strong argument for this case is that Wood's films look extremely well today—in fact look better as the years progress—which is of course another litmus test for what is enduring art.

RAUSCH: *Why did you decide to write a book about Wood?*

CRAIG: I decided to write about Ed Wood for several reasons. First of all, I love his films. They have baffled, intrigued, and amazed me for years. They are so narratively unhinged, so expositionally surreal, so delightfully non-linear in many respects, they come across almost as art films. Since I had previously gotten the opportunity to write about another favorite filmmaker, Larry Buchanan, I knew that Ed Wood would benefit from similar treatment. I had discovered, with Larry Buchanan, that taking a serious critical look at a group of films is always an adventure and a journey. Even though I was intimately familiar with Buchanan's TV movies—the "Azalea Pictures"—when I actually got down to a close reading of them, so many things started to pop out at me, like the constant presence of a heroic "super-couple" who saved the world, Homer-like, from all evil, within a grimly realistic, deeply depressed, suburban setting. I knew that the same would be true with Ed Wood, and it was.

There is a lot going on in Ed Wood 's films—whether anybody cares to pay attention or not—and I knew it would be fascinating and rewarding to take a closer peek. I began with *Glen or Glenda?*, and that film in itself took almost six months to write about. It's really Wood's masterpiece, as well as his back-handed autobiography, and it says so much about shifting gender roles, and the always-precarious nature of personal identity, in the post-war era that it really wowed me. The rest of the book was comparatively easy, but I discovered so many wonderful things about Wood's art, and philosophy, along the way. Even if every theme, motif, narrative template, and character archetype in Wood's films was inserted subconsciously, they still resonate in the films today, and this to me is very exciting. Even a supposedly bad filmmaker like Wood has, if you care to look, a lot going on in the films. Of course, many disagree—most of the reviews of the Wood book accused me, rather predictably, of over-interpreting, hallucinating, or just plain making things up in the films in order to create a pseudo-academic critical analysis of a bunch of bad films which should by no means be looked at seriously. (My favorite review was in *Video Watchdog*, which suggested I should "go outside and get some fresh air!")

But I stand by my conclusions in the book, and I stand by the basic premise that any interesting artist, in any medium, may create works which contain within them certain recurring themes, plotlines, characters and concerns which are valid to see and valid to enjoy. This is the old auteur theory, greatly oversimplified of course, and considered passé today, but it is a great way to look at these iconoclastic low-budget filmmakers like Wood, Buchanan, and Andy Milligan, who proved to be an veritable treasure trove of thematic constancy. I believe that any films which fascinate me to a degree to which I keep going back to revisit them has to have something going on deep within its textual heart—no simple melodrama could have that kind of power over a viewer to warrant such devotion and repeated visitation. Ed Wood's films are fascinating to me in that way, and from their increasing popularity, I would imagine there are others who think so.

Although I've certainly enjoyed the pastime, gawking at the flaws in a "bad movie" only gets you so far, and "bad" is such a subjective term, acting primarily as elitist censorship tool, declaring certain films, genres or filmmakers to be unworthy of respect or thoughtful viewing. By and large, the "bad film" movement tended, at least initially, to target very low-budget genre melodramas made by obscure and eccentric independent filmmakers, a prejudice which suggested that "bigger" films were by definition better than smaller ones—a thesis with which I wholeheartedly disagree.

For instance, if you asked me what are the worst

movies ever made, I would unhesitatingly start with *Star Wars* (1977), *Ghostbusters* (1984), and *E.T.* (1982). These movies, and their ubiquitous brethren, are "bad" because even with the advantages of corporate sponsorship, bloated budgets, large crews and ostentatious production values, they commit two deadly cinema sins: they are boring, and they are stupid. They are utterly predictable, and they insult the intelligence. To me, that is truly "bad." An Ed Wood or an Andy Milligan, working alone for peanuts, was nonetheless able to make bizarre, exciting melodramas which were unpredictable and intellectually intriguing—feats a Spielberg or a Lucas couldn't achieve even with a trillion dollars or an army of flunkies. I guess you could say I prefer championing the under-dog!

RAUSCH: *What are some misconceptions you feel that people have about Ed Wood's work?*

CRAIG: I don't know that there are misconceptions about Ed Wood as much as dismissal or under-appreciation of his work. I doubt that Wood fancied himself an artist—although we can never know what he thought in his heart of hearts—but the films and writings stand for themselves as strong, unique, in fact quite extraordinary cultural texts. They are eccentric to be sure—raw and primitive—and so can easily be dismissed as "bad." The sheer awkwardness of Wood's films make them easy targets for perfection-oriented souls who don't like to see any missteps or incongruities in their film narratives, preferring squeaky-clean, predictable corporate product. But there are others—and I might suggest *many* others—who enthusiastically embrace these apparent "flaws" and find in *Plan 9*, *Glen or Glenda?*, or *Orgy of the Dead* (1965) true expressions of the industry "outsider," someone who forged entirely unique—if rough—products using only his wits and immediate resources, and playing entirely by his own rules. This is what I always found fascinating about Wood, and I know there are others who feel the same way.

Another reason I think that Ed Wood deserves further study and scrutiny is that the films look better as they age. Outside of their original time, films like *Plan 9* and *Jail Bait* and *The Sinister Urge* look shockingly modern today—maybe even post-modern, although I still can't get a clear handle on what that overused term signifies when dealing with cinema—and of course, this is the true test for art in general. Any cultural text which resonates and entertains (i.e. "holds up") years after its manufacture has something going on which cannot be ignored. A good deal of commercial cultural product that was designed for quick consumption and disposal (film, TV, and pop music are three major genres) date badly, and look positively embarrassing today (take, for example, most mystery movie series of the 1940s, such as the "Boston Blackie" films; any TV situation comedy produced in the 1970s; virtually all popular music of the 1980s). Yet "timeless" cultural product endures and resonates with each new generation, boasting a certain immortality by seeking and capturing new audiences (examples: "golden age" Hollywood films; popular music of the 1960s; and some independent "counter-culture" cinema of the 1970s). Wood's films stand today completely severed from their time; although they mimic and acknowledge their pulp fiction 1950s origins, their bizarre radicalization of the themes, tropes, and motifs of that time make them alternately absurdist and allegorical, and they come across—more than anything—as abstract *parodies* of that time period and those genre conventions. In this way, Wood was either ahead of (or outside) his time. Artists ahead of their time rarely get recognition during their lifetimes, this being basically the definition of that phenomenon. If, however, the works are substantial and meaningful, if they have a message to relate to subsequent generations, they may be "discovered" in the future and finally appreciated. I absolutely think this is true with the films of Ed Wood, who has managed to gather an entire cult of devoted acolytes, a fiercely devoted fan base which started almost at the exact moment of his death circa 1978, and which now grows exponentially, possibly without end. At the end of recorded time it may be revealed that Ed Wood was one of the true geniuses of cinema, on a par with Orson Welles and D.W. Griffith and Alfred Hitchcock. To paraphrase Criswell, "Can You Prove It *Couldn't* Happen?"

Interview: Brenda Fogarty

Actress Brenda Fogarty made her screen debut in the 1975 comedy
If You Don't Stop It... You'll Go Blind!!!. She next appeared as the lead
in the cult film *Trip with the Teacher* (1975). Her other films include
The Candy Tangerine Man (1975), *Chesty Anderson U.S. Navy* (1976),
and *The Happy Hooker Goes to Washington* (1977). She also appeared
in two Ed Wood-scripted Stephen C. Apostolof films, *Fugitive Girls*
(1974) and *The Beach Bunnies* (1976).

Today the actress performs in one-woman show (which she also
wrote) called *The Lesbian Monologues*.

ANDREW RAUSCH: *How did you originally hook up with Stephen
C. Apostolof and his group?*

BRENDA FOGARTY: Through Tallie Cochrane and Patrick Wright.
I'm sure it was them. They turned me on
to a lot of stuff. They were good friends of
mine. I think the first movie I ever did was
If You Don't Stop It... You'll Go Blind!!!. I
think I had two scenes in that one. And
little did I know back then when I was
twenty-seven or twenty-eight, however old I
was when I started, that I'd be sitting here
someday in the park with eight dogs and a
cat. [Laughs.] Life is good!

RAUSCH: *What were your impressions of Steve Apostolof?*

FOGARTY: He was a mad Hungarian director. He was just crazy. He was mad on the set. He was always yelling. He'd wear the big hat, and he had the personae of the mad director. He was nice to me, always nice to me, but he was very nervous and high-strung. He did a lot of yelling. "I don't want that, I want this!" A lot of the stuff was shot MOS [meaning without a soundtrack] and then they'd add that in later, so he could yell all he wanted! [Laughs.]

RAUSCH: *Did you ever meet Ed Wood?*

FOGARTY: I don't think so. At the time I didn't know who he was. Just like nobody knows who Brenda Fogarty is...yet! [Laughs again.]

RAUSCH: *Were you surprised later on to learn that this now-famous man had written two of your films?*

FOGARTY: Yes. I didn't even know about it until just recently when a friend of mine, Eddy Detroit, told me about it. I didn't know. I said, "Really?" Life has its twists and turns, doesn't it? It's full of surprises.

RAUSCH: *You worked on* The Fugitive Girls *as an extra. What do you remember about that?*

FOGARTY: We shot that at a Boy Scout camp up in Frasier, California. They rented the whole camp, and what I remember is I knew everybody who was in the movie. We all had a good time on that.

You know, I watched *Fugitive Girls* last night on YouTube. I had never seen it. That was great. I was just an extra in that, a campfire girl. I didn't have any lines. It was a last minute deal. They needed people or something, I can't really remember. But

I'm in there for quite a long time. It was fun.

RAUSCH: *What are you memories of working on* The Beach Bunnies?

FOGARTY: I remember I had poison oak on my forehead. I think I got it in the middle of the shoot, which probably lasted a week. It was a short shoot. It was all itchy and red, and I was like, "What?" I think we ran to Rite-Aid, so I could get some poison oak medicine. That's why I had my hair down over my face in some of those scenes. I also wore a scarf in some of them. I'm not sure how I got poison oak; I just got it.

I liked doing what I did, and the cast and crew was really friendly. Making *The Beach Bunnies* was just a fun thing to do. I liked starring in it, because I knew I'd be a star. I've almost always been the lead in the movies I've done, and then when you go online you see that I'm doing a one-woman star show now... I just really liked working on that.

I remember the wardrobe lady—I think her name was Nancy Youngblood—called me about two weeks after the shoot wrapped. She said, "Hey, Brenda, I'm the associate producer on *The Happy Hooker Goes to Washington*. The actress we had lost her passport, and she can't do the picture. Can you do this? I told the director I knew someone who could fill in. Oh, and we shoot tomorrow morning." I said, "Sure!" So I went in the next morning, and that was when I got the script. We shot in a high-rise in Century City on the tenth or twelfth floor. And I did it. I was the editor of the main character's movie magazine. And the director, William Levey, came over and said, "You know, I've never cast anyone before without seeing them first, but you're wonderful. You did a fabulous job."

RAUSCH: *You are by far the best thing about* The Beach Bunnies. *You're very funny in the movie.*

FOGARTY: Do you remember the scene where I spray the fire extinguisher? Well, that was probably the second or third take. I usually do things in one take because I'm always prepared. That's why if you see my one-woman show on YouTube, you'll see that my memory is great. I just go over the lines over and over again... So I always did everything in one take. But I remember I sprayed the fire extinguisher too much and they yelled cut! "We can't see anything, Brenda!" The cameras couldn't see the actors. [Chuckles.] After that I was a little bit more careful.

RAUSCH: *It looked like a fun movie to make. You had that great scene where you pretend to be eaten by a shark...*

FOGARTY: And that scene with the bellboy. And I remember the scene where I was dressed as a maid and I was trying to get into the star's bathroom. I just made up some of that as I went... But I haven't seen that for probably thirty years.

What I do remember is that a lot of people didn't use their real names on it. Even the cameraman. I remember him saying he didn't want to put his name on it. I remember that conversation... A lot of young girls start out in those sexy movies and they don't use their real names because they want to be a star.

RAUSCH: *You had the funniest, strangest line in the movie, too. "I've got to find out if Rock Sanders has a cock!" That line always gets a laugh.*

FOGARTY: [Laughs.] Oh, god! That's right. Oh my gosh. And then I have that scene where I make it with the bellboy. I remember that... He was as scared as I was. Well, I wouldn't say scared, maybe 'reluctant.'

RAUSCH: *You strike me as a very progressive person. What did you think of Wood and Apostolof's handling of the rape in* The Beach Bunnies?

FOGARTY: What do you mean?

RAUSCH: *It feels a lot like a rape justification fantasy in that the woman who gets raped on the beach ends up liking being raped and then later says she's now sexually awakened thanks to the rape.*

FOGARTY: Steve Apostolof, all his movies, had dancing, production, women who liked to have sex. He was trying to sell what he thought the audience wanted to see. I think he downplayed the rape stuff because then it would be a whole different genre of movie. He was about no means yes, because he made the girls like it. Today that's rape, but back then if the woman liked it, sure, rape me again... That was just the kind of audience Steve was playing to—the kind of person who would go out and see a movie like that. He was selling to that market, and I'm sure he sold it all over the world. They downplayed rape in those movies because those were supposed to be feel-good films.

RAUSCH: *One of the most blatant instances is in* The Cocktail Hostesses *when Forman Shane's character basically says, she's a whore, what does she care if she gets raped?*

FOGARTY: That's terrible, but some males really think that way. And they buy the movie. These weren't message movies. They weren't very evolved; in fact, they were pretty primitive. But then my character was raped in *Trip with the Teacher*, and they played it well. They played it the right way. And there was actually more to that scene than what ended up in the final cut. Thank god it ended up on the cutting room floor. And in that film, I got to kill the guy, which was the ultimate revenge.

Interview: Rudolph Grey

There is perhaps no one who can be said to be more responsible for the public's appreciation and knowledge of Edward D. Wood, Jr. and his films than author and film historian Rudolph Grey. His seminal 1992 work *Nightmare of Ecstasy: The Life and Art of Edward D. Wood, Jr.* remains the pinnacle of Wood studies. Grey was one of the last people to speak with and document the stories of many of Wood's associates before they passed away, so his book is unlikely to be rivaled any time soon.

Grey's book served (somewhat loosely) as the basis for the 1994 Tim Burton biopic *Ed Wood.* Grey is also known as the man who located the "lost" Wood films *Take It Out in Trade* (1970) and *Necromania* (1971). He is widely considered the foremost expert on all things Ed Wood.

ANDREW RAUSCH: *How did you first learn about Edward D. Wood, Jr.?*

RUDOLPH GREY: My original exposure to Ed Wood was through *Famous Monsters of Filmland*, where they did a feature on *Night of the Ghouls* (1959), which I think at that time was still called *Revenge of the Dead*. It was very intriguing. The Black Ghost, the White Ghost, the giant Lobo... Forry Ackerman got those great stills directly from Ed Wood.

RAUSCH: *When did you get to see your first Wood film?*

GREY: That would have been around 1961, when the local television station here, WPIX, premiered *Plan 9 from Outer Space* (1959) and *Bride of the Monster* (1955).

RAUSCH: *What were your first thoughts on the films?*

GREY: I was totally transfixed; Bela Lugosi, Tor Johnson, Vampira, Criswell… Wonderful, iconic characters. Who else used Vampira in her Vampira guise? Or gave Tor a co-starring role?

RAUSCH: *When did you decide you were going to write a book on Ed Wood?*

GREY: Going even back to 1978, my best friend, the artist-musician Sumner Crane had a connection to a San Francisco magazine called *Vacation*. We were going to do a series of interviews. I think we did one or two… But on the list was Sumner's favorite cartoonist, Bob Powell, and we learned he'd died in 1969. And I wanted to interview Ed Wood. Of course little did I know that around that time he was probably being evicted. So that was that. And I had no idea how to contact him. I didn't think he'd be in the phone book, which he was. But that was the beginning of my interest in writing about Ed Wood.

RAUSCH: *How long did it take you to write* Nightmare of Ecstasy?

GREY: About ten years. It was really triggered off when they used to have a thing here on St. Marks Place called the Monster Movie Club. They would show films every week. And one night Frank Henenlotter

was there. I forget what movie they were showing
that night. But, from Richard Bojarski, Frank got a
copy of Ed Wood's resume. A colleague of Bojarki,
the writer/artist Don Fellman, had been calling
Wood, and insisted that he get a list of his credits.
So Richard got that valuable document from Wood
when he interviewed him, which I believe was in
April 1978. So when Frank Henenlotter started
reading off all these credits—especially that he'd
written all these paperbacks, which nobody knew—
I said, "Wow, I'd like to see those." So through
Frank Henenlotter I got in touch with Richard
Bojarski. His book on the films of Bela Lugosi
came out around 1980, so this must have been 1980.
It was obvious that he had written and spoken to
Ed Wood. Bojarski was very helpful. He gave me
the names of all these people to contact out in Los
Angeles. I became a good friend with David Ward,
and I stayed over at his place during some of those
early trips. That saved me a lot of money. I pretty
much sold my entire poster collection to fund these
early trips to LA, which were maybe about a month
long. It had to be done. You had to be out there in
Los Angeles to talk to and find these people.

So it took about ten years—from about 1982 to
1992.

RAUSCH: *A lot of the Wood crowd was supposed to be somewhat
eccentric. Do you have any interesting specific memories
regarding any of them?*

GREY: I'd really have to go through the list of all the people.
[Laughs.] But my one regret is that I never got to
meet John "Bunny" Breckinridge. We were all set
to visit him, but we got a call from his lawyer
telling us not to do that. They were afraid he was
mentally unstable. But I was going go up there

with Vampira and with David Ward driving. But, unfortunately, that never happened. But he would have to be the most eccentric of all the Ed Wood cast.

And he did love it when I told him he was well-loved for his performance in *Plan 9*. [Chuckles.] Evidently he had never heard that! "Oh, my movie...!"

RAUSCH: *What made you decide to use the so-called oral history format when constructing your book?*

GREY: I had just read a book by Jean Stein and George Plimpton titled *Edie: American Girl*, about the Andy Warhol actress and socialite Edie Sedgwick. I said to myself, "Wow, this reads so well." Just the way it was constructed. I said, "This is the way to go." I had tried the normal biographical approach, but it just wasn't working. I thought that documentary-like oral history format was the way to go. I interjected quotes from books and newspapers and magazines, so it's not strictly oral. It all fits together pretty well, I think.

RAUSCH: *In your book, Dolores Fuller claims that Loretta King paid for her role in* Bride of the Monster. *King, of course, denied this until the day she died. We can never know definitively what happened there, but what are your thoughts on this? Did King pay her way into the movie?*

GREY: I think Ed had to come up with an excuse for why he wanted to use Loretta for the lead role in the film. I think he probably told Dolores that, but Loretta told me that wasn't the case. I think he just told that to Dolores to take the heat off of himself.

RAUSCH: *As you know, some members of Bela Lugosi's family have come forward and said that Ed Wood was just using Lugosi, and that they were never really friends. What is your take on this?*

GREY: That's definitely not the case. At one point Wood was practically managing Lugosi's career. He even took care of his bills for him. So he helped Lugosi out, and they were really good friends. There's no doubt about that.

Lugosi was always one of Ed Wood's favorite actors. He had always referred to him as "the great man." He wanted to "do right by the great man."

RAUSCH: *Since your book was released twenty years ago, there have been a lot of things written about Wood. Some of it was true, and some of it I suspect to be false. What are some of the things you've read that you feel are inaccurate?*

GREY: What I really dislike is when they say he was untalented. There's this endless repetition of that— "he just had no talent." You know, look at the films. You can watch them over and over again, which is the mark of a work of art. The "so bad it's good" cliché doesn't work either. Something can't be bad and good at the same time.

RAUSCH: *Since your book is really the Bible of Ed Wood studies, do you feel a responsibility to protect Wood's legacy from people like the Medved crowd?*

GREY: Well, to be fair, Harry Medved, Michael's brother, helped me out in L.A. He did set me up with some contacts. And he really liked Ed Wood's films, but possibly for the wrong reasons. And when the book came out, he was very effusive. He said it was better than anything anyone could have dreamed could be made about the subject. I did give him an acknowledgment, but I did so under his pen name, "Harold Bear." I had to do that, or else Kathy Wood would have killed me! [Laughs.] You know, they stuck Ed with that "World's Worst Director" title, and she saw that. They did speak to her, and she felt betrayed.

RAUSCH: *Since Wood wasn't as big a name back then as he is now, did it take you very long to find a publisher?*

GREY: Well, Research out of San Francisco wanted to do it, but my friend Jimmy McDonough, put me in touch with Adam Parfrey at Feral House, and Adam Parfrey saw the potential for that right away. Adam was an Ed Wood aficionado, and he really appreciated the films, and in the right way.

RAUSCH: *I'd like to ask you about the film* Take It Out in Trade. *Obviously you've seen it—you talk about it in some detail in your book. Do you know why that "lost" film has never been released to the public?*

GREY: I'm negotiating with the person who owns it. That's all I can say.

RAUSCH: *So there's a chance we might see it one day?*

GREY: Yes.

RAUSCH: *Now that some of these films have resurfaced, which of the remaining lost films would you consider to be sort of the Holy Grail of lost Wood films?*

GREY: Wood did something called *The Night the Banshee Cried.* It was a short half hour thing made for television.

RAUSCH: *Right. Do we know as a fact that that project exists as an actual film and not just as a screenplay?*

GREY: I believe it does exist. Through my research I found he wanted to release that along with *Final Curtain.* He wanted to shoot another segment and release it as a feature, but he could never get that third film done. So where is *The Night the Banshee Cried?* I suspect scenes from that were used in *Night of the Ghouls.*

RAUSCH: *You obviously possess one of the most complete Ed Wood collections around. What are some things in your collection that people may not even know exist?*

GREY: Well, that will be in the expanded version of my book! [Laughs.]

Interview: Aris Iliopulos

Aris Iliopulos is a writer, director, photographer, painter, and sculptor. His early influences from punk rock, Federico Fellini, Ingmar Bergman, and Edward D. Wood Jr. are always present in his work. An accomplished traveler, Iliopulos is fascinated by and follows the Masai tribes in Kenya and photographs their vanishing world. He spends his time between homes in New York City and Joshua Tree in the Mojave Desert.

In 1998, he produced and directed the Ed Wood-scripted silent film *I Woke Up Early the Day I Died*. The film features many, many top-notch actors such as Billy Zane, Christina Ricci, and Tippi Hedren. Unfortunately, the film has been hung up with legal problems and has not had a DVD release in the United States. (It is available in Europe.)

Iliopulos hopes to one day direct Wood's screenplay for *The Ghoul Goes West*, and promises that his next film will be very much in the spirit of Wood, as well.

ANDREW RAUSCH: *How did you first encounter the work of Ed Wood, and what were your initial thoughts?*

ARIS ILIOPULOS: Ed Wood was one of the first artists I encountered when I first came to the United States. I saw Ed Wood on channel 13, which is a PBS channel. I thought he was so avant-garde, and I had to follow up with his work. However, it was pretty difficult to find it back then. In New York you can find a lot of the stuff, but not everything. I basically saw the four classic films of his, and then I became a really big fan of his work.

RAUSCH: *Do you feel there's a misconception about Ed Wood's work?*

ILIOPULOS: I think everybody has their own point of view, but it seems really easy to say that he was naïve or that he was really not careful in his work. But I believe he's quite the artist there. I mean, yes, he's a cult director, but at the same time I see his work as more of an artistic effort. I find his work to be very innocent and artistic rather than that of someone who was just trying to make a cult movie like a lot of people do.

Kathy Wood always said she hated it when people called him stupid, or when they said his movies were bad. She really hated that.

I must say, there is some work there that I've never seen, like *Orgy of the Dead* (1965) and that kind of work. Have you seen any of that kind of work?

RAUSCH: *Yes, I've seen all of them that are available. We're covering all of the sex films in the book, as well.*

ILIOPULOS: And what did you think of that work?

RAUSCH: *Those films are different from the films he's best known for. A lot of the same themes are present, though, and the classic Ed Wood dialogue is definitely there. The dialogue in some of those—especially* Orgy of the Dead—*is unmistakably Wood's.*

ILIOPULOS: Right. [Laughs.]

RAUSCH: *One thing that's interesting about Ed Wood is that he made a film titled* The Sinister Urge, *which decried pornography. In that film, he made no bones about the fact that he looked down on the makers of those films. It's sad that Wood himself was making pornography only about five years after that.*

ILIOPULOS: Well, he was really poor, and I think there were money reasons there. And I think he was drinking a bit too much there at the end of his life, which made it difficult for him to focus on his work.

Also, I think the whole system has changed. There in the 60s, I think Ed was kind of into free love and those kinds of movies were completely new. Kathy told me that Ed had a few movies that screened around Hollywood that no longer exist. In fact, the Woods' lawyer confirmed it for me that there are certain movies that just no longer exist. And they were a little bit on the sexy side, we'll put it that way.

We all make mistakes in life, or we make masterpieces and mistakes. [Laughs.] You could certainly say that about Orson Welles! He did some horrible things in the 60s. But, you know, *Glen or Glenda?* (1953) and *Plan 9 from Outer Space* (1959)—that stuff is incredible! And I'm still puzzled how he pulled those films together.

Which film is your favorite?

RAUSCH: *I'd say* Plan 9 from Outer Space *is my favorite of the films he made while he was alive. However, your film,* I Woke Up Early the Day I Died, *is my favorite of the entire canon.*

ILIOPULOS: Really?

RAUSCH: *It's our assertion that* I Woke Up Early *is his masterpiece. It's the film that Wood always wanted to make, but just didn't know how.*

ILIOPULOS: I'm glad to hear that. I tried to follow his style. And to tell you the truth, he gave me tremendous freedom. Trying to follow a certain style gives you a kind of freedom, that without that, you would never experience the certain liberty I took in filmmaking. There will always be obstacles; you never know what's going to happen at the end of the day. Some stuff happened on two or three takes. For instance, at one point we lost our location. But a lot of the other stuff, it was very comfortable to shoot. I had three weeks to shoot, and you know, that's more than Ed Wood ever got in his entire life. It was always something like ten days for him.

RAUSCH: *How did you become involved with* I Woke Up Early the Day I Died?

ILIOPULOS: I was at the right place at the right time. I was out with my production office one day for lunch, and Bob Weinberg, who is the lawyer that represents the estate, was there. When I heard the name Ed Wood I was like, "Oh, my God." And I was really wanting to make a picture at that time. I wanted to make a picture, but I wanted it to be something that was according to my own personal tastes. I'm not a gun for hire.

So Bob Weinberg made everybody sign a confidentiality agreement; if someone was going to read the script, he had to know about it. So I went right to the office, grabbed the script, and I read it. And I thought, great, this is my picture! Then I found the courage to call them up and say that I really wanted to do this picture. "Let's get into business here," you know? I said, "I know you have all these contracts, but why don't you give me a shot?" I then set up a meeting with Kathy Wood.

We went to Kathy Wood's house there in Hollywood, and we just had a great time. I brought her flowers and started joking with her. She said, "Aris, you're the right guy for this picture. You do it. I did not trust anybody to do this picture because everybody wants to put dialogue in it." She said, "You have to promise me you won't put dialogue in it." I said, "I promise you." But you know, that's what I really liked about the script in the first place—that there was no dialogue.

Kathy really guided me through the process a little bit and shared a lot of stories about Eddie. She gave me inspiration, and I felt Eddie had a sort of spiritual involvement with the project. She told me this was Ed's favorite script, and that it took him ten years to write it. Of course he died without making it because nobody wanted a picture without dialogue. For Ed, that was his masterpiece. She said, "He never put it down. He said, 'This is my masterpiece.'" Kathy told me one day there was a fire at the apartment, and he jumped out of the window. She said he was naked, clutching that screenplay. It meant that much to him. It was the only thing he grabbed out of that room.

He may have been doing these other kinds of movies, but that was his passion. Kathy said he would revisit the material every year, and he would just rewrite it and rewrite it and rewrite it. I find his writing to be quite fascinating. One of the decisions I made on the film—I made it with Billy Zane— was to put excerpts from the script on the screen at times throughout the film. I just find his writing to be super-entertaining.

RAUSCH: *What were some of the goals you wanted to achieve with this film?*

ILIOPULOS: Well, I had actually found a script that I wanted to do. At that point it was sort of like there was no stopping. When I believe in something, just in general, it will happen. When it's the right moment and the right time, it will happen. In fact, just six months after I signed the contract I was shooting the picture.

I got some of my friends to sign on; like Christina Ricci, who was shooting *Buffalo '66* (1998) at the time. A few other people signed on, as well. I think Billy Zane was working on *Titanic* (1997) at the time. He read the screenplay and he called me. He was shooting in Mexico, and I could not go to Mexico at the time. So he came down here, and we spent a whole week talking about this and just getting an idea of the situation. And that's how the whole thing started. Once Billy came onboard, the process went very quickly.

RAUSCH: *You had a ridiculously talented cast.*

ILIOPULOS: Things just happened so fast. There was a moment when people were fighting over parts. "Give me a part. I want to be in that picture. I don't care what the part is." I feel that Eddie had a lot to do with the casting. [Chuckles.] I was at a party in New York and I ran into Eartha Kitt. I went over to her and I said, "I'm making this picture, and you've got to be in it." She said, "Send me the script." I sent her the script, but I said, "Your part is not written. It's there, but it's not written." She said, "What do you mean?" I said, "It's an Ed Wood picture." She

said, "You know, I've been in an Ed Wood film
without being in an Ed Wood film." I said, "What
are you talking about?" She said, "If you watch
Glen or Glenda?, when he comes to the movie
theater, it says 'Eartha Kitt performs tonight at
9:30,'" or something or other. So she was aware
of Ed Wood. And she was just great. She even
wrote the song she performs in the movie for me,
which I thought was nice. Also, it was her last
performance.

For the Tippi Hedren part, I had three people
in mind—Zsa Zsa Gabor, Kim Novak, or Tippi
Hedren. Tippi called me right away and said she
loved the idea of being in an Ed Wood picture.
So a lot of the actors just loved the idea of being
in an Ed Wood picture. Then there were some
people who didn't like the idea of there being no
dialogue. And of course I have to thank my casting
director on the project. She helped a lot. She had a
tremendous amount to do with the casting.

But I think it was the right moment and the right
time. A lot of people liked the idea of a movie with
no dialogue, and I think a lot of people really like
Ed Wood, believe it or not. But the fact that there
was no dialogue confused a lot of people.

Interview: Jason Insalacco and Jonathan Harris

Jason Insalaco and Jonathan Harris are responsible for finding and restoring the once "lost" 1957 Edward D. Wood, Jr. television pilot *Final Curtain* for Wood's proposed series *Portraits of Terror*.

Insalaco, the nephew of the late actor Paul Marco (Kelton the Cop of *Bride of the Monster*, 1955, *Plan 9 from Outer Space*, 1959, and *Night of the Ghouls*, 1959), first began his quest to find the lost Wood film after hearing about it from his uncle. Years later, he eventually located the film and brought it to his friend Jonathan Harris, an avid Wood fan, to assist him in its restoration.

Insalaco works as a district director for a state legislator and has a twenty year background in media. Harris, an American Film Institute graduate, works as Director of Video at Sony Pictures' online streaming channel Crackle. Neither of them had restored a film before prior to their adventures with *Final Curtain*.

ANDREW RAUSCH: *Jason, how aware of your Uncle Paul's involvement with these films were you when you were growing up?*

JASON INSALACO: It was talked about a little bit. I first saw *Plan 9 from Outer Space* at a screening in Los Angeles in the early Eighties. My uncle was there, he was a part of the screening. I didn't fully understand at that time what all of this was, but then when the *Ed Wood* movie came out in 2004, it really seemed to solidify everything that my eccentric uncle had told me. There was the Rudolph Grey book and all this stuff, and it really seemed to validate this incredible world and it has opened it up for exploration ever since.

RAUSCH: *How long did your hunt for the film last, and what did that entail?*

INSALACO: Well, when my uncle died, he was kind of a... Well, I don't want to call him a hoarder, because that's kind of a derogatory term for that, but he was at least borderline hoarding. He saved *everything*. We cleaned out his apartment, and it took quite some time. And in cleaning out his nightstand, we found original documents about *Final Curtain*. And he had told me about *Final Curtain* and how Wood had planned for Bela Lugosi to be in it, and the whole thing. I'd heard about it, but it hadn't fully resonated much. My uncle was full of a lot of stories. But here we found, in his nightstand, this original contract signed by Ed Wood concerning *Portraits of Terror: The Final Curtain*.

So I was like, "Wow, this is a real film. It must exist. Certainly it must mean something if it's in his nightstand." So I hunted around, and posted things, and looked around for a couple of years.

RAUSCH: *How did you wind up finding the film?*

INSALACO: I went around and spoke to collectors and film people. I even went to Kansas City and spoke with the gentleman who's sort of been the Ed Wood guy. He had been the one who had found *Plan 9* and these other films and had brought them to prominence in the Eighties. I came to mostly dead ends, or people hadn't heard of it, or they just didn't care. Then I heard that a gentleman who was a film collector had just acquired a bunch of films and there may have been some Ed Wood stuff involved. That was all I knew. I went through the cans with him, and they reeked of vinegar. I don't know a thing about film restoration or anything like that, but I had no idea if it was even salvageable. I bought the cans from him. I was very excited, but I had no idea what I had. For all I knew, it could have been just some vinegar and it might have been mislabeled. So I brought it to Jonathan and he worked on it painstakingly to restore the print.

RAUSCH: *While you were hunting for this film, did you get any leads on what was apparently the second episode of* Portraits of Terror *titled* The Night the Banshee Cried? *This has long been referred to as a lost film, but I was wondering if you had ever heard anything about whether or not Wood had actually even filmed this?*

INSALACO: I've heard about it. I haven't seen it, and in my search for this film I didn't come across it or any part of it.

RAUSCH: *Did you happen to come across anything else of a Wood nature?*

INSALACO: Not in terms of the films, but in terms of the people I met, certainly. [Laughs.] There were some very interesting people—interesting characters in their own right. Passionate people about Ed Wood and about this genre of film. Since we've come forward with this film, we've received some inquiries by people who claim that they have something. There was a recent pornographic film of Ed's that just came to light in Canada… People reach out to us about that, but nothing came up during the search, no.

RAUSCH: *What were your reactions the first time you saw* Final Curtain?

JONATHAN HARRIS: Well, the first time we saw it had no sound. So it was kind of weird with no sound. I remember seeing this long shot of a pipe and thinking, "What is this movie about? What kind of movie features long shots of plumbing?" [Laughs.] Without the sound, it has kind of an eerie, creepy feel to it. It just wasn't the same without the sound; the sound sort of augments the story. So we got the whole thing, and it was very interesting to watch it with no sound because you notice that it sort of relied on D-roll. There are so many shots of inanimate objects. It was sort of unusual for a film that was longer than two or three minutes to have one actor in it, so little dialogue, and so many inanimate objects. It was kind of bold. Wood kept cutting from his actor to his subjective view of things. And there is something kind of creepy about these things as he's looking around this empty theater. The movie is unusual, and somehow it's less funny with the sound off. The overwrought narration sort of makes it more comic. Without sound, it seemed a little more serious.

INSALACO: It's really interesting compared to Wood's other films, because he really lets things breathe for a long time here. The overwrought narration is one thing, but the shots seem longer... He kind of meditates on the stage and the backstage area and the stairs. There isn't a lot of scene changing there, and it doesn't look like his other stuff in that way. It's completely different. He's not afraid to just kind of let the story sit there. There weren't a lot of non sequiturs like there are in his other films; in this one, he just sort of rolls with it.

HARRIS: It's really interesting when the mannequin shows up. That mannequin is such an unusual person. At first we weren't sure if it was a man or a woman. It's a very strange moment there where finally another person shows up. That's a very surprising part of the movie.

INSALACO: At first we weren't sure if that might have been Ed Wood in drag there. I think that has since been refuted, but at the same time, Janet Stevens, who is credited with that role, is a mystery to us. We did some preliminary research and we've asked around—no one seems to know who she is. I believe it's her only credit on IMDb, or at least last time I checked. We don't know anything about her. Who is this person? Wood tended to work with a lot of the same people—especially at that time; people like my uncle, Conrad Brooks, he had the same guy doing the musical scoring... There was Duke Moore, who appears in other Wood movies. So who is this person? We don't know. We have no idea if she's still alive.

RAUSCH: *How long did it take you guys to restore the print?*

HARRIS: I'd say it took about a year and a half.

RAUSCH: *What were some of the most difficult aspects of the restoration process?*

HARRIS: We had to learn about a bunch of these things. The movie had a vinegar smell, which indicates that there was some deterioration. So we had to get the movie assessed and cleaned before we could get it transferred. We were very lucky to have someone at Warner Bros. to transfer for us, but they wouldn't transfer it if the movie was not in good shape. We had to get it into a better condition before we could do that.

INSALACO: What do you think of *Final Curtain*?

RAUSCH: *I was kind of surprised by how good it was. I was really impressed with how Wood used what little he had on-hand to attempt to make horror. I mean, there was a light turning out that's supposed to be scary and a scene where Duke Moore thinks the railing is turning into a snake. I rather enjoyed it.*

HARRIS: I'm guessing that you've seen the YouTube version of the film?

RAUSCH: *Yes, that's right.*

HARRIS: The YouTube version of the film is a copy of our version... I mean, it's the same running time, and so forth, but our version is really pristine. A lot of the other Ed Wood movies are in various states of disrepair, or they're copies of copies. The thing that's really unusual is that the copy we have really looks great, but someone else put this one up on YouTube at about the same time we had ours. Jason tried to get that taken down, because we're interested in trying to do something with our copy. But we've been unable to do anything about that.

INSALACO: What happened was, we were able to debut it with much fanfare and enthusiasm at Slam Dance in 2012. Then this appeared on YouTube about four or five months later. I don't know what happened, if it fell into the wrong hands or during the transfer process they ended up with an inferior copy. The good news was that we were able to show it at

Slam Dance before anyone had seen it. We thought we were quite discreet about who handled it before that screening, but...

There was a lot of press and audience interest in it, and we've received messages from all over the world from people wanting to see it or asking questions about it. It's been quite the story in the sense that it kind of keeps on going. I think the people who do watch it are sort of surprised that there are several levels to it... Jonathan and I have watched it maybe six or seven dozen times, at least, and there are different things you see in it every time—some of it's campy and you're like, "I can't believe I missed this mistake or continuity problem," but then you'll also say, "There's some subtext here that I hadn't caught before." And you can't say that about many television pilots. Here we are fifty years later, and it still holds up and gives us a lot to analyze and debate about what it's really about.

RAUSCH: *What were the audience reactions like at the screenings you've held for* Final Curtain?

HARRIS: The screening at Slam Dance was fantastic. The crowd was enthusiastic. They were very excited. There was a lot of anticipation. They really seemed to enjoy it. There was a lot of laughter, but it was good-natured laughter. Nobody was booing or anything. People were just having a really great time. The movie went by very quickly. There was such excitement in the room. And afterward, everyone applauded. There was something about having a big, packed room full of people laughing together that was just great.

INSALACO: We didn't know what to expect. The interest was high. The intrigue was there, but we didn't know if it was going to deliver. We didn't know what the reaction was going to be, but it was a pleasant surprise that made it feel even more like it was worthwhile.

RAUSCH: *Is there anything else you'd like to talk about regarding* Final Curtain?

HARRIS: I've always referred to this as Ed Wood's version of *The Twilight Zone*. It was a half-hour, black-and-white supernatural-themed show sort of like that. I just sort of told everyone about it with that line as a handle. Then we happened to look up the dates and we found out that this had actually been made before *The Twilight Zone*! That sort of surprised me. I had always thought, this is sort of like *The Twilight Zone*, and it probably inspired Ed Wood to try and make something like that. But that was not the case. Ed Wood actually came up with this concept before Rod Serling. And history has shown us that that was a pretty good idea. Maybe Ed's execution wasn't all that it could have been, but he didn't have CBS behind him like Rod Serling did. This was actually something that was quite cutting edge at the time Ed made it.

INSALACO: When you think about television of that era, it was largely influenced and based upon radio. Wood had Dudley Manlove provide narration that now seems comical and overdone, but television was then derivative of radio. It was radio with pictures. And Dudley Manlove was a longtime radio announcer, so I think that's why it kind of sounds like a radio play when you listen to it. If you looked at this in a historical context, these television programs were radio-based shows that had been made into television programs.

Interview: John Johnson

John Johnson made his first film at the age of eight. By the time he finished college, he had completed five feature-length films, a television series consisting of twenty one-hour episodes, and nearly fifty short films. He is the founder of Darkstone Entertainment, an independent film company based out of Charlottesville, Virginia, and the director of films such as *Shadowhunters* (2004), *Skeleton Key 2: 667 Neighbor of the Beast* (2008), and *Skeleton Key 3: The Organ Trail* (2011). He is also the writer and director of the forthcoming remake of Ed Wood's *Plan 9 from Outer Space* (1959), simply titled *Plan Nine* (2014).

ANDREW RAUSCH: *How did you first become acquainted with the work of Ed Wood, and what were your initial thoughts on it?*

JOHN JOHNSON: When I first saw *Plan 9 from Outer Space*, I was around ten years old. When cartoons wrapped up on Saturday morning, *Grandpa's Monster Movies* would come on. It was all Hammer films and Godzilla flicks! Then came Ed's opus. Since I was so young I didn't notice the film's blemishes so much and just took it as another epic with aliens *and* zombies!

RAUSCH: *As you've gotten older, how has your view of the film changed over the years?*

JOHNSON: As most, when Tim Burton's *Ed Wood* came out I had seen the comical side of the film and those involved with the production. But it wasn't until I met Conrad Brooks that I bonded with the story of the creators and saw similarities in the crew I work with on a daily basis.

RAUSCH: *How did you meet Conrad Brooks?*

JOHNSON: I was working on a western in the early 2000's and the producers knew him. They said we should meet and work together. So we did! I shot four films adding Connie to the cast and then, finally, *Plan 9*, my remake of Ed's film.

RAUSCH: *In what ways, if any, was your connection with Conrad integral to your eventually deciding to remake the film?*

JOHNSON: It had everything to do with the remake. Conrad had told me the story of Ed and his crew. It was a much sadder story of how they made "the worst movie of all time" than Tim Burton's take. I felt the remake as well as being a fun film could be a way to redeem their work instead of mocking it, because at the end of the day there *are* worse films out there—I have made some myself—and it truly is a fun idea and concept.

RAUSCH: *What are some of the things you most like about the original film?*

JOHNSON: Well, of course the obvious goofs are fun to giggle at. But on a much deeper level, I loved the mix of celebs and actors all coming together for the film. I, in the remake, followed those steps. And then on the story side, a fun take on the alien invasion concept. Even [George] Romero said he was influenced by the concept.

RAUSCH: *I read that you intentionally set out to make a zombie film that didn't adhere to the old Romero rules. Do you want to talk about that?*

JOHNSON: Sure. When you make any zombie movie in this age, you are essentially making a film in Romero's creation. To be honest, even *Walking Dead* can be an unofficial sequel to *Night of the Living Dead* (1968). But *Plan 9 from Outer Space* was much older and did not follow the rules we have all come to love and adore in pop culture. So when I wrote the script I took a lot from the ideas Ed had and broadened them. Although in this universe the Romero films do exist and the characters take note of them as they are dealing with their zombie problem.

RAUSCH: *I like that. What elements from the original screenplay did you know immediately that you wanted to keep?*

JOHNSON: A lot of imagery. There are fifty-four nods to the original film in the remake; maybe more. They would be fun to watch back to back. Also, the concepts are similar but presented very differently. The characters are all there in both films. And while expanded, still have a general design that stays the same.

RAUSCH: *Tell me about the process of adapting the screenplay.*

JOHNSON: It was a fun experiment to begin. I had never written a remake prior. Stressful is a good word to use, as well. It's difficult trying to pay respect and not upset those who love the original, but at the same time present a film in the vein of what I wanted to see and love about film. At the end of the day it will be up to the audience to decide, but I can say I have never worked harder on a project, and it is the best and strongest piece of all my other works.

RAUSCH: *It must feel pretty good sharing a screenwriting credit with Edward D. Wood, Jr.*

JOHNSON: Absolutely. He is without a doubt a part of film history. To be in his ranks is humbling and truly an honor.

RAUSCH: *Having now walked in his shoes, so to speak, do you feel a kind of special bond with Wood?*

JOHNSON: Sure. I think it already existed before the remake. Our passions for the work are very similar, and in his honor I did wear pink angora on the first day of production. But he probably looked better in it.

RAUSCH: *Is that true?*

JOHNSON: Yep. There are pics somewhere and television interviews documenting it. Also, there is a feature length documentary on the idea and production that covers that as well.

RAUSCH: *It seemed like from the very get-go there were a lot of people criticizing this project without really knowing much about it and without having seen a single frame of the picture. Why do you think that is?*

JOHNSON: Remakes in general are frowned upon. And rarely...rarely...exceed the original. I think people are tired of them. So when they hear this, a big "what?" is exclaimed to the gods. That's why we shot the teaser. So people could see what we were really hoping to do with the production. Since then the inter-webs have been a lot friendlier to us.

RAUSCH: *That teaser came out four years ago. What are some of the factors that led to the delay of the film?*

JOHNSON: Money. Raising it. The teaser alone cost a small bundle. I knew I couldn't half-ass this movie. It needed to be all I could do and have the proper funds to make it what it deserved to be. So I would not go forward until we were truly prepared.

RAUSCH: *Tell me about the casting for the film.*

JOHNSON: There are about fifty speaking roles in the film. And the cast is an awesome mix of all generations of horror icons, as well as some new talent to the scene. YouTube played a large role in the casting as well. We had a few celebrities coming in and playing roles to kind of create that original cast Ed had put together

RAUSCH: *I understand that Criswell is an actual character in this film, and not just the narrator. Is that correct?*

JOHNSON: That is correct. He's played by another horror host, Mr. Lobo. I thought it would be a fun twist and spice things up.

RAUSCH: *It sounds like you've done some really interesting things in this film. How did you land Brian Krause?*

JOHNSON: Pretty simple as it were. We pitched his agent, he read the script, we talked and got along really well. He was on set two days later. And he truly made the film better. He's an extremely talented guy

RAUSCH: *I understand you had the premiere of the film about a month ago. How did that go?*

JOHNSON: Fantastic! Lots of love. However, a plush crowd of

three hundred. Everyone there knew or was a part of the production in some way. The true test will be when it hits the streets.

RAUSCH: *What elements of the film are you the most proud of?*

JOHNSON: I think the film has a strong feeling and design of small town horror; Stephen King's neck of the woods. Granted the humor of the film differs quite a bit from his works, but the small town horror I believe truly comes across, and I am very proud of that creation.

RAUSCH: *What do you think open-minded viewers will get from* Plan 9?

JOHNSON: Hopefully they'll have a fun ride. It's a love letter not only to *Plan 9 from Outer Space*, Ed Wood and his crew, but as well as a love for the Eighties' and Nineties' horror films I grew up on. There is a lot of influence that many will pick up on I think.

Interview: Larry Karaszewski

University of Southern California graduates Larry Karaszewski and Scott Alexander have established themselves as a talented writing duo—especially in regard to writing biopics. After film school, the two made a name for themselves as the screenwriters of the comedy films *Problem Child* (1990) and *Problem Child 2* (1991). They quickly found success, but also found themselves trapped in what looked like a future of writing movies they didn't want to write. However, they had a dream project—they wanted to make a motion picture based on the life of Edward D. Wood, Jr. After Rudolph Grey's book *Nightmare of Ecstasy: The Life and Art of Edward D. Wood, Jr.* was released, they then adapted the book into the film *Ed Wood* (1994), directed by Tim Burton and starring Johnny Depp and Martin Landau. The film received rave reviews and won two Academy Awards for Best Supporting Actor (Landau) and Best Makeup.

Karaszewski and Alexander have since written such acclaimed films as *The People vs. Larry Flynt* (1996), *Man on the Moon* (1999), and the Stephen King adaptation *1408* (2007). They have also co-directed the comedy *Screwed* (2000) and have produced such films as *Auto Focus* (2002) and Tim Burton's *Big Eyes* (2014).

ANDREW RAUSCH: *What was the genesis of your film,* Ed Wood?

LARRY KARASZEWSKI: The genesis started back when Scott and I were film students. That was sort of back in the early Eighties, when the Medveds were kind of traveling around with their *Fifty Worst Movies of All Time* and *The Golden*

Turkey Awards. So Ed was on our radar at that point. Scott and I were both film junkies—sort of odd film junkies. We actually became friends when we were standing in line somewhere freshman year, talking about Herschell Gordon Lewis movies. I grew up in the Midwest where those movies played all the time. Scott grew up out here [in California] where they really didn't. So I was sort of the only person around here who was kind of expert on them. [Chuckles.]

The more you heard about the stories of Bela Lugosi and Ed Wood, you knew there was something there; there was a story to be told. Scott actually wrote a treatment for a documentary called *The Man in the Angora Sweater* when we were at USC.

Then we kind of had some success with *Problem Child* (1990), and because of that success people only wanted us to make that kind of movie. Whenever we would pitch an idea they would say, "That's a really great idea, but you guys aren't good enough to write that idea." We were sort of in a situation where they didn't think we were good enough to write our own ideas. Even though we had had some success, we both wanted to take our careers in a different direction. We wanted to make an independent film and really make something from the heart. So we decided to revisit the Ed Wood story. Right about then the book *Nightmare of Ecstasy* came out, so that was a beautiful source. Our original idea was to make it as a one or two million dollar indie film. We had another friend we had gone to film school with named Michael Lehmann. He directed a movie called *Hudson Hawk* (1991), which was kind of reviled as a terrible movie. We always thought it would be funny if the screenwriters of *Problem Child* and the director of *Hudson Hawk* made a movie about the worst filmmaker of all time. "Hey, we know what we're writing about." So we brought Michael in as director and we wrote a treatment. Then he decided he was going to make a different movie, so he said, "Maybe I can help you get this made." A producer he had worked with on *Heathers* (1988) was now working with Tim Burton. "Maybe we can get it to her and you can get it made as 'Tim Burton Presents' or something like that." That would make it easier for us to get that million dollars, and it seemed like the kind of material Tim might dig.

We did send it to her. Tim kind of flipped out over it, and Michael recognized that excitement and said he would step aside completely if Tim wanted to make this as his next movie. He told Tim, "I'll produce it and you direct it." So that's how Tim Burton came on board.

RAUSCH: *That had to come as tremendous news at the time.*

KARASZEWSKI: Absolutely. I remember we met with Tim very briefly. At the time he was going to make a movie called *Mary Reilly* (1996), but he had like two months to make a decision. At that time we only had an outline, and he said, "I'll make the decision when I see the script." So we just burrowed away and wrote a script in six weeks. It was a little longer than it should have been, but we gave it to him. Then we got the message that changed my life when Tim called and said he loved it. He wanted to make it and he was leaving *Mary Reilly.* He didn't want any notes, any development... He just wanted to go and make the movie. So we basically shot the first draft.

RAUSCH: *That's quite a responsibility bring Wood's life to the screen. I mean, a lot of people knew Rudolph Grey's book, but the majority of people that you talk to only know about Ed Wood from your film. I think it was a great decision to just focus on the making of those three films. Was there a lot of thought that went into that?*

KARASZEWSKI: I wouldn't say a lot of thought went into that. Scott and I had talked about this project for a while, but there was never any more than that. The project came in our minds pretty much fully-formed. We saw this as a love story between Bela Lugosi and Ed. It was about a guy who gets to meet his hero and then sort of use him and give him a reason to exist. Once we did that—once we knew that that was what we were passionate about—it all came together quite easily. So with that in mind, it was a natural decision to just focus on those three movies. You had sort of the ups and downs of their relationship. Would Ed be able to carry on with Bela? It never occurred to us that we would carry the story on to things like *Fugitive Girls* and the Stephen Apostolof films. I'm not saying there's not a story there... There might be a whole other movie there, but that wasn't the story that came to our minds.

RAUSCH: *I love how you guys sort of summed it up at the end of the film, saying Ed went on to make "nudie monster movies."*

KARASZEWSKI: Back then, around 1993, those were sort of the Video Search of Miami days... I remember those video companies would always claim films were of a certain genre; "nudie-cuties," or "roughies," or "nudie monster movies." [Laughs.] It was like, "Do these genres really exist, or are you guys just typing?"

So that's where that sort of came from.

RAUSCH: *Now that you guys have for all intents and purposes become his biographers, do you feel a sort of kinship with Ed Wood?*

KARASZEWSKI: Oh yeah. I think the big turn from when we were in college talking about an Ed Wood movie to when we actually made one was the *Problem Child* experience. When you write movies and they don't get produced, there's still this picture playing in your mind. When we wrote *Problem Child*, we were trying to write—I know it sounds silly to say this—a Billy Wilder *Fortune Cookie* (1966)-type movie about yuppies who wanted a kid and wound up with a bad one. And what we envisioned was not what came out. So what we'd do when we examined Wood was we realized that no one sets out to make a bad movie. Ed Wood loved his movies. He was putting his heart and soul in these things. This was the kind of movie he wanted to see, so he was trying to make something for himself. Actually his movies are quite personal; *Glen or Glenda?* (1953) is personal independent filmmaking. So we decided we weren't going to back away from anything, but we didn't want to focus on his failures; we wanted to show him as a guy who succeeded. Most people look at him as a failure, but we're saying, he came out here and wound up writing, directing, producing, starring in a number of movies. His dream actually came true. Particularly when we're not going into the alcoholic porno years, he was a happening guy. We wanted to celebrate the passion. Once we decided to celebrate the passion of Ed Wood, the tone for the whole piece fell into place. Through sheer force of personality, this guy is making films.

I think that's changed the way some people look at his films. In the 1980s, it was very easy to laugh at his films as being incompetent. I think what our film has done, since you now know the man's story, is make it more difficult to laugh at him. It's a very *avant-garde* movie about a man bearing his soul.

RAUSCH: *As far as Wood's life went, did you feel that you had to pull any punches? Was there anything you made a conscious decision not to include?*

KARASZEWSKI: I don't think so. Ed was probably a bit more of drinker than what the movie portrays. But whenever you take someone's life and turn it into two hours, you're gonna miss some things. It's impossible to cover everything. People will always think you're trying to whitewash things. They're like, "Well, why'd you leave out the guy's third wife?" We've done enough of these biographies that we've seen that time and again. "Hey, Bela Lugosi had big dogs, and you've got him with small dogs!" [Laughs.] You know, it's not a conspiracy here. You make a movie and decisions get made. We have scenes of Ed sitting in a bar, drinking by himself. We just don't have him falling down drunk.

RAUSCH: *I love the scene with Orson Welles. Tell me how you came up with that.*

KARASZEWSKI: That was interesting. We knew the ending was going to be the making of *Plan 9 from Outer Space* (1959) and Ed's battle with the Baptists. But we felt like it needed something else. It wasn't quite there. It didn't feel enough like the end of a movie. And Ed Wood was obsessed with Orson Welles... I don't remember exactly, but I have a vague idea that maybe Scott and I were in a car. It might have been Scott who said, "What if the worst filmmaker

of all time met the greatest filmmaker of all time?"
I'm not saying those labels are true, but here you'd
have what legend says are the greatest and the worst.
And it was just one of those moments where, *bam!*
We both knew that was it. Here they are at complete
opposite ends of the spectrum, but they're the exact
same person. They have the exact same problems.
They're constantly having trouble raising money,
they're having their movies recut by other people.
You know, they'd start filming something and then
have to stop and then start filming again three years
later... They both had to compromise at every turn.

Scott and I don't like to take huge liberties with
someone's story, but when something like that
presents itself...that poetic meeting...we loved it.

RAUSCH: *There for a number of years it seems like a lot of
Wood's old cohorts had complaints about the movie.
What are your thoughts on that?*

KARASZEWSKI: I think the people who did get involved with the
movie appreciate the movie and had a good time
working on it. We always went out of our way to
try to include people like Paul Marco and Conrad
Brooks...The real people. You know, they all have
parts in the film. Vampira, Kathy Wood, Dolores
Fuller. All of those people were brought into the
team. I know that some people said they have had
a sort of re-think afterward. I know Dolores Fuller
always had some sort of beef with Sarah Jessica
Parker, saying she was a bad actress or something
like that.

Then in the marketing of the movie, a lot of us
didn't want to appear that we were making fun of
Ed Wood, so we didn't want to market it as "This
is a movie about the guy who made the worst

movies of all time." We didn't want to do that kind of thing. But when you remove that, what do you have? [Laughs.] You know, "a man with a passion." Well, what makes him interesting? Ed had spent so many years being made fun of... We didn't want to make fun of him for being a bad movie-maker; we didn't want to make fun of him for being a transvestite. But when you remove those things from the marketing materials, all you have left is a guy in a director's chair.

RAUSCH: *Do you have any interesting stories from the making of the film?*

KARASZEWSKI: Do you know the story about how Kathy Wood came to the set? We were kind of shooting in the area of Los Angeles where Ed Wood really lived. We were shooting right off of Hollywood Boulevard. I wasn't on the set, but Scott was there. I guess someone from the crew came over and said, "There's a woman over there waiting for a bus, and she says she used to be married to Ed Wood." We were like, "Whoa!" So he went over there, and she was carrying her groceries, and it was Kathy Wood. We had not met her yet. She said, "Ooh, I sure would like to come over and say hi and meet everyone."

She wanted to meet Johnny Depp since he was playing her husband. So Scott brought her over to Johnny's trailer. So Scott brought her over to Johnny's trailer. It was the day they were shooting the Orson Welles scene. Someone told Johnny that Kathy Wood was out here and that she wanted to meet him. Johnny was in drag—and not even nice drag; it's where his hair and his lipstick are kind of messed up. He said, "I can't meet her like this! She's gonna think we're making fun of Ed!" He was horrified. He wanted to meet Kathy Wood, but he was afraid it would look like we were all just making fun of his legacy.

Well, at that time Tim called Johnny to come out to the set, so he couldn't avoid walking out of the trailer. She was right there. He was not happy about it. And he walked out and she said, "Ah, you look just like my Eddie!" She loved it. She actually went home and brought back Ed's wallet with his driver's license and things like that in it. She gave it to Johnny, so in most of the scenes Johnny is actually carrying Ed's real wallet.

Interview: Gary Kent

Actor and stuntman Gary Kent has made quite a name for himself in an impressive career that has spanned more than fifty years. Kent, whom director Quentin Tarantino has called the "greatest living stuntman," made his debut in the 1958 film *Legion of the Doomed.* He later appeared in Ray Dennis Steckler's cult film *The Thrill Killers* (1964). He then did stunt work and some acting for Monte Hellman's classic Westerns *Ride in the Whirlwind* (1965) and *The Shooting* (1966), doubling for a young Jack Nicholson. He also appeared in Ted V. Mikels' *The Black Klansman* (1966). That same year he appeared in frequent Ed Wood collaborator Stephen C. Apostolof's film *Suburban Confidential.* He appeared and performed stunts in the Richard Rush features *Psych-Out* (1968) and *The Savage Seven* (1968). Kent performed in and handled special effects for Peter Bogdanovich's directorial debut *Targets* (1968). He appeared in a couple of schlockmeister Al Adamson's films, even serving as assistant director on *Dracula vs. Frankenstein* (1971).

The focus of this interview, however, was his appearance as Olaf, leader of the cavemen, in the Ed Wood-scripted sexploitation romp *One Million AC/DC* (1969).

ANDREW RAUSCH: *How did you become involved with* One Million AC/DC?

GARY KENT: Gary Graver, who was a really good friend of mine, directed it. And he called me up and said, "Hey, I want you to do this film. Will you do it?" Graver and I worked together along with a bunch of other guys through-out the years. We were all friends and we just helped each other with our films. So, you know, I would do just about anything for Gary. But when he sent me the script, it was about thirty-two pages maybe. I didn't know that it had been written by Ed Wood. It just said Akdon Telmig, which was Vodka Gimlet all mixed around.

RAUSCH: *What did you think of the script?*

KENT: It was kind of funny, kind of goofy.

Well, we shot it back in the Bronson caves, up above Hollywood. A lot of films have been shot there. When we got up there, Gary would just say, "If you feel like doing something, just improvise it." So a lot of this stuff was stuff we just made up as we were shooting. For instance, the line about the grapes—

RAUSCH: *"Save me some grapes."*

KENT: Right. "Save me some grapes." I just made that up.

RAUSCH: *That's my favorite line in the movie.*

KENT: And then that song about the lizard—we made that up, too. We just did that to be funny, and Gary said, "Let's shoot it. Let's put it in." So we did. And it just became kind of a campy film that took off in a weird sort of way on its own. We all knew he was going to use a little hand puppet for the monster, so we just said, okay.

RAUSCH: *So Gary Graver was Ed De Priest?*

KENT: What do you mean?

RAUSCH: *The director's credit is listed as "Ed De Priest."*

KENT: Gary directed the film, but Ed De Priest was a producer of nudie-cuties. I think Ed put up the money for the film. If Gary used his name, he must have. I wasn't aware that Gary didn't use his name on that.

RAUSCH: *Did you ever meet Ed Wood?*

KENT: Well, Ed Wood showed up on the set maybe twice while we were shooting. At that time, I wasn't aware of his background. I hate to say it, but I didn't know about *Glen or Glenda?* (1953) and all of those films. He showed up, and I was told he was the writer. He was kind of just this nice guy who looked like a thin, aging Bobby Duvall, at least at that time.

It was only after the shoot, when they were editing the film and I went by the editing room, and there was Ed Wood, Jr. working there as an assistant editor. I forget who was editing it. I think Gary sometimes, and sometimes Bob Jones. But that was when I got to sit around and kind of observe him. I would drink coffee, and I thought Ed was drinking coffee, too. He always had a little Styrofoam cup, but his was full of vodka. He would sit there and be pleasant... He was just a pleasant, nice guy; not assertive or anything like that. You would never know that he had done a lot of film or that he had much of an opinion about anything. He was just sitting there and smiling, talking with Jones and Graver.

RAUSCH: *Did Gary Graver ever tell you any stories about Ed Wood?*

KENT: No, not really. He would kind of be tongue-in-cheek whenever he mentioned Akdon Telmig. Gary would say, "Akdon may come to the set today, blah, blah, blah." And he would do that little smile of his. Gradually Gary told me who Ed Wood was, and I had no idea. He said, "Didn't you see *Glen or Glenda?* or *Plan 9 from Outer Space* (1959)?" And I had not.

I got the distinct feeling that Gary was rather fond of him.

RAUSCH: *Have you seen those films since?*

KENT: I have. I've seen both of them—*Glen or Glenda?* and *Plan 9 from Outer Space.* And now somebody has sent me a copy of *One Million AC/DC.*

RAUSCH: *I find it fascinating that in 1969 you worked on both* One Million AC/DC *and* The Mighty Gorga, *which sell together today as a single-disc double feature.*

KENT: Is that right? I didn't realize that. *The Mighty Gorga*...another one where they used a fake monster! [Laughs.] I think Dave Hewitt directed that, and if I remember right, half the time Gorga was Dave Hewitt in an ape suit. He would just run around and jump around in that suit.

RAUSCH: *I'll bet you guys had a real laugh over the toy dinosaur that's used in* One Million AC/DC.

KENT: We did. We constantly made fun of that, and the ape taking the girl into the cave. We just laughed and laughed about that. I think that might have been Gary's idea. At least I don't think it was scripted to happen over and over again in the movie. Gary said, "Let's do it again. Let's do it again." And then when the monster comes out, that was Gary. It was a hand puppet, and Gary was doing it. I can't remember who was behind the camera, but Gary wanted to do the puppet himself.

RAUSCH: *What were your thoughts on the final film? Obviously it's supposed to be silly, so you can't really take it too seriously.*

KENT: That's what I thought. I just thought it was very campy, and I enjoyed it because I liked some of those people very much. Gary... And of course Maria Lease was a good friend of mine. We did several films together, but we never dated. She dated all my buddies, but nonetheless we were good friends. She was in it, and another really good friend of Gary's named Glenn Jacobson. He was the guy who was doing the painting, the artist... I liked him a lot. Don Jones was on the crew. He was good friend of mine, and he was doing sound and editing. And I knew Ed De Priest, the guy who financed the movie.

RAUSCH: *Are there any specific memories you have about the movie?*

KENT: I just remember that it was fun. It was just always fun going to work. It was a laugh a minute. And, as you can see, we didn't take it really seriously. I never thought it would get distributed, let alone find any kind of following. But I know people who like it. It's amazing.

Interview: Casey Larrain

In 2014, an obscure Ed Wood sex picture titled *The Nympho Cycler* showed up on the scene. The film, which was a sexploitation biker exploitation soft-core porno, starred a young ingénue named Casey Larrain. To say that Larrain is the best thing about that film would be an understatement of tremendous proportion. A quick scan of Larrain's film credits shows her working in a number of other Wood films, but according to Larrain, she only worked with Wood once. Apparently Wood took footage from *The Nympho Cycler* and integrated it into some of his later nudie films.

We caught up with Casey Larrain the week Alpha Blue released The Nympho Cycler to DVD to find out what she remembered about working with Wood. At the time of our conversation, Larrain had still never seen the film.

ANDREW RAUSCH: *How did you meet Edward D. Wood, Jr.?*

CASEY LARRAIN: I met him through one of my modeling agents. At that time, as I recall, I really hadn't been working in the industry for a while. This was 1970, I believe, and everything had gone hardcore. I wasn't interested in doing that, so I hadn't been working. One of my old agents called me and said there was this fellow—and I had never heard of him—who was interested in having me appear in this little soft, nudie film. The reason he requested me was because I knew how to ride a motorcycle.

So, I went and met with him. At first he was talking about doing a semi-serious film. [Laughs.] He was telling me that he had had a film in the Venice Film Festival. I think that was *Glen or Glenda?* (1953). So I said, "Okay, sure." That was it.

RAUSCH: *What was he like to work with?*

LARRAIN: He was a very fun, very sweet man. Very nice. Really working with him was sort of insane! There was no coherent story. I don't think there was a script of any kind; he would just tell us what he wanted us to do and say in the scene. We would do that. But it was impossible to tell what kind of story he was wanting to tell.

I rode a bike in the film, and he contacted some motorcycle club to shoot film of me riding with these people. He actually had me ride on of their bikes. So we shot some motorcycle footage; we shot some stuff in Griffith Park; we went down to Venice one day, and found a bunch of fellows who appeared to be elderly winos. These were homeless people who lived on the beach. He got a large bottle of jug wine of some kind, and had us all sit around in a circle, drinking this wine and talking. This was real wine, so of course I got smashed! [Laughs.] Then there was all sorts of stuff we shot at various houses in the valley. There was some footage we shot in a car. He had us shoot some footage at his house up in the Hollywood Hills at one point.

When we were out in the world, he wore normal clothes. But when we were shooting indoors, he was always dressed in drag. He had us do some very camp stuff. At one point, he and I are together in a hot tub, conversing about something. He's dressed as a woman. I don't know if he was shooting this as any kind of serious… At the point when I worked with him, he was definitely older and a bit puffy. You know, I had a friend who knew a lot about movies. When I mentioned to him that I had worked with this fellow who used to direct in drag, he said, "That must have been Ed Wood." And I said, "I don't really remember his name." And my friend said, "Very handsome fellow?" And I said, "Oh, no, that can't be the same guy. He was so much older by that point. He was not the Johnny Depp Ed Wood. He was sort of older and looked bloated and alcoholic. He had a lot of stubble on his face. So, dressed in drag, there's no way anyone would have taken him for a female. So, we're doing this scene in the hot tub, and talking, and he's dressed as a woman. Then he pulls off his wig and says, "After all, I am your husband." [Laughs.] He said it as if this supposed to some kind of big reveal! [Laughs again.]

I don't know if he intended that to be completely camp, or if he intended it to have a note of seriousness. He did later invite everyone to a screening. I assumed it was going to be some sort of edited version of what we were doing. We still had no idea what the story of this film was. He ended up just screening pieces of random footage from the shoot that he had shot them. There was something wrong with the sound equipment, so there was all this footage with no sound. That was all I ever saw of the film.

RAUSCH: *You said that was the only time you ever worked with Wood?*

LARRAIN: Yes. Friends have told me that they've seen pieces of me in films with different titles. On his film listings on IMDB, I'm listed as being in several of his films. I only worked with him the once, but he apparently cut that footage up and used in all kinds of different projects.

He was a funny guy, but like I said, very sweet. He was kind of surreal to work with.

RAUSCH: *How long was the shoot?*

LARRAIN: I really have no memory of how many days we shot, but with all the locations involved I'm thinking it was a week-and-a-half to two weeks.

RAUSCH: *How many takes did Wood generally take for each scene?*

LARRAIN: I don't remember him ever doing more than one take, but then he was so vague about what he wanted that there was really no way you could do it wrong.

RAUSCH: *Once you found out who he was, were you surprised to find out that Johnny Depp had played him in the movie?*

LARRAIN: I did see that after the fact. My friend just kept telling me for years that I must have worked with Ed Wood and that he was handsome. This guy I had worked with was old and puffy and not in particularly good shape at all. I think he did die fairly young, didn't he?

RAUSCH: *Yes. He was apparently an alcoholic.*

LARRAIN: He definitely had that alcoholic air about him. He never drank on the set though. Of course he could have been half lit up, but I never saw him drink on the set. I do also remember that he spoke often of Bela Lugosi, with whom he had worked and who he considered a dear friend. He talked about how very addicted Bela had been—and how when they were out together for any length of time he couldn't maintain without a fix and that Ed would then shoot him up under the table.

But my friend kept telling me Ed Wood was attractive. Then he pulled out this movie book he had about this guy, and in the back were some pictures of the older Ed Wood. I took one look and said, "Yeah, that's him." My name was actually in the index of the book as someone who had worked with him. So I then watched the Johnny Depp movie. I think I rented a couple of his movies. One of them was *Glen or Glenda?*. I had seen *Plan 9 from Outer Space* years before, but I had no idea who made it.

So now one of my claims to fame was that I worked with Ed Wood.

Interview: Andre Perkowski

New Jersey filmmaker Andre Perkowski has directed three Ed Wood adaptations—one short film, *To Kill a Saturday Night* (2008), and two features, *Devil Girls* (1999) and *Tomb of the Vampire* (2013). The first two projects were adapted by Perkowski from a short story and novel by Wood. *The Tomb of the Vampire* was based on an unfilmed Wood screenplay. He has also adapted the screenplay *The Ghoul Goes West*, but has not filmed it due to legal entanglements surrounding the ownership of the project.

In addition to these projects, Perkowski has made many other films including a three-hour adaptation of William S. Burroughs' *Nova Express* (2009). Most recently he directed a "Super-8 gutter kung fu epic" entitled *A Belly Full of Anger* (2012), which was dubbed by Phil Proctor, Bob Odenkirk, Joel Hodgson, and Trace Beaulieu.

ANDREW RAUSCH: *How did you first discover Ed Wood, and what were your initial thoughts of his work?*

ANDRE PERKOWSKI: I grew up hearing my father rave about a little film that he saw at a drive-in called *Plan 9 from Outer Space* (1959), along with competent Tor Johnson impersonations, so naturally I had to find this thing. It's safe to say that I wasn't disappointed, and it opened a window into a parallel filmmaking world I hadn't really been aware of. Despite boldly proclaiming "MADE IN HOLLYWOOD, U.S.A.," this was some other sort of

Hollywood. This was a Hollywood that lived deep inside the unique brain of one very quirky individual—Edward D. Wood, Jr. The fascination began, though most of what I found about him were sneery Medvedian tropes. I tracked down his scant filmography that seemed to grow and mutate every couple of years as rumors of Wood ghostwriting a script spread.

What really did it for me was reading Rudolph Grey's *Nightmare of Ecstasy*, just as John Waters blurbed on the back, all night with my mouth hanging open. *Wha? Wha? Whaaaat!?* On and on it went into delirious detail, layers of *Rashomon*-like tale that described a life of a man born to put his nutty visions on screen. Of course, I had to track down as many of his books as I could find—which inevitably led me to *Devil Girls*.

Being overly ambitious and youthfully deranged, I looked at the book's appendix of lost Wood projects and it broke my heart... Maybe I could do something about it! I know: a trilogy! I'll make three of these! That crazy enthusiasm carried me through two features in two years before I realized I should probably work on my own stuff. You can't manufacture cult, and I cannot stand faux camp or winking at the audience. It embarrasses me that some of the actors tried to be cutesy with the material, since the only way to do it is totally deadpan. But since I was a 22-year-old goofball working on a four-day schedule, I couldn't exactly be Robert Altman with the actors and gently guide their performances. So instead I tried to recreate the aroma of Wood by shooting as fast as possible and not thinking, leaning into it and embracing accident, chance, and crummy weather.

RAUSCH: *I'll be honest, that was my primary problem with the film—that you had actors who were basically bad actors pretending to be worse actors, whereas Wood's performers played everything straight.*

PERKOWSKI: It's definitely a good lesson to learn early on, and boy did I learn it. I tried to tell the actors this, and a few of them at least understood what I was going for and did it straight. The problem was a lot of them were theatre actors used to playing material to the seats in the back, being cute with the audience and being above the material. You can't be. I loved this crazy writing, this lurid purple prose. I just wanted to bring some of his fevered visions to life. Nowadays I would approach it all differently... You should see the stuff I had to cut due to this problem.

I think what happened was they all saw Tim Burton's *Ed Wood*, which is a wonderful movie and everything, incredibly inspiring and gorgeously shot, but not really good homework for the actors. Perhaps if I had presented it as a straight script and had not even mentioned Ed Wood it may have worked better.

RAUSCH: *Had you made other films by that point, or was* Devil Girls *to be your first?*

PERKOWSKI: I shot a lot of Super-8 and 16mm collage films and Burroughsian cut-ups. I even did a ridiculous Mexican masked wrestler feature to warm up and test the camera—then I leapt in.

RAUSCH: *Once you started reading* Devil Girls, *how quickly did you realize you wanted to make it into a film?*

PERKOWSKI: Honestly, I decided to make it before reading the novel. My initial plan was to do *The Vampire's*

Tomb, a juvenile delinquent epic, and then end with *The Ghoul Goes West*. The title *Devil Girls* was wonderful, and I'm a big fan of *The Violent Years*. I waited patiently for the book to arrive, and once it did, it did not disappoint. I laughed like a madman and typed up a draft quickly, weaving in fragments from his sex magazine stories and pulp novels for extra Woodian "grace notes."

RAUSCH: *How many of Wood's novels have you read now? They say there may be as many as 100 of them since he used so many different pseudonyms...*

PERKOWSKI: About 50 of them, and there are some doozies. *Security Risk* would be a fun production.

RAUSCH: *I've never read it, but I hear it's fun.*

PERKOWSKI: Cold war commiesploitation in Hollywood. How can you resist? It's hardly sexy though... I wonder how disappointed his readers were.

RAUSCH: *That's like* Jail Bait. *You know the title made people think it was going to be sexy instead of just being about a gun.*

PERKOWSKI: Then suddenly you've got some plot about an old guy and plastic surgery...and Lyle Talbot strutting around to that friggin' flamenco music.

RAUSCH: *It's an awesome mess. I wonder if that story from* Nightmare of Ecstasy *about James Cagney almost appearing in it is true. I mean, how different would that film have been?*

PERKOWSKI: It would have been pretty surreal.

RAUSCH: *But the novels...*

PERKOWSKI: Right. The autobiographical details of his novels
               are what hooked me. There is always angora. There
               is always a Shirley. There is always a washed up,
               bitter film director.

RAUSCH: *Which of Wood's films is your favorite?*

PERKOWSKI: *The Sinister Urge* (1960). Those fragments of Ed
               Wood battling Conrad Brooks from his unfinished
               teensploitation epic are worth the price of admission.
               Then you add Kenne Duncan sneering, Duke Moore
               being Duke Moore, and Jean Fontaine's raspy
               incarnation of Gloria peeling the paint from the
               walls with her voice, and you're in for a quality
               film experience.

RAUSCH: The Sinister Urge *is interesting because Wood takes
               such a judgmental stand against pornography, but
               then only years later he was writing and directing
               pornography himself.*

PERKOWSKI: That almost heartbreaking moment when Johnny
               Ryde melodramatically intones the words: "I look
               at this slush...and try to remember...at one time I
               made good movies." I love it when an author puts
               himself into his work.

               Although so many aspects of his life are a great
               tragedy, the worst is that he didn't live just a bit
               longer to bask in the warped acclaim. He would've
               been shooting horribly shot-on-video crap along
               with everyone else, chuckling behind the camera
               and adjusting angora caps on actresses.

RAUSCH: *That would have been fantastic, although I'm afraid
               he might have gotten lost in the mix had that happened.
               He would have been just like everybody else.*

PERKOWSKI: Us writer-types do like a nice narrative, huh? Yeah, the story works as is. A singular, warped vision that somehow managed to burrow onto celluloid for a while—and when he couldn't do that, he poured it into dozens upon dozens of books.

RAUSCH: *It's crazy to think how many books he wrote; especially when you take into account how broke he was in his later years. I guess being a writer didn't pay much even back then.*

PERKOWSKI: You can take his story so many ways. Is it inspiring? A cautionary tale? Ah yes, my friends, gaze into the eyes of Ed Wood and tell me what *you* see...in the future.

RAUSCH: *So you mentioned Ed Wood regular Conrad Brooks earlier. How did you hook up with him, and what was he like to work with?*

PERKOWSKI: I met Conrad Brooks and Ted V. Mikels at a Cleveland convention we were guests at. We spent a Saturday morning there shooting a 16mm short of Wood's story "To Kill a Saturday Night," which he intended to use for an anthology film. Ed may have wanted John Carradine for the lead, but I had Conrad Brooks. It's a bleak bit of business about two drunks getting sloshed and discussing murdering a prostitute. Ed does Bukowski and nobody wins. It sparked off a friendship with Ted...and months of collect calls from Conrad Brooks—once while I was having sex. I actually answered the call... [Laughs.] Oh, but I did make Conrad Brooks drink half a jug of Sangria at nine in the morning and he looked like he was about to puke!

I remember he wanted money up front from me for the film. I said, "Can't we wait until lunch?

Let's make some art!" And Connie said, "Fuck art! Your last name may be Perkowski, but I think there's a little Jew in you." Ah, to be called cheap by an associate of Ed Wood's was like an anti-Semitic merit badge!

RAUSCH: *So you paid him to be in the short?*

PERKOWSKI: It couldn't have been more than $20. I was poor... I think I bought some of his videos. Such a presence, that guy. I was fascinated by his weird purple-ish hair strands that emerged from his cap.

RAUSCH: *So whatever happened to that short film you made?*

PERKOWSKI: It's on the *Devil Girls* DVD. It's not very good... just silent black-and-white footage of them, not synced to a reading. Just a little thing.

RAUSCH: *I rented the movie on Amazon, so I didn't get the short.*

PERKOWSKI: Well, at least it paid for a small coffee for me then.

RAUSCH: *Enjoy your coffee, sir.*

PERKOWSKI: Extra cream, please. [Laughs.] But you know, I never expected to make money on these, or in fact any film I've made. I'm just compelled and feel incredible amounts of self-imposed guilt when I'm not making stuff.

RAUSCH: *So what came next for you—adapting the script for* The Ghoul Goes West *or making* Tomb of the Vampire?

PERKOWSKI: I shot *The Vampire's Tomb* about eight months later without even finishing editing on *Devil Girls*. This began a horribly tragic pattern in my life of shooting features and keeping them in a closet to edit on a rainy day. I think I have about seven unreleased features I'm still working through and putting out slowly...with titles like *El Cerebro de Hitler* and *The Man Who Couldn't Lose*.

RAUSCH: *Do you have any more Wood-related projects?*

PERKOWSKI: That's it, although one day I might shoot *The Ghoul Goes West* anyway, despite legal problems surrounding it, when everybody is dead and I can barely walk, much less look through a viewfinder.

RAUSCH: *When you see or hear about Wood now, do you feel a sort of kinship after having worked on these projects?*

PERKOWSKI: It's impossible not to. During that period I felt like I was some sort of twisted medium, channeling a ghost with very strange sentence structure. I tried to keep most of my sense of humor and obsessions out of it and just give in to his. These days I look back fondly at the whole thing, and I understood what he went through to get his work out there. I gained a lot of respect for anybody who dares to pick up a camera and say, "Let's make a movie," and actually finish it. Even a terrible piece of shit is somebody's dream. When I met Joel Hodgson, he summed it up with a sigh: "It turns out that making a movie is really, really hard." The critics might scoff, but my sympathies are with those with peculiar fetishes and preoccupations they are burning to share with the world onscreen.

RAUSCH: *Making a movie is hard. I wrote one that I was really, really proud of, and it got universally bashed. [Laughs.]*

Getting it out there is hard enough, but then you have to deal with the critics. At least Wood didn't have to deal with the critics so much since most of his stuff flew beneath the radar.

PERKOWSKI: You know, I don't think I've heard of any contemporary reviews. I wonder if *Daily Variety* mentioned some of his pictures.

RAUSCH: *I say this about reviewers after having picked on your movie in this book a bit. But on the upside, I was very much taken with the way you did your Ed Wood homework. I could tell it was a film made out of genuine love and respect. And you can hardly make the next* Ben-Hur *on a budget of $500.*

PERKOWSKI: No, but I can probably pull off *Ben-Hur Meets Son of Hercules* for $250! [Laughs.]

RAUSCH: *I understand you met Ed's widow, Kathy Wood, once. Where was that, and what was that experience like?*

PERKOWSKI: I got to meet the Wood femme fatales in 2001 or so, and Kathy Wood told me, "Eddie would have been very proud." This was a nice boost and had me grinning stupidly.

Dolores Fuller was also wonderful to chat to, although mostly we talked about her songwriting for Elvis. I did make her crack up by bursting into "Rock-a-Hula, Baby." Vampira ended up grabbing me by the lapels and intoning the words: "Darling, forget Ed Wood. Criswell! That's who you have to write a book about...Criswell!" I wish I had the detective skills to pull that off; he was a fascinating fella.

RAUSCH: *So just an observation here, but the Criswell in your movie* Devil Girls *looks like he's about 19-years-old. Is this a prequel?*

PERKOWSKI: Ha! I'm sure Rob Gorden will be pleased he came off that young. In the follow-up film, *The Vampire's Tomb*, we ended up going with the actual Criswell. It's hard to beat that eccentric phrasing. The only thing that sticks out in my mind about quickly taping those faux Criswell segments at the end of an exhausting day where we nailed about 30 pages of script was the fact that the hairpiece was only a tiny little spit-curl piece that meant he couldn't move his head up, down, or to the side. "Don't move your head is always priceless motivation for an actor. I'm told John Hurt operates under the same principle!

RAUSCH: *I read that much of that film was shot at the University of Chicago campus. How did you pull that off? Were you a student at the time?*

PERKOWSKI: No, Christine Malcom managed to get us access for both films. You'll notice in the classroom destruction scene, those vicious juvenile delinquent thugs are incredibly careful not to actually damage much and gingerly toss desks and erasers around. Everything else was just shot on the streets guerilla-style. I just used what I had or could scavenge. Ideally with a budget I would have kept the Texas setting of the novel. Also, I'd probably avoid Toyotas appearing in the background.

RAUSCH: *I produced a micro movie, which also featured Conrad Brooks, and was shot almost entirely on the grounds of a college. We are kindred spirits, my friend.*

PERKOWSKI: The campus police are definitely much easier to bamboozle. I find striding around purposefully like you own the place works well.

RAUSCH: *That's the only way if you want to do it right.*

PERKOWSKI: I think there is one shot where the police did chase us away, and I just included them in the background and kept shooting until the very last second. "Ooh, free uniforms!"

RAUSCH: *What format did you shoot the two Wood features on?*

PERKOWSKI: Um, all of them? Except for 35mm obviously. But you know, mini-DV, DV cam, Super-8, 8mm, 16mm...

RAUSCH: *It's just like a little* Natural Born Killers (1994). *[Laughs.]*

PERKOWSKI: I would have loved to do it all on film, and I wish I wasn't seduced by the "DV revolution" gibberish of the 90s. It looks like cheap porn! Film-look isn't the look of film, folks. I learned my lesson and subsequently tried to keep my features all shot on film, which means it takes years to finish anything as you'll notice the cost of that stuff is absolutely ridiculous. I'd do things like buy boxes of outdated Soviet-era black-and-white, giving those film sequences from *The Vampire's Tomb* such a spooky, age-fog glow.

I'm obsessed with grain, scratches, dirt...so I would unspool the film onto the ground to pick up dirt and bits of cat hair.

RAUSCH: *Interesting. So if you're to continue on your career in the vein of Ed Wood, you have to make sex pictures and porno next. Is that the trajectory you're headed on?*

PERKOWSKI: Thankfully not! I try to keep things weird and make a full one-eighty each time around. The next project that absorbed my life was a three-hour found footage adaptation of William S. Burroughs' cut-up novel *Nova Express*.

RAUSCH: *Very eclectic.*

PERKOWSKI: I suppose it would probably help to just do the same thing over and over, but it's the spiteful stubbornness to keep doing different stuff that has kept me incredibly obscure and frequently panicked over power bills. I want to end up with a filmography that makes you go, "What the *hell?*" Unfortunately, some of the entries in that filmography are better off imagined or kept as titles.

RAUSCH: *See, in some ways you are following the Wood path—you're broke.*

PERKOWSKI: On the plus side, I'm actually paid for art and comedy now and don't have to do wedding videos. My last flick was a deranged shot-on-film Hong Kong homage entitled *A Belly Full of Anger*, and I managed to rope in Bob Odenkirk, Phil Proctor, and some of the *Mystery Science Theater 3000* guys to voice it, so that keeps me amused. He may be broke, but damn, he's amused!

RAUSCH: *That's all that really matters.*

PERKOWSKI: Coming up next is a 16mm black-and-white animated feature of Alfred Jarry's 1896 play *Ubu Roi*. I expect this to have an audience of about 32, so this broke thing will probably continue unless pataphysics make a huge comeback.

RAUSCH: *You could rename it* Ed Wood's Ubu Roi! *Think of*

the possibilities.

PERKOWSKI: Woodsploitation: from here to obscurity.

RAUSCH: *That could be the name of your autobiography.*

PERKOWSKI: *Pop Culture Frankenstein.* I'm just all the bits of my favorite artists sewn together into a shambling, horrible mess.

RAUSCH: *What difficulties did you face when rewriting Wood's scripts for* Tomb of the Vampire *and* The Ghoul Goes West?

PERKOWSKI: Difficulties? None. I've never written a script faster. I didn't want to put too much of myself into it so it was more of an editing process to get *more* of Wood's language in there. Also, I was young and stupid. That tends to free you up.

RAUSCH: *Was that experience as fun as it would seem to be?*

PERKOWSKI: It was pure fun, an exhilarating ride. The idea that I could shoot a film on the same sort of timetable with what, 1/50th the money, not even accounting for inflation, was delightful. You know that Orson Welles line about it being the biggest electric train set a boy ever had? That's about right. Unfortunately I'm not Orson Welles. Damn! It turns out that nobody cares how quickly you shot something or for how little money; they just want to be entertained by a film. A pretty sensible enough request. Who really cares about technical exercises? So the pendulum swung wildly in the opposite direction, and my next film, *I Was a Teenage Beatnik and/or Monster from the Literal Underground!*, took a breezy five years to shoot.

RAUSCH: *Micro films don't get much respect.*

PERKOWSKI: Because we've all sat through abomination after abomination in the search of a little gem. The downside of the low cost of entry into this deranged game are low-quality products. The ugliness of video gives things such a nasty, cheap look that even the worst 70s flick doesn't have. I suppose it's getting better with HD, but I'm still not convinced. Dammit, cameras need to be huge, metallic, and as loud as a coffee grinder!

RAUSCH: *Everything shows up on DV and it often looks terrible. Ethan Hawke once told me it was like the Emperor in* Amadeus (1984) *said: "Too many notes."*

PERKOWSKI: Exactly. Ethan Hawke is probably a swell guy, but I don't want to see his pores blown up on the screen. I don't want to see individual nostril hairs.

RAUSCH: *Did you dress in angora and pumps when you directed these films?*

PERKOWSKI: Not even once! Perhaps this explains the lack of proper Shirley-ness.

RAUSCH: *I think it was a missed opportunity.*

PERKOWSKI: I think my eyebrows are too terrifyingly Eastern European to pull it off.

RAUSCH: *All jokes aside, do you feel that making these Wood adaptations has given you any sort of insight into Ed Wood the man?*

PERKOWSKI: Of course. Those several years researching every scrap I could find about the man, tracking down the survivors of his circle to ask questions they hadn't been asked a thousand times before, forming a band of dedicated freaks to pull off this caper on no budget only to be released into a generally uncaring world... I learned that you should pursue these things because you *have* to; because you mean it. That's what makes an interesting film—people who care no matter how strange and pointless it seems.

It may not be quite your cup of tea, but it's hard not to respect single-minded dedication and drive like Wood displayed. He was far from "the worst filmmaker of all time," as his works are infinitely more interesting than cookie-cutter projects from the passionless. They are unique, hard to compare to anything else—utterly *him*. Even when you try to copy and emulate the style, like I did as a young goofball, you're not going to hit on the proper alchemy to transmit shit into purest gold. So learn from dear ol' Eddie; follow your crazy dream, find like-minded friends, and do what makes you happy. Above all else, take a chance and pull the string. After all, one is always considered mad when one perfects something that others cannot grasp.

RAUSCH: *Okay, my last question: you die one day and you go to heaven and you meet Ed Wood. What would you like him to say to you, and is there anything you'd want to say to him?*

PERKOWSKI: I just hope his ghost didn't think I was making fun of him or anything. I adored his quirky take on things...it's charming and kinda sweet. I would ask one thing, though. "What the hell was the buffalo stampede all about, my good sir?"

Afterword
by David C. Hayes

I have been immersed in Wood-ian study and fandom for quite a few years now. I was introduced to the films of Wood at a young-ish age without appreciating them; just another 'bad' movie hosted by our own Count Scary on channel 50 in Detroit. We all had one of those UHF smorgasbords of schlock; that channel that dared to show the passion products of desperate filmmakers eager to break into the big time. *Robot Monster, Planet of the Vampires*. Them and any number of former drive-in scare pics played out in black and white melodrama on Saturday nights in the 1970s and 80s and kids like me just couldn't get enough. But, through all the horrible films, a single light did shine and it wasn't until I had grown a bit and moved far away from that UHF signal before I could appreciate it.

Living in Chicago, I answered a casting call for a film called *Devil Girls* and met Andre Perkowski. I was the only fat guy around willing to shave my head to play Tor Johnson's Lobo so the hiring was a no-brainer. Regardless, Perkowski was the man that really impressed into me the import that Wood had. He wasn't simply some Hollywood hack job, Ed Wood had a voice. His films had their own language and he was actually SAYING something. What that something was and how important it would be to humanity was up for debate but it was something. This was the late 1990s and post-Golden Turkey awards so Wood was, at that time, being regarded as the worst director ever (based, mostly, on *Plan 9 from Outer Space*). Nothing could be further from the truth.

This volume (along with my earlier book and Rudolph Grey's *Nightmare of Ecstasy*) should stand as testament to Wood's stature as a filmmaker of some repute. There are innumerable filmmakers from the same era that did not have the longevity, or vision, to be so well regarded in modern thought. Were his films well-made by standard definitions? One really couldn't say that. Were they box office winners despite their flaws? Well, no. Were they critical successes pushing the envelope of theme and message? Not really. What the films of Wood were, from the most base to the most perverse, was unique. No one could ever accuse Edward D. Wood, Jr. of world building that was boring. Hampered by time, budget, cast, crew, era and talent to certain extent, Wood's films always had that unique voice. Each of them, including the later smut pieces, expressed Wood's unique worldview.

I'm not quite sure what that worldview was, but if I could sum it up using the trials and tribulations of Wood's protagonists as metaphor for an artist's intent I would say that worldview was "never say die." Like Wood, his heroes and heroines (of all three genders) never gave up. They fought to be individuals and fought to be unique. Whether it was watching the dead dance, having copious amounts of sex in a haunted house or stopping an alien invasion, Wood's characters embodied the spirit with which he used to create film after film, book after book. Like their father, the Glens and Bucks and Shirleys and all the rest refused to give up even when faced with insurmountable odds.

Just like Ed.

Selected Bibliography

BOOKS

Craig, Rob, Ed Wood, *Mad Genius: A Critical Study of the Films*, Jefferson, NC, McFarland & Company, 2009.

Crouse, Richard, *Son of the 100 Best Movies You've Never Seen*, Toronto, Ontario, E.C.W. Press, 2008.

Faust, M., "A.C. Stephen," *Shock Cinema*, issue 14, 1999.

Fuller, Dolores, *A Fuller Life: Hollywood, Ed Wood, and Me*, Duncan, OK, BearManor Media, 2008.

Grey, Rudolph, *Nightmare of Ecstasy: The Life and Art of Edward D. Wood, Jr.*, Portland, OR, Feral House, 1992.

Hayes, David C., *Muddled Mind: The Complete Works of Ed Wood, Jr.*, Vancleave, MS, Ramble House Publishing, 2009.

Schiff, Laura, "Orgy of the Dead," *Femme Fatales*, June 1998.

Wood, Jr., Edward D., *Hollywood Rat Race*, London, Four Walls Eight Windows, 1998.

FILMS

Carducci, Mark Patrick, *Flying Saucers Over Hollywood: The Plan 9 Companion*, 1992.

Copner, Michael, *On the Trail of Ed Wood*, 1990.

Newsom, Ted, *Ed Wood: Look Back in Angora*, 1994.

Ross, Jonathan, *The Incredibly Strange Film Show: Ed Wood*, 1989.

Thompson, Brett, *The Haunted World of Edward D. Wood Jr.*, 1995.

WEBSITES
Cinema Head Cheese (www.cinemaheadcheese.blogspot.com)

The Hunt for Edward D. Wood, Jr. (www.edwoodonline.com)

Internet Movie Database (www.imdb.com)

Acknowledgments

We would like to thank the following individuals for their assistance: Ben Ohmart, Tony Schaab, David C. Hayes, Mike White, Rudolph Grey, Andre Perkowski, Larry Karaszewski, Aris Iliopulos, Rob Craig, Fred Olen Ray, Brenda Fogarty, John Johnson, Gary Kent, Jason Insalaco, Jonathan Harris, Frank Henenlotter, Casey Larrain, Gary Graver, Stephen C. Apostolof, Conrad Brooks, Herschell Gordon Lewis, Alpha Blue Archives, Chris Watson, and Joe Ziemba. We would also like to thank our friends and family for their love and support on this (and every) project.

CPSIA information can be obtained
at www.ICGtesting.com
Printed in the USA
BVOW06*2151211117
501054BV00005B/19/P